AUSTERITY BITES

For my husband, Colin and my sister Lisa
who are always there for me

AUSTERITY BITES

A journey to the sharp end of
cuts in the UK

Mary O'Hara

First published in Great Britain in 2014 by

Policy Press
University of Bristol
6th Floor
Howard House
Queen's Avenue
Bristol BS8 1SD
UK
Tel +44 (0)117 331 5020
Fax +44 (0)117 331 5367
pp-info@bristol.ac.uk
www.policypress.co.uk

North American office:
The Policy Press
c/o The University of Chicago Press
1427 East 60th Street
Chicago, IL 60637, USA
t: +1 773 702 7700
f: +1 773 702 9756
sales@press.uchicago.edu
www.press.uchicago.edu

British Library Cataloguing in Publication Data
A catalogue record for this book is available from the British Library

Library of Congress Cataloging-in-Publication Data
A catalog record for this book has been requested

ISBN 978 1 44731 560 5 hardcover

Cover design by Soapbox Design.
Printed and bound in Great Britain by TJ
International, Padstow.
Policy Press uses environmentally responsible
print partners.

Austerity:
a definition

... difficult economic conditions created by government measures to reduce a budget deficit, especially by reducing public expenditure: a period of austerity/[as modifier] austerity measures.

(Collins Dictionary)

* * * * *

"No matter how often it repeats that its actions are fair, this government is making a political choice to attack the public sector and, by doing this now, damaging the whole of the economy long into the future." (Derek Simpson, Unite General Secretary, October 2010)

"Austerity has failed. It has failed in the UK and it has failed in the Eurozone. Its failure was predictable and, by some at least, predicted. It turned a nascent recovery into stagnation. That imposes huge and unnecessary costs, not just in the short run, but in the long term as well: the costs of investments unmade, of businesses not started, of skills atrophied and of hopes destroyed." (Martin Wolf, columnist, *Financial Times*, May 2013)

"Cutting the welfare state in the name of producing more growth and opportunity is an offensive canard.... Austerity is not just the price of saving the banks. It's the price that banks want someone else to pay." (Mark Blyth, author of *Austerity: The history of a dangerous idea*, 2013)

"Your society's broken, so who should we blame? Should we blame the rich, powerful people who caused it? No, let's blame the people with no power and no money and these immigrants who don't even have the vote – yeah, it must be their fucking fault." (Iain Banks, author, spring 2013)

"Austerity is not a medicine. It's a cancer; a cancer at the heart of society." (Jack Monroe, blogger, November 2013)

"Austerity is not working. It isn't working anywhere it's being used. I do not know why anybody with a so-called intelligent mind would attempt to bring austerity in when they can see it isn't working anywhere else." (Maria McGee, resident, Cookstown, Northern Ireland, January 2013)

"We never imagined we'd read about children, disabled and non-disabled being left without food.... They say there is no money but if they stopped tax evasion and tax avoidance they wouldn't have to make the cuts." (Linda Burnip, Disabled People Against Cuts [DPAC], autumn 2013)

"I've got no TV. I've got no fridge running, I'm not using the heating at all yet. To me it just looks so gloomy. I've done my best. I've got two degrees. I'm afraid to put the light on at night because of the cost of energy. It makes me very angry but there's not the support out there. I'm just so stuck." (Lynne Middleward, South Tyneside)

"I can't think straight when the government cuts certain things. I don't know how they come to these decisions.

I don't think they live in the real world. They're cutting benefits people need to survive." ('Annie', Birmingham)

"There's people that are suicidal. There's people with mental health issues – and if they didn't have mental issues before, they have them now because they are being so degraded. They are being so run down in life. I'm not saying I want a life of luxury. I don't want a life of luxury. Do you know what I want? A life." ('Dec', Luton)

"I think the moral test of any government or of anyone with any humanity is ... do you look after the people who are sick, who are lonely and depressed? That ain't happening. People are scared stiff." (Jackie Gallagher, Citizens Advice manager, Derry, Northern Ireland)

Work Capability assessor: "Are you suicidal?"

Benefits claimant: "Yes"

Assessor: "Well then, why haven't you achieved it?"

Contents

Acknowledgements

Authors always say this because it is a truism: a book is the product of the efforts and talents of many people. This book is no different. A lot of wonderful people showed incredible faith in me during the writing of this book, including a small army of friends and colleagues, and I owe them all deep thanks. First I want to thank the team at Policy Press. Alison Shaw believed in this project right from the start and was instrumental in not only making the book possible but in encouraging and supporting me to take it on despite extremely tight deadlines. To Jo Morton and the production team I owe a debt of gratitude for forensically picking up on errors, reshaping where necessary, and making suggestions that have made the book much better than it would otherwise have been.

I consider myself very lucky indeed that the people who read and critiqued my earliest drafts were not only generous with their time but also with their ideas, insights, and guidance. Thanks to Professor Danny Dorling who, as well as reading and critiquing, was always on hand as a friend with advice, and to Baroness Ruth Lister and Professor Simon Duffy for their candid and sage contributions. To Alison Benjamin, my long-time editor at *The Guardian* who also critiqued early drafts, I am inordinately grateful. Thanks too to Josie Long and Janine Gibson for their support for the book and to Mark Thomas for carving out time to write the foreword. Longstanding thanks to Alan Rusbridger who as editor of *The Guardian* put his faith in me many years ago, giving me my break in journalism.

To the Joseph Rowntree Foundation and the charity Locality whose dedication to promoting a wider understanding of poverty and of austerity provided the catalyst for the project from which this book was derived, there are many thanks due. Most of all I wish to thank the people I worked with directly from the start on the multi-media reports I compiled during

2012 and 2013 that would go on to form the bedrock of this book. Abigail Scott-Paul, Paul Brook, Emma Stone, Julia Unwin and the whole JRF team were a joy to work with. A group of more professional, warm and engaging people it would be hard to imagine. The same goes for Steve Clare, Steve Wyler and the team at Locality. To Steve Clare in particular a very big thanks is owed for helping with the complicated task of coordinating my travels and interviews around the country. Equally, my thanks to Quintin Oliver for his role in helping set up interviews across Northern Ireland. In addition, many thanks to Chris Kaboli who did such great work on the videos for the project.

Then there is Alexis Harvey. I first worked with Alexis in my mid-20s when we both ran departments at *The Guardian* and I was in utter awe at her skills as a writer and editor. The fact that she agreed to help research and sub-edit this book was my very great good fortune. There is no one who could have done a better job at knocking me and the copy into shape or who could have helped with everything from tidying grammar to shoring me up when the process became daunting – which it frequently did.

Finally – to every individual who shared their views and experiences and to every organisation where someone made time to talk to me or contributed in some way to this project, my sincerest and deepest thanks go to you. No one knows more than those on the frontline the despair generated by austerity, and if this book plays any kind of part in making sure you are heard then that is what matters most of all. This book is therefore a tribute to all of you and to all in the United Kingdom whose lives have been so radically affected by the tragedy of austerity.

A quite rude foreword

by Mark Thomas, comedian and political activist

19 May 2014: Budget Day, though not so much a Budget as class war waged with a calculator. Chancellor of the Exchequer George Osborne stands outside Number 11 Downing Street posing for the traditional photo call, holding the famous red briefcase containing his speech with a slightly awkward expression on his face, the look of a man lifting his own luggage for the first time. Arm rigid and knuckles white around the handle he seems about to ask, "… Er … Whose job is this? …" He smiles, nods at the press and confidently leaves to deliver his fiscal medicine in the House of Commons.

Every Budget speech ever given in Parliament is subject to the principles of reverse technology: if you look at who benefits from a Budget then you can see the voters the Chancellor is trying to woe. Osborne's is no different but when he announced a cut in bingo tax and 1p off the price of a pint of beer he revealed his limitations as well as his aspirations, and those of his party. Conservative Party Chairman Grant Shapps MP infamously tweeted: 'Cutting the bingo tax and beer duty to help hardworking people to do more of the things they enjoy.' Oh uncontained delight! Bingo and beer. Let every flat cap on every whippet be thrown into the air with gay abandon. Let every walrus moustache on the lip of every hardworking man be wiped clear of foaming ale so all may cry, "Gawd bless Mister Osborne!" He could not have been more patronising if he announced a tax break on racing pigeons.

Class is what defines this Coalition Cabinet above all else, its massed ranks of millionaires and ex-Etonians who have no grasp of everyday reality for working people. It is almost as if we have returned to the 1930s where the rich were our masters and betters, and the poor knew their place. In the 21st century we are governed by people who think Downton Abbey is a documentary. In a world of millionaires and Etonians it must be effortless to use the two classic Conservative strategies deployed in the face of rising poverty: (1) deny the facts; (2) blame the poor.

The explosion of people using food banks was greeted with derision by Lord Norman Tebbit, who insinuated that this was an example of a something-for-nothing culture, implying that there is no poverty, just greed. That those in crisis and facing destitution are just greedy kids running after free sweets thrown into the air in a playground.

Privilege and dogma have framed the Conservatives' thinking as they mount the greatest ever assault upon the welfare state and the poor since World War II. The poor simply do not matter; they are casualties of ideology. If the facts don't fit the credo, the facts are wrong.

It does not even seem to matter to Osborne that the one task he asked the electorate to judge him by has been beyond his reach, namely to eliminate the budget deficit by 2015. On 19 March 2014 he announced new predictions for the elimination of the deficit by 2019 and more public spending cuts. Maybe the one real task he is judging himself by is the Tories getting elected with a working majority in 2015, this time without the hindrance of having to help the Lib Dems put up some bunting every now and again.

We are in the middle of cult-based economic experiment where the rich have fixed their world but not ours.

So I am delighted to scribble these ill-constructed words for the author Mary O'Hara. This book contains things the Conservative-led Coalition hates. It has facts. The author actually made the unforgivable faux pas of listening to the unheard voices, the poor, the huddled masses; those who would in a better world seek shelter beneath the wing of a caring state. This book gives voice to those at the bottom of the heap, those who struggle to just exist.

This book is ammunition. Use it.

Salut!

Introduction

This book tells the story of the (all too often) voiceless, invisible people who have been the victims of one of the most radically regressive and destructive economic experiments the UK has ever seen. Drawing on interviews conducted all over the UK in 2012 and 2013 with people at the sharp end of the Conservative-led Coalition government's unprecedented 'austerity' programme, it examines how savage cuts to public expenditure have been needlessly and shamelessly[1] unleashed on the country, and the ways in which they have scarred individuals, families and communities.

The book demonstrates how, despite government claims that drastic cuts to public spending and sweeping reform of the welfare state were necessary and 'fair', this was, in fact, a fallacy. What was implemented was a regime that disproportionately affected the most vulnerable people in society while leaving the well-off unscathed.[2] By examining the lived experience and 'real-time' reactions of those most affected by a whole raft of bruising austerity measures – the poorest and those most reliant on public services – the rest of the book lays bare the extraordinary damage inflicted during what has become known as 'the age of austerity'. And it looks too at one of the most important factors explaining how austerity was so forcefully applied: the fact that policies were deftly propped up by a shrewd political narrative which both painted cuts as inevitable and depicted people who were living in poverty, out of work or who were victims of austerity as 'scroungers', to blame for their own predicament.[3] As the New Economics Foundation (nef) succinctly put it:

> Well-framed, well-crafted and often repeated, the austerity story is the dominant political narrative in Britain today. The Coalition has an economic narrative that is the textbook definition of a powerful political story. They have developed a clear plot, with heroes and villains, and use simple, emotional language to make their point clear. Repeated with remarkable discipline over several years, their austerity story has gained real traction with the British public. The government has successfully framed all economic debates on its own terms, but what is most powerful about their narrative is how resilient it is to different circumstances. If the economy is strong the medicine is working; if the economy is weak we need more medicine.[4]

If you found yourself walking around some parts of the UK during the so-called 'age of austerity' (I say 'so-called' because awarding it such an epochal epithet serves to imbue it with an undeserved legitimacy), say, a bustling shopping mall or a busy high street in an affluent part of London, you'd be forgiven for thinking everything was ticking over nicely. Even when the country was in the midst of a recessionary slump of historical proportions[5] it wouldn't have been difficult to find a place where people appeared to be doing okay. But this would have been a mere veneer. Yes, some people had money to spend. And yes, not everyone was in financial difficulty. But just beneath the surface, austerity in the UK was wreaking havoc on the lives of millions while storing up even more misery for the future as the Chancellor, George Osborne, repeated that he would stick to his guns and keep cutting for years to come.

There may have been some tentative (if patently uneven and precarious) signs of a return to economic growth by the end of

2013[6] – London's economy was where most of the growth was concentrated – but this arrived five full years after the 2008 global economic crash and was much lower and later than, for example, growth in the US. And besides, years of economic stagnation had already meted out plenty of damage to UK citizens.

This is what austerity in the UK really looked like. By the end of 2013 – three-and-a-half years after austerity was introduced – tens of billions of pounds had been wiped from public expenditure (estimated to be more than £64 billion by 2015)[7] at Osborne's behest, with a further 20 per cent cut scheduled for between 2014 and 2018.[8] At recurring intervals from 2010 departmental budgets were slashed across central and local government, meaning many vital public and community services ranging from libraries to clubs for children with disabilities were eradicated, reorganised or pared down as a result.[9] And, as The Centre for Welfare Reform pointed out, the distribution of cuts was staggeringly disproportionate:

> If we exclude the areas of growth and protected services there are in fact cuts of £75.2 billion. And of these cuts over 50 per cent fall on just two areas, benefits and local government, despite the fact that together they make up only 26.8 per cent of central government expenditure. Most people do not realise that local government's primary function (over 60 per cent) is to provide social care to children and adults.[10]

Meanwhile two thirds of a million public sector jobs were lost by the end of 2012 as a result of austerity, with a further quarter of a million expected to disappear by 2015.[11] Wage freezes for remaining public sector workers were introduced. There was a fundamental shake-up of the welfare state,[12] including eradicating or reconfiguring a number of key benefits that had primarily assisted the working poor, while the introduction of a new tier of excessively punitive sanctions into the social security system thrust hundreds of thousands of people into extreme financial difficulty, destitution and in some cases, mental breakdown.[13]

For the first time ever in the UK there were more people in working families living below the poverty line than in workless or retired families combined – 6.7 million in 2013, according to the Joseph Rowntree Foundation (JRF) and the New Policy Institute.[14] There was also an unparalleled squeeze on average household incomes. Living standards plummeted. Wages decreased by 14 per cent from 2008 to 2013, according to the GMB union,[15] while the independent Institute for Fiscal Studies (IFS) projected living standards to be lower in 2015 than in 2010.[16] So dire in fact was the situation with wages that the Director General of the main UK business body, the Confederation of British Industry (CBI), uncharacteristically used his 'New Year message' at the beginning of 2014 (ordinarily a platform calling for cuts to business taxes) to tell companies to share profits and start paying workers more to help those 'stuck in minimum-wage jobs without routes to progression.'[17]

Along with benefits cuts and an accelerating pattern of low-paid, unstable work, whole swaths of the population were propelled headlong into serious debt. Hundreds of thousands of families were using debt to pay for basic needs, pushing them to breaking point.[18] And the unthinkable was happening: more than half a million were regularly turning to food banks for hand-outs of essential supplies.[19] Some groups including people with disabilities, women and children and people from black and minority ethnic backgrounds were disproportionately affected by all of this, meaning many were enduring inexplicable suffering on top of existing disadvantage. And meanwhile, the UK enshrined its place as one of the most unequal nations in the Western world, with income gaps between those at the very top and those at the bottom widening with each passing year.[20] According to the think tank the Resolution Foundation, while FTSE 100 bosses saw record-breaking pay rises, the super-rich were growing ever richer despite the economic crash. The top 1 per cent in 2012/13 pocketed 10p in every pound earned in the UK just as the majority saw their incomes deplete rapidly.[21]

All in all, austerity translated as a very bleak reality indeed for a considerable proportion of the British population – especially the poor and especially those living in deprived or disadvantaged areas. And yet to listen to politicians (of all hues – the Labour opposition, while less enthusiastic about austerity, were nonetheless committed to cuts should they get elected in 2015), the economic medicine simply had to be stomached. The thing is – it didn't. Austerity was a choice made by the British government. As Mark Blyth pointed out in his book, *Austerity: The history of a dangerous idea*,[22] austerity was not imposed by an outside body, as was the case with the International Monetary Fund (IMF) in Greece after 2008 or during the notoriously flawed and counterproductive 'structural adjustments' foisted on a number of Latin American countries in the 1980s and 1990s.[23] Neither was it the only option. It was a domestic political decision to 'shrink the state'.[24]

When it came to power in May 2010, the Coalition government, headed by Conservative Prime Minister, David Cameron, and his Liberal Democrat Deputy, Nick Clegg, took great pains to convince the British public of the fallacy that, rather than neoliberal ideology masquerading as 'fixing' the economy,[25] the wholesale dismantling of the welfare state they had in store was essential if the UK was to tackle its budget deficit.[26] Paraded in the language of 'fairness', step by step, the government undermined six decades of core social security protections such as Child Benefit and support for people with disabilities. The previous Labour administration had got away with profligate public spending, the Coalition cried (to barely a whimper from a timorous Labour Party which feared – correctly – that public opinion blamed them for the deficit). The global economic crisis and banking catastrophe of 2008 was unprecedented and therefore warranted an exceptional response, the austerians declared. Austerity was right, necessary, unavoidable and (most memorably false) the population were 'all in this together'. However, as Blyth and others argued, rampant public spending was not the primary culprit in the UK's difficulties, as the austerians insisted. Rather, it was the billions of taxpayers' cash pumped into bailing out a failed global banking system:

> We need to remember that the crisis that brought us here was a private sector crisis [Blyth wrote]. Their debts landed on the balance sheet of the public sector through bank bailouts, recapitalisations and unlimited quantitative easing. In other words, taxpayers bailed bankers and the price was a ballooning deficit.[27]

According to Blyth, Professor of International Political Economy at Brown University in the US, the logic underpinning austerity – that growth and competiveness would be restored by reducing public spending quickly and drastically – has been proven wrong so many times throughout history it's a wonder anyone continues to take it seriously. 'The policy of austerity is more often than not exactly the wrong thing to do precisely because it produces the very outcomes you are trying to avoid.'[28]

If, as surveys suggested,[29] the British (and European) public and many within the political and media classes had bought into the austerity narrative, that did not mean critics of austerity stood silent. They may not have been reaching wide audiences, or have manufactured the kind of emotionally powered narrative nef alluded to, but they were there. They included trade unionists, charities and many people directly affected, as well as some corners of the press but many of them were economists and academics too,[30] challenging the perceived wisdom of necessary austerity from a number of very important structural fronts. And one of these was on the basis of human rights. Throughout 2013 there was a clear momentum building around challenges to austerity as a violation of basic human dignity. In the UK (and indeed in Europe, where countries such as Greece and Spain had endured a much more extreme incarnation of austerity) UN representatives[31] and other international organisations including UNICEF[32] were increasingly vocal in their criticism of not only which policies were being implemented, but how, and of their evident disproportionate impact on vulnerable groups such as the poor, women and children.

The core critiques tended to be economic, not rights-based, however (perhaps explaining why the public in 2013 had yet to be divested of their acceptance of the 'austerity is necessary' myth). One of the central economic springboards for the discrediting of austerity (just as the UK government was ploughing ahead with even more drastic cuts) came with the extraordinary development that the paper written by two Harvard economists, which austerians wheeled out at every opportunity to justify cuts, was exposed as fundamentally flawed methodologically.[33] There was also evidence of austerity resting on ever-shaky ground when the IMF cautioned Osborne about the extent of austerity in early 2013, having previously backed his strategy.[34]

A number of prominent economists, including 2008 Nobel Prize winner Paul Krugman, argued vociferously that the case for austerity had crumbled on multiple levels. In his 2012 book, *End this depression now*,[35] Krugman took to task the idea that the private sector would magically rescue the UK economy after cuts. The 'confidence fairy' that would supposedly generate growth courtesy of the private sector as the public sector retreated, and on which Cameron, Osborne and co had pinned their economic dreams when they came to power, proved to be spectacularly elusive.

Writing about the first two years of austerity in the UK, Krugman said: 'Did consumers and business become more confident after Britain's turn to austerity? On the contrary, business confidence fell to levels not seen since the worst of the financial crisis, and consumer confidence fell even below levels of 2008–09. The result is an economy that is deeply depressed ... there is a real sense in which Britain is doing worse in this slump than it did in the Great Depression.... One could hardly have imagined a stronger demonstration that austerians had it wrong.'

Meanwhile fellow Nobel Prize winner in Economics Joseph Stiglitz was repeatedly warning of the damage austerity was wreaking, calling the policies underpinning it 'stagnation by design'. Placing it in the context of numerous and serious underlying structual problems with the economy, and criticising the post-crash response of policy-makers 'on both sides of the Atlantic', Stiglitz highlighted how growth had been stymied: at the beginning of 2014 he wrote: 'Before leaders who embraced austerity policies open the champagne and toast themselves, they should examine where we are and consider the near-irreparable damage that these policies have caused.'[36]

By the end of 2013, when something resembling sustained growth finally appeared to be returning to the UK (the economy grew for three consecutive quarters, according to the Office for National Statistics [ONS], albeit at low levels)[37] – and the austerians were (naturally) claiming that they were right all along and their medicine had begun to take effect – critics were quick to puncture the government's self-congratulatory posturing about the rebound. John Cassidy, in *The New Yorker*, was one. Referring to the Chancellor's claims that austerity had worked as 'hogwash', and calling it an 'effort to cure the patient by subjecting it to the equivalent of leeching', Cassidy concluded that the Coalition's 'pre-Keynesian' cuts in public spending and increases in regressive taxation had failed 'abysmally',[38] with growth slowing significantly after austerity was introduced.

Summing up the overall impact, he wrote that after the global economic crisis, Osborne 'subjected his countrymen and countrywomen to three more years of slump-like conditions, and it produced a dearth of public-sector and private-sector investment that will hobble Britain for years to come'.

Significantly, Cassidy wrote that for all the pontificating from the Chancellor (or as Cassidy refers to him, 'the patron saint of austerity enthusiasts') about 'Plan A' working, the government had actually failed to meet its own self-imposed target of 'reducing the budget deficit and bringing down Britain's overall debt burden'.[39] What, many critics were therefore reasonably asking – other than ideology, was the point of the whole exercise if deficit reduction targets weren't even being met?

In the *Financial Times* columnist Martin Wolf[40] wrote that while any recovery was to be welcomed – especially for those personally struggling with the fallout of the prolonged economic slump – the UK's economic performance since Osborne had become Chancellor was 'dismal' (to say nothing of the fact that the Eurozone – the UK's single biggest export market – was still teetering on the brink[41]). Wolf pointed out that in the second quarter of 2013 GDP was still 3.3 per cent below the pre-crisis peak, and '18% below its 1997–2007 trend'. Wolf also stressed that the recovery that appeared to be under way by the end of 2013 needed to be understood firmly in the context of lost economic output. He wrote:

> Whatever the causes of the crisis, it has bequeathed huge headaches. But the biggest, by far, is how to reduce the permanent losses of output. Even if the economy grew at a sustained rate of close to 3 per cent a year, the present value of lost output would be close to five times annual GDP. This is why a delayed recovery is not much of a triumph.[42]

Indeed, what recovery there was as 2014 approached was weak, fragile and piecemeal (in part fuelled by a boost to mortgage lending that was on track to overheat the housing market in the South East of England once again because of a Help to Buy scheme[43] introduced by the Chancellor, igniting concerns that any rise in interest rates could plunge thousands into paralysing debt as their mortgages became untenable[44]). Meanwhile, polls confirmed the public's view that if a recovery was happening, they were certainly not feeling it in their wallets.[45] And as austerity cuts continued apace —with much more to come in 2014 and beyond – the outlook for millions remained grim whatever the government preached about growth.

By the time David Cameron stood up in London at a Lord Mayor's banquet in front of the financial elites of the UK in November 2013 and ostensibly admitted (from an ornate golden throne, no less) that austerity was not an emergency response to testing economic times after all, but a permanent disassembling of the state, neither longstanding critics nor the people at the sharp end of three-and-a-half years of cuts were surprised. Bombastic and buoyed by the recent news of an economic upturn, Cameron revealed his true colours. He talked of forging "a leaner, more efficient state", and uttered the words many felt he had been holding back since 2010: "We need to do more with less. Not just now, but permanently."[46] There it was – a declaration of permanent austerity. It was the dream even Margaret Thatcher hadn't dared to dream.

Taken in the context of the ongoing suffering of millions of UK citizens and when compared to Cameron's 2010 'New Year message', it was clear as crystal that any prior allusions to the fairness and economic necessity of austerity belonged in a box marked 'We are not, and *never were*, all in this together'.

"I didn't come into politics to make cuts. Neither did Nick Clegg. But in the end politics is about national interest, not personal political agendas", Cameron had protested back in

2010. "We're tackling the deficit because we have to – not out of some ideological zeal. This is a government led by people with a practical desire to sort out this country's problems, not by ideology."

But as George Eaton wrote in the *New Statesman*[47] the day after the speech at the Lord Mayor's banquet, 'By making it clear that he believes the government can do "more with less", Cameron has paved the way for a dramatic reduction in the size of the state. For those reliant on public services and the welfare state to maintain an adequate standard of living, it is a foreboding prospect.'

At the end of 2013 it was unclear if, despite the damage wrought, Cameron and co would get to form the next government in 2015 and see their goal of 'perma-austerity' realised. For the people living at the sharp end of austerity, whose lives were being wrecked, nothing could have been more important than winning the moral, political and economic argument for halting austerity in its tracks.

Structure of the book

This book is made up of seven chapters and a conclusion. **Chapters One**, **Two** and **Three** examine some of the most visible totems of austerity, including the vast rise in food poverty that emerged after 2010. They also look at the enormous pressure on household incomes and wages, far-reaching social security changes such as the 'Bedroom Tax', benefits sanctions and the crippling personal debt that resulted. **Chapter Four** tackles the political narrative that underpinned austerity – the so-called 'striver versus skiver' debate – and assesses the harm this was doing across society, while **Chapter Five** explores the changing face of work in the UK as radical 'back-to-work' policies contributed to a further destabilisation of employment in an increasingly 'no pay, low pay' economy. In **Chapter Six** some of the most disproportionate impacts of austerity are evaluated – namely, those directed at people with disabilities and the long-term sick – putting paid to any suggestion of fairness in the application of austerity measures. **Chapter Seven** continues on this theme, looking at some of the worst fears induced as austerity took root, including the emotional and psychological price being paid by vulnerable people, the wholesale devastation caused by local government budgets being slashed, and the danger in which women and children were being placed as a result of cuts to legal aid. Finally, in the **Conclusion**, the grassroots and community response to austerity is assessed along with the myriad groups and individuals who, by 2013, were coalescing to form an anti-austerity movement as well as what all of this might herald for the future of the welfare state in the UK.

Scope of this book

This book is not intended to be a comprehensive guide to or overview of austerity in the UK or elsewhere, and neither is it a macro-economic analysis. Rather, it is concerned with the direct impact of austerity policies on people's lives, and with the ramifications of its implementation on wider society. It therefore addresses some of the most prominent and damaging policies, their implications and the reactions of those people most affected.

Out of necessity, due to the sheer scale of austerity and its impacts, some very important austerity-related policies and their effects are not covered in detail here, in particular, the impact on the National Health Service (NHS) and education services. Both budgets had been ring-fenced in theory, although the reality was that tightening budgets and redundancies were commonplace and escalating.[48] Reforms such as unbridled moves toward privatisation and the controversial out-sourcing of contracts to private firms such as Serco and G4S were also having an impact on these services.

The scope of this book had to be restricted to those health and education issues that were specifically raised by interviewees – for example, rising tuition fees, the eradication of some grants for poorer students and, in the case of the NHS, pressures on mental health services directly related to austerity. There are other areas I wish there had been room for, too. Cuts to the police, fire and prison services and the privatisation of some of these services were another vital component in the austerity landscape. The disproportionate impact of austerity policies on certain parts of the UK and on specific sectors of society would merit a book each, as would the impact of housing benefits changes. I hope that the detailed notes at the end of the book will direct readers to good sources of additional information. Finally, there is some inconsistency in how individual interviewees are referred to. A number of people opted for a pseudonym or wished to remain anonymous. I respected their wishes.

One more thing. This book was incredibly challenging to write. Each day, as I sat down and turned on my laptop in the second half of 2013, there was a deluge of information/ misinformation, reports, studies and opinions about how austerity was affecting people. It was as fast-changing a terrain as I've ever encountered, and at times it was overwhelming. Short of this book being thousands of pages long, there was simply no way to reference all of the facts, figures and analyses that would better inform our understanding of the many and complex issues tied up with such a dramatic shift in the economic and political direction of the country. That said, the book does its best to leave readers with a genuine flavour of what life was like in the initial years of 'Austerity UK'.

Background

This book was borne out of a year-long project I undertook in the autumn of 2012 for JRF and the charity, Locality. I was asked to travel around the UK and report back at regular intervals on how people were experiencing austerity on the ground, and to document the impact of policies as they were being introduced in 'real time'. There was no prescribed narrative I was expected to adhere to and no preordained philosophy to follow. Rather, it was about providing a conduit through which the experiences, views and insights of people on the front line of cuts could be recorded – as they happened.

I did this by going into communities, conducting interviews and then producing a series of print and audiovisual packages online, outlining what I was finding, and broadcasting conversations with the people I spoke to about their take on austerity. The multi-media reports can be viewed at www. jrf.org.uk/topic/austerity. The people interviewed had either been directly affected by austerity policies or were supporting those who were. In addition to publishing online accounts, I wrote about some of my findings as the project progressed in publications such as *The Guardian* and the *New Statesman*.

As the months passed a few things crystallised for me. One was the mushrooming intensity of the financial and mental strain inflicted by austerity with each passing month. Another was the depth of the fury people felt at the political classes. Many spoke of having been abandoned by mainstream politicians and of the visceral anger they felt at MPs in Westminster for having written off those people who were struggling or who objected to the cuts. Many said it was as if, as citizens, they didn't live in a democracy at all, and as if their votes served no purpose.

This democratic deficit and shared sense of anger and dislocation from national politics I observed was evidenced in a number of broader ways during 2013, including the rise in popularity of the anti-Europe party UKIP, which had been tapping into working-class disillusionment with those in power. The extent of the fury and disenchantment was also apparent in a survey carried out by the polling group ICM[49] just before

Christmas that showed the degree to which trust in politicians had sunk to a new low. The survey found that almost half the electorate (47 per cent) said they were angry with politicians while 46 per cent said the reason they wouldn't vote was because they believed politicians were 'on the take'. Sixty-four per cent said politicians didn't keep their promises. Only 2 per cent were 'inspired' by politicians.

Another thing I encountered travelling around the country was the utter bewilderment that a government in the sixth richest nation on earth was eviscerating the social safety net for its poorest citizens. I also witnessed the tremendous resilience, hope and defiance people demonstrated even when cut after cut was affecting their capacity to manage from day to day, and the degree to which people clung to their dignity while the media and politicians were painting them as 'skivers'.

In 2012 and 2013, as I went from place to place, I watched as the social security system that had protected much of the population from the worst vagaries of inequality was being ripped from its foundations. And I saw at first hand how destabilised and fearful it was leaving people. What I observed during my travels was a society in deep existential as well as economic and political flux. It seemed to me that austerity was generating social and economic schisms faster than they could be tracked, never mind adequately countered. There was a sense of an expanding segregation of the rich and poor, the entrenchment of a 'them and us' view of the world that produced not only a lack of social contact but also a political gap so wide as to seem unbridgeable. Everyone spoke of how the rich seemed to keep getting richer at the expense of the poor. The most vulnerable people of all often seemed to be completely at sea, lost in a tidal wave of upheaval and relentless vilification by those in power.

As the hours of interviews began to mount up it occurred to me that the 18 separate reports I was originally commissioned to write couldn't possibly house all of the prescient material I'd accumulated. Nor could they offer it a wider context. The people I interviewed had a lot say and they wanted to be heard. Many of them felt that they were helpless in the face of the government's enormous PR machine (which to many included much of the media). This book is an attempt to help those people be heard and to do a little to redress the balance.

One afternoon in early 2013, as a group interview was drawing to a close in Northern Ireland, a woman turned and looked me straight in the eye and said: "I hope whoever in power reads this or hears what we have to say is really listening. Because this is people's lives we're talking about." I hope they're listening too.

A short note about the author

In a special edition of *Prospect* magazine that posed the question 'Poverty in the UK: can it be eradicated?' published at the end of 2013,[50] the economist Diane Coyle hit on something that resonated with me. In the article she wrote: 'Unfortunately, it is hard for those who are not poor – which includes economists – to understand fully how social exclusion affects people. The poverty trap is not just financial, not just a matter of material access to services or housing, but a social and emotional trap too. Even if you think you appreciate that point, it is all but impossible to put yourself in another person's shoes.'

One of the lesser-discussed facts about reporting on poverty or austerity is that the media, like politics, is largely populated by people who are not from poor backgrounds.[51] This may go some way to explaining why so much coverage is negative, and why journalists are so quick to propagate what Professor Danny Dorling called 'the homogenising myth of our times' – that the poor are so because it is their own 'undeserving' fault.[52] It is an obvious point to make, but first-hand experience of issues is in no way a pre-requisite for journalists – if it were, hardly anything would get covered. But for me, in the case of writing about poverty and the welfare state, my first-hand experience has informed my work.

When I go into deprived communities and talk to people who are struggling, it feels almost like going home. I don't have to put myself in someone else's shoes because those *were* my shoes until, at the age of 18, I escaped 'the poverty trap' Coyle referred to. Thanks in part to outstanding teachers and visionary schools that taught my fellow pupils and I that we had as much right to aspiration and achievement as people from wealthier backgrounds, I was the first person from my family to go to university, and the first in my inner-city comprehensive to get into Oxbridge. Because of this it matters deeply to me that young people from disadvantaged backgrounds are given opportunities on an equal footing with their wealthier counterparts. It matters to me that the current and future generations of poor children are not relegated to the margins of society and made to feel like they or their families are skivers – as was so vigorously being preached by austerians and neoliberal elites in Austerity UK.

When I was 10 my father, a 36-year-old bricklayer who had worked every day since he left school at 14, became unemployed due to health difficulties within the family. He never worked again. Despite our family's misfortune, thanks to the welfare state I was able to live in a home fit to be lived in because we were provided with a council house that meant we had basic amenities like an indoor toilet and bathroom. Thanks to the welfare state I had libraries to go to and a nutritious free meal at school every day. I had free eye tests and a subsidised school uniform. I was able to fulfil my potential because the welfare state provided me with some of the essentials in life. It gave me a fighting chance.

What is so rarely understood – and what was under direct attack during austerity – is that the welfare state is not about dependency: it is about opportunity. Done well it is a life raft when times are tough and is a springboard to better things.

The social safety net envisaged at the end of the Second World War and supported and upheld by successive governments over many decades was designed for that purpose. It was a potent signal that we had moved on from less enlightened times, and that fairness and justice had a central place in our government and our society.

I consider myself to be a graduate of the welfare state – and I am proud of it. I know the crippling shame of poverty and what it feels like to internalise that shame, but I also know the liberation of moving beyond it and therefore why supporting those less fortunate within our society is not just desirable, but necessary. We all do better if our poorest citizens do better – it is the most fundamental riposte to neoliberal individualism and to austerity.

In the course of researching and writing this book and observing the impact of the welfare state being systematically dismantled, I have become more convinced than ever of its importance, its nobility and its role as a force for good. Yes, it could be improved. Yes, it needs to adapt. But to lose it? That would be an indictment of us all, and an inexcusable betrayal of future generations.

ONE

Money's too tight to mention

Food poverty: austerity made visible

The austerity drive in Britain isn't really about debt and deficits at all; it's about using deficit panic as an excuse to dismantle social programs. (Paul Krugman, recipient of the Nobel Prize for Economics, in *The New York Times*, May 2012)

"As far as I'm concerned if you have to go to a church and ask for food it's going back to Victorian times. I've never stolen anything in my life but I think I'd rather steal than have to go, cap in hand. It's begging for food!" (Debbie, Croxteth, Liverpool, Spring 2013)

Rapid rise of food banks

The women hovering outside St Peter's Church Hall on the Braunstone estate on the outskirts of Leicester are chatting among themselves, corralling boisterous children and clearly enjoying some rare sunshine on a chilly autumn day. They are waiting to be called inside, where they'll be able to enjoy a cup of tea and talk some more. However, for all the congeniality in the churchyard, this is not an afternoon club or a church fete the

—

women are waiting to get into. It's a food bank. And they are here because, like hundreds of thousands more all over the UK, they are struggling to make ends meet and are turning to food banks for essential items to help feed themselves and their families.

It's October 2012, right at the beginning of my journey through Austerity UK, and a few months after the proliferation of food banks began to attract widespread news coverage and debate. This particular food bank was operated twice a month by a local voluntary organisation, The Braunstone Foundation. The food being packed into bags by the bustling volunteers inside the church hall was supplied by FareShare,[1] a national charity that sources and distributes supermarket food that is earmarked for landfill and redistributes it to those in need, with the help of a variety of grassroots groups.

The women gathered at St Peter's are only too happy to talk about why they find themselves queuing in the cold for food. They are open and forthright, telling of how they never thought they'd see the day this would happen – never mind be commonplace – in one of the richest countries in the world.

'Eileen': "With not much money about if you're on benefits, you're [living] hand to mouth. And if your bills come through? Sometimes you're trying to pay your bills as well as buy your food. And what's happening with the housing ['Bedroom Tax'], you're going to have to [pay] your rent and then end up in arrears. But your biggest thing is food. Rent comes second. It's horrendous what [the government] are bringing in.... But if your kid needs a new pair of shoes?"

'Angela': "A lot of people live on the poverty line so [the food bank] does help them out a bit. It's a really good thing that there is a Food Share."

'Deirdre': "You're left to fend for yourself. There's a lot of people who can't get out and so we go and deliver the food to them which is good."

Inside the church hall the bags go swiftly. Some people enter, pick up supplies and leave right away, embarrassed expressions on their faces. Others stay and chat, eating cake made by the vicar's wife. Two young teenage volunteers helping to lay out bags of food on the wooden trestle tables explain that they don't want to be formally interviewed because they are humiliated at needing to fetch food for their mother. They volunteer, they explain, because by doing so they feel the food has been earned. It is not a hand-out that way, they say. And it helps mitigate some of the stigma of what could be seen as begging. There is no sign whatsoever of people taking food (as ministers repeatedly alleged) not out of need but because it was available.

The vicar, Chris Burch, talks about how, largely due to £50 million in cash pumped into the community under the previous government through its New Deal for Communities,[2] much of the 15,000-person-strong estate has been regenerated and spruced up over the previous decade. It was (and remains) an area of considerable deprivation, he says, but the government grant had helped to re-energise the community. He goes on to explain that in 2010 worries began to emerge about how the economic downturn and government policies were affecting people's budgets. In essence, he wanted to know "whether we were going to be looking at food poverty" – which wasn't an issue previously. Within months of setting up the food bank demand was soaring, with more than 300 local people using the services regularly by October 2012. "I had no idea we'd be doing this," Burch says. "It's hard that it has to happen but it's good that we are able to make it happen."

The Braunstone food bank was just one of hundreds that sprang up all over the UK following the economic downturn that began in 2008. They became ubiquitous in some communities and were regarded by many people as one of the most potent manifestations of austerity and the hardship it wrought. The mushrooming need for food banks was brought up by interviewees in almost every location visited for this book, with many of them stressing that it wasn't only people who were unemployed or officially below the poverty line using them, but also people in work who were underemployed or on low pay.

According to Angie Wright, chief officer of The Braunstone Foundation, the multiple factors prompting people to turn to food banks and the speed with which demand was soaring caught even the most experienced community workers off guard. "It's not just people who are on benefits who are struggling. People are coming in and saying 'we are stuck, we need a bit of help'." She added: "I've been shocked. I've not seen anything like this before."

Food banks unquestionably became one of the most visible totems on the austerity landscape – what one voluntary sector chief executive remarked was fast becoming "the new normal". So common had they become by December 2012 that the UK Prime Minister, David Cameron, lauded food bank volunteers as exponents of his 'Big Society' initiative,[3] but critics countered that they represented nothing short of a return to a 'Dickensian' model of welfare, where the state retreats from its most basic responsibilities and charities and churches are left to pick up the pieces.[4] (David Cameron's 'Big Society' vision was to devolve central decision-making to local areas and to 'empower' local people and communities to take responsibility for their own services. This 'localism' agenda coincided with the drastic reduction in funding to local authorities – and the resulting reduction in funding to local charities and service groups. The policy has been criticised as simply a means of justifying reduced government spending on services.)

—

Use of food banks had snowballed thanks to mounting pressures on household finances caused by, among other things, job cuts, wage stagnation, spiralling utility and shopping bills, and a panoply of austerity-driven benefits changes including the application of sanctions. There were, of course, people in need prior to the financial crisis and the Coalition government's cuts programme, as the government's own statistics bear out,[5,6] as well as a considerable body of research on poverty by JRF and many others.[7,8] And while there is evidence that under the Labour government inroads were being made on child poverty in particular,[9,10] and that tax credits went some way towards alleviating at least some financial pain, many people nevertheless had to survive on very low incomes. Indeed, food banks existed pre-recession to help some of the people for whom poverty and pecuniary anxieties were part of everyday life, as well as for people with temporary problems who slipped between self-sufficiency and need because of temporary unemployment, for example.

However, the growth of food banks – especially during 2012 and 2013 as cuts really began to bite – was as startling as it was exponential. While the general economic outlook was slightly better by the end of 2013 compared with a year earlier,[11] growth was still well below post-recession historical trends, and the real 'growth industry' in the UK, it seemed, was food poverty. Throughout 2012 and 2013 numerous reports appeared documenting how hundreds of thousands of people were turning to food banks out of desperation. One early article in *The Guardian*, published in July 2012, highlighted the plight of people resorting to food banks in Coventry, one of which ran out of food so high was demand.[12] It reported:

> A man arrives in the rain, very distressed to see the No Food sign. This afternoon he has walked three miles from his home to collect a food parcel, arriving just after the session began,

—

but because he had no ID on him, he then had to walk a mile into the centre of town to get a letter from a charity certifying that he is who he claims to be, and then walk a mile back to be issued with some food. His benefits have been stopped for reasons that are not clear to him, and he faces the prospect of a three-mile walk home again, with no food and no money, until volunteers agree to let him join the crowd of 30 people still waiting in the church's cafe, and promise to find him something to take away. "There's nothing at home. If I don't get this food I'll end up shoplifting," he says.

An article in the tabloid *Mirror* two months earlier titled 'Our hidden poor'[13] reported on the grim circumstances pushing more and more people towards food charities:

> The young couple trudge into the church hall looking gaunt, meek and beaten. They have walked for three miles in heavy rain, their thin clothing so drenched it sticks to their skin as they huddle by a radiator for warmth. Across the room, a 34-year-old mother weeps into her hands as her shopping trolley is filled with food which will stop her two children going to bed that night with hunger pains. Over by the racks of second-hand jackets, shirts and jumpers on sale for 20p each, sit two jobless men without a penny in their pockets, pondering how the three-day emergency rations they've just been handed can last a week-and-a-half.
>
> Behind them a smartly dressed couple who've never been on benefits before suffer the indignity of explaining how they have lost their jobs and home and cannot feed their three kids.

If the *Mirror*'s report seems hyperbolic, the figures suggest this is not without justification. In the months that I travelled across the UK there was a marked escalation in demand with people in need being referred to food banks in alarming numbers by a whole range of statutory agencies, from GP surgeries to jobcentres.[14] In the 12 months to April 2013, even before the government's most drastic benefits changes were formally rolled out, approximately 3,400 tonnes of food were donated to food banks, according to the UK's largest emergency food provider, The Trussell Trust. (Over 90 per cent of donations come from members of the public.) By March 2013 the charity was running 345 food banks, with an average of three new ones opening every week. On the eve of April 2013, just as a plethora of major welfare reforms began to roll out, including caps on some benefits, The Trust reported staggering increases in demand.

There was a 76 per cent surge in the number of new Trussell Trust food banks, while established food banks reported 'significant rises' in footfall. The Trust published figures showing the biggest leap in requests for emergency food since it was established in 2000. Almost 350,000 people were in receipt of at least three days' worth of emergency food from the food banks in the 12 months to March 2013, more than three times the number assisted in the previous 12 months (128,697) and 100,000 more than anticipated. Since 2009/10 the number of people helped had jumped more than eight-fold, from a base of 41,000.[15]

And it wasn't just The Trussell Trust reporting rises in demand. Research for Church Action on Poverty with Oxfam in May 2013 warned that the numbers using food banks was already as high as half a million and was likely to increase further; it called the trend 'a national disgrace'.[16] And in August 2013 Citizens Advice published a report revealing that there had been a 78 per cent leap in enquiries about food banks at their offices in every region of the UK in the previous six months.[17]

Meanwhile FareShare, the organisation supplying food to the Braunstone food bank for distribution, was also publishing stark figures. In May 2013 the organisation reported what it referred to as 'shocking new figures' showing that it had fed over 43,700 people daily during the previous 12 months – 7,200 per day more than the preceding year.[18] Even more ominously, it found that more than one third of the charities it distributed food through were reeling from funding cuts themselves, and over two thirds (70 per cent) feared demand would surge in the year ahead.

Releasing the results, Lindsay Boswell, FareShare chief executive officer, said: "Last year we fed more people than ever before but we know the demand for our services is increasing at an alarming rate. The recession, rising cost of living and unemployment all mean there are more people turning to charities for food than at any other time in FareShare's history."

Trussell Trust's chief executive, Chris Mould, called the skyrocketing demand his organisation had seen 'a wake-up call'. This is how he summed up the situation:

> "The sheer volume of people who are turning to food banks because they can't afford food is a wake-up call to the nation that we cannot ignore the hunger on our doorstep. Politicians across the political spectrum urgently need to recognise the real extent of UK food poverty and create fresh policies that better address the underlying causes."[19]

Crucially, he continued, the variety of people needing help was much broader than in the pre-austerity, pre-banking crisis past:

> "Incomes are being squeezed to breaking point. We're seeing people from all kinds of backgrounds turning to food banks: working people coming in on their lunch breaks, mums who are going hungry to feed their children, people whose benefits have been delayed and people who are struggling to find enough work. It's shocking that people are going hungry in 21st-century Britain."

Food poverty: a public health crisis in the making?

The ballooning of food banks came against a wider backdrop of concerns about food poverty throughout the UK and the shocking practice of parents increasingly sacrificing their own nutritional needs in order to feed their children as money became tighter and inflation put upward pressure on food prices.[20] As 2013 progressed, the disturbingly dystopic phrase 'heat or eat' became common parlance as the levels of desperation increased.

Research has documented patterns and trends in food poverty in the UK over time,[21] but a formidable body of evidence built up during austerity proved that the situation had been made markedly worse by austerity and its fallout.[22] A study conducted by the Centre for Economic and Business Research for Kellogg's, published in March 2013, suggested a significantly deteriorating situation.[23] It found that people in the UK were spending 20 per cent more on food but eating less, with the poorest in society cutting down on fresh food to make ends meet. It estimated that 4.7 million people in the UK lived in food poverty and projected that worse lay ahead, with the average annual UK household food bill set to rise by £357 over the five years from 2013–18.

By the end of 2013 the situation with food poverty had become so bad that a group of leading public health experts wrote a letter to the *British Medical Journal* saying it had 'all the signs of a public health emergency that could go unrecognised until it is too late to take preventative action'. The signatories, who included academics and scientists from University College London's Institute of Child Health and the Medical Research Council, said that a delay in the publication of government research on the impact of rising demand for emergency food led them to conclude that the cause was related to the rising cost of living and 'austere' changes to social security. They called for urgent monitoring of the effects of austerity policies on the health and nutritional status of vulnerable groups. Referring

—

to the narrow range of foodstuffs consumed by people on low incomes, they warned: 'Malnutrition in children is particularly worrying because exposures during sensitive periods can have lifelong effects.'[24]

Despite such warnings ministers blamed increased media coverage and the growing number of food banks, not strains on incomes, for the rise in the numbers using them despite frontline workers repeatedly telling them this was not the case. When it surveyed users of its services, Trussell Trust acquired specific feedback on the real reasons so many were in need in 2012/13 compared to 2011/12 – and it wasn't because of greater media coverage. The figure below shows the reasons people gave The Trussell Trust for needing emergency food supplies in the 12 months to April 2013. Low incomes and debt accounted for a significant proportion (almost a third of all cases cited these reasons), with 14.65 per cent attributing the spur to changes to the benefits system and 4.29 per cent to being refused emergency loans ordinarily available from government funds to tide them over. By far the largest single category was delays in payment of benefits – at 29.69 per cent – resulting from the complex overhaul of the benefits and jobseeking systems.

This was clear proof that it wasn't just a *lack* of money compelling people to turn to food banks but additional austerity-related pressures pushing people into food poverty. A sizeable portion were forced to turn to emergency food because of late payment of benefits to which they were actually entitled and (increasingly) sanctions, whereby claimants could be without benefits for weeks on end if they did not comply with strict new regulations on jobseeking. The new benefit sanctions regime came into force on 22 October 2012 and introduced a four-week sanction of benefits for the first offence with up to a maximum of three years' sanction of benefits for 'higher level' offences.[25] On 19 September 2013 the government announced the appointment of an independent reviewer into benefit sanctions, Matthew Oakley, due to report in Spring 2014.[26] There was a great deal of confusion and distress about the circumstances under which sanctions could be legitimately handed down, how harsh the new regime was, and considerable bewilderment at how to appeal against sanctions once given. Organisations such as Citizens Advice were inundated with panicked people who had been santioned and left without vital cash. When the government announced its intention to introduce a seven-day delay before qualifying for benefits payments in June 2013,[27] this was seen as yet another way to pummel the poor – a kind of 'pre-emptive sanction' – and one that would only increase food poverty further.

Voucher distribution by type of crisis

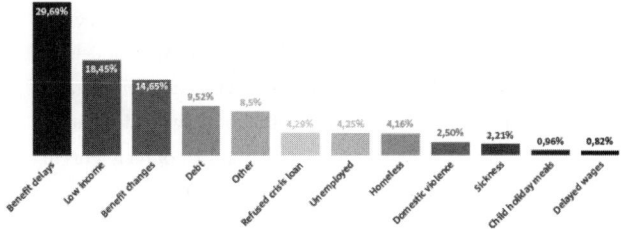

Source: The Trussell Trust, April 2013

However, if food poverty and the food banks that resulted were sensitive issues prior to April 2013, once the biggest tranche of changes to social security were introduced in 2013, they became even more so. As the numbers using food banks rose to historic levels, ministers appeared more out of touch than ever as they avoided attributing this to benefits cuts. In July 2013 in the House of Lords the tone was firmly set by Work and Pensions Minister, Lord Freud, who claimed disingenuously that there was no link between the floods of people turning to food banks and the government's welfare changes, saying that if free food was available, then of course people would seek it out.[28] The assumption was promptly refuted and the minister was accused of ignoring the evidence from multiple sources, including The Trussell Trust. Freud (who had also served as a minister in the previous Labour administration) was castigated as being spectacularly out of touch by a host of critics.[29] Not long after Lord Freud's intervention, The Trussell Trust published a new set of figures, for the first quarter of the new financial year 2013/14. This was the three months that immediately followed the massive rolling out of benefits cuts and social security reforms. The outcome? A 200 per cent increase in the number of people receiving help from food banks. This is how *The Guardian* reported it:[30]

> More than half of the 150,000 people receiving emergency food aid from Trussell food banks between April and June were referred because of benefit delays, sanctions, and financial difficulties relating to the Bedroom Tax and abolition of council tax relief, it said. The total number of recipients in the same three months last year was 50,000.

It goes on:

> Trussell's first-quarter findings challenge the government's insistence that there is no link between welfare changes and the rapid increase in food bank use.... Nearly one in five (19%) of all referrals to Trussell food banks in the three months to June related to benefit changes – up from 12% during the same period in 2012, the trust said. Benefit delays accounted for 33% of referrals, up from 31%.

A few months later, the *Daily Mail*, ordinarily a cheerleader for the Conservative Party and paper-in-chief when it came to disparaging people on benefits, outed the Education Secretary, Michael Gove, for blaming poor people for their circumstances, and set off a Twitter storm of condemnation about how removed from reality ministers were.[31] The only reason people were going to food banks, Mr Gove said, was because they weren't managing their personal finances well enough. The paper reported:

> Mr Gove had said: "I appreciate that there are families who face considerable pressures. Those pressures are often the result of decisions that they have taken which mean they are not best able to manage their finances. We need to ensure that support is not just financial, and that the right decisions are made."

In response, Labour politician and Shadow Minister for Public Health, Luciana Berger, 'vehemently' disagreed with Gove, saying "People I have met are ashamed to have to turn to food banks. I vehemently disagree it is because they have mismanaged their finances. This government has got no answer to the millions of parents that are really struggling to get by." And Citizens Advice chief executive, Gillian Guy, said: "It is appalling to suggest the rise of food banks is due to poor financial management."

Just a few months later in Wales, where use of food banks had risen considerably, Tory MP for the Vale of Glamorgan, Alun Cairns, also found himself in the firing line when he claimed people turned to food banks for "a variety of reasons", including mismanaging their finances and due to drug and alcohol addictions.[32]

The front line of food poverty: a new normal?

As I travelled the country there was a growing awareness that something unprecedented was taking place. People who had lived on or near the poverty line their whole lives were telling me

—

they had never seen anything like it, and how every week there seemed to be a new food bank opening up. It appeared to many that a creeping normalisation of food poverty was taking place and that the state was abdicating any responsibility for it. Indeed, by the end of 2013 an article in *The Independent* by Luciana Berger[33] challenged such normalisation. Its headline declared:

> We must not normalise food banks. Their proliferation is a mark of shame on this country.

Earlier in the year Tim Lang, Professor of Food Policy at City University and a former adviser to the Department for Environment, Food and Rural Affairs and the World Health Organization (WHO), warned that ministers could allow charitable food banks to become 'institutionalised' as an alternative to state support: 'The rise of food banks risks eroding the state safety net as politicians endorse a "Dickensian" model of welfare'.[34]

In Croxteth, Liverpool, in spring 2013, long-time local residents and community workers gathered in a local community centre spoke of the multiple ways austerity was hitting them and their community, and the spread of food poverty was one of their primary concerns. Croxteth, ranked 12,615 out of 12,775 parishes in England in terms of poverty,[35] is hardly new to financial adversity, but once the government's cuts programme began there was a palpable sense that austerity was having a corrosive effect on daily life and on people's ability to manage financially and, in some cases, their ability to feed themselves and their children. There was considerable anger at any suggestion by politicians or the press that the need for food banks was down to anything other than poverty made worse by austerity. This is what one of the women, Debbie, had to say:

"I've always been aware of radio appeals for toys at Christmas, always been aware of people needing help and charity donations. But I've never ever come across anybody who had to access it personally, or who had to use a food bank. I think in this day and age, its just quite appalling that anybody has to go and ask for food to feed their children because of the cuts that are happening...."

She goes on:

"As far as I'm concerned if you have to go to a church and ask for food it's going back to Victorian times. No one is a scrounger who goes to a food bank. I've never stolen anything in my life but I think I'd rather steal than have to go, cap in hand, where there's a chance you'll see someone you know. It's begging for food! Everyone's got a basic right to live. And its not just people on benefits who are struggling, it's people who are working."

According to staff and volunteers at food banks,[36] the likelihood of yet greater numbers of people turning to them – and straining limited resources – was a growing concern after April 2013 and particularly as benefits sanctions, delays to payments and the disappearance of crisis loans began to seriously hit home.[37] Evidence mounted that escalating numbers of benefits claimants and people on low incomes were being referred to food banks by statutory bodies that would previously have been able to offer monetary assistance (or refer people to agencies that could provide it) in the form of interest-free loans or grants to purchase food in an emergency.[38]

And there was another dimension to the phenomenon. Many observers were pointing out that while people given financial assistance in the form of a crisis loan could at least choose what food to buy and when, with the vouchers (generally) provided to attend food banks, people tended to be more or less stuck with what was handed out, thereby having no say over the nutritional balance. Here's how one report in Scotland put it:[39]

> Vouchers provided by the trust are now used instead of crisis loans to give people an emergency three-day supply of food. Crisis loans, which as part of the ConDems welfare cuts, were quietly 'devolved' to local authority control in April of this year.
>
> The harsh reality is that cash-strapped local authorities now distribute vouchers for the Trussell Trust instead of a small amount of money which an individual could use to choose the type of food they would like to eat.

Politics of food poverty

Another worry for those handing out emergency food – and remember that these were voluntary or church-run organisations that largely relied on public donations – was the fact that everyone was being told that yet more pain was in store as further cuts were scheduled for the years ahead. The wider economic and political backdrop to food poverty and emergency food provision was crucial to how things were unfolding. At the beginning of the financial crisis, politicians were tripping over one another to remind people that real economic recovery was a long way off, and to brace themselves for the worst. For the first two years it was a matter of the then Labour government engaging in damage limitation, with the former Chancellor, Alistair Darling, taking steps to 'save' the banking sector and pursuing a policy of stimulating the economy with a £20 billion spending package funded by efficiency savings and increased government borrowing.[40]

After the election of the Coalition government two years later, the electorate was told that the only way to 'fix' the country's problems was to cut, cut and cut some more rather than deploying an ongoing stimulus, as was the case in the US, and even after the economy began to grow.

To the despair of many people – and most certainly the poorest, including low-paid workers in receipt of benefits, thousands of whom found themselves standing in queues at food banks they never dreamed would exist – this austerity song was still being sung three-and-a-half years on. So long as the Eurozone remained in the doldrums, so long as so-called 'scroungers' found a way to dupe the benefits system into paying them to live the life of Riley, so long as the Coalition was 'cleaning up the mess left by the previous government',[41] or whatever other reason was touted for the stagnation of the economy and the scale of the public debt, times would be tough.

And it wasn't as if the Labour opposition was providing reassurance that things would be dramatically different if they came into power.[42] If anything, Labour remained timid for the first three years of austerity, tamed by the Tory 'austerity is the only way' juggernaut and a political blame game by the Tories that was remarkably effective. At the beginning of austerity, Labour's mantra that the government was cutting 'too deep, too fast' was nothing more than a rudderless sound bite that provided zero solace for those people rapidly running out of money to feed their families. Labour shadow ministers condemned the rise in food poverty and food banks, but in places like Braunstone this rang hollow because what people struggling to subsist were actually being told by the main opposition party was that austerity was inevitable – it was only a matter of degree.

Even when in the autumn of 2013 the Labour Leader, Ed Miliband, stepped up the focus on falling living standards, declaring that if elected to government the party would freeze energy prices,[43] the Coalition continued to haul the nation towards a wholesale culling of the welfare state with only the most feeble of retorts from Labour. If it wasn't for some individual

MPs and shadow ministers who went out of their way to highlight specific issues such as food poverty and who stood up to Tory jeers in Parliament about the extent of the problem,[44] there would have been a total void in mainstream national politics. (A recurring criticism against Labour at the time from those on the Left was that it was easy to criticise food poverty or individual austerity policies, but the Party was failing to offer a robust economic alternative or overarching case for adequate investment in the welfare state to protect vulnerable people.)

As if he deliberately wished to add to the general sense of despair among all but the very rich, the Chancellor of the Exchequer, George Osborne, with his evident eagerness to leverage political capital from any indication of economic improvement,[45] as a sign that things were heading in the right direction (or to use the Chancellor's own term, the economy was 'out of intensive care'), couldn't resist drumming home the fact that the cuts would keep on coming. In the same breath as declaring growth had returned and that areas such as the property market were on the up, he pontificated about how people (meaning poorer people) would have to pay a personal price for dealing with the deficit. But what was the point of growth if people still couldn't afford to put food on the table?

A Patrick Collinson pointed out in *The Guardian*: 'No amount of upbeat economic assessments and reports on rising house prices can disguise the cost of living crisis bewildering households across the country.'[46]

In September 2013, on the back of some good news about the economy, the Chancellor proclaimed in a bullish speech in the City of London that austerity was working, growth had returned and that his detractors were wrong – despite caution from some analysts on the type and extent of growth and being rounded on by critics for the fact that the small upturn had no impact on average earnings and did not represent a 'national' upswing, leaving whole chunks of the country behind.[47] But just in case he sounded too upbeat, he reminded people on the sharp end of cuts day in day out that, yes, more pain was yet to come: clearly teeing up for the election in 2015.[48] "More tough choices will be required after the next election to find many billions of further savings", he declared.

To the people I was interviewing it seemed as if the Chancellor and his political cabal were living, as one woman in the North East of England put it, "in a complete bubble", with no real grasp of what it meant to go hungry. I spoke to a mother in Newcastle who was trying to rebuild her life after fleeing a violent relationship and turning to a women's refuge. Her criticism of all the political parties was particularly adroit:

> "They live in a bubble. All of them. That kids have to go and get food parcels? It's unbelievable. They all sit down there in the House of Commons with their subsidised food and drink and yet people like me can't get emergency crisis payments. The mental strain is unbearable at times. Now I have to rely on food parcels. Government just doesn't get it. It's a miserable, hideous existence. It's not living; it's existing. And this is going to get so much worse."

But it wasn't just the government trumpeting the need for sticking with 'Plan A', regardless of the stunning degree to which people were being affected. There was the right-wing press[49] and there were right-wing think tanks.[50] And there were economists too, champions of austerity who piped up (some even declared that austerity had gone nowhere near far enough). In July 2013, the country's top civil servant (who, in theory, should be neutral), Cabinet Secretary Jeremy Heywood, warned that austerity was 'not a two-year project or a five-year project', but rather a 10- or 20-year 'generational battle' to restore the economy.[51] Addressing other senior civil servants at an event in London, he said:

—

"There is a very, very long way to go. We were reminded only last week that the economy as a whole remains about 4 per cent below the size that it was in 2008. Five years on from the bottom of the recession we have still not even near recovered all the output we lost in that terribly deep recession that we suffered in 2007–08. Those are really daunting numbers that just show the size of the challenge; there is no alternative."

In this context it is perhaps not surprising that Chris Mould referred to the situation with food banks as "a wake-up call". Indeed, by the autumn of 2013 there came further ominous signs of just how big the problem was becoming. The Trussell Trust released yet another report, this time for the six months from April 2013 to September 2013, which documented further rises in demand – up threefold on the same six months in 2012, prompting the charity to call for a formal inquiry.[52] A few weeks earlier – and for the first time since the Second World War – the Red Cross announced that it would be distributing food to Britain's needy that winter and that it was working with FareShare to collect and distribute food. The move came on the back of a report from the Red Cross that found a 75 per cent rise in the number of people across austerity-charred Europe turning to it for food aid for the year until October 2013.[53]

When the announcement was made, Chris Johnes, UK Poverty Director for Oxfam, told *The Independent* newspaper he was "genuinely shocked". "[The Red Cross] don't do things for reasons of grandstanding at all," he said. "The fact that they are doing this ... is a very clear signal how serious things have become." And, as if to crown off a year of unprecedented need, Citizens Advice reported in December 2013 that by the end of the year it would have given out more than 100,000 vouchers for emergency food – rising by a quarter every six months. A key reason for the increase? People being left without money due to benefits sanctions.[54]

—

As is often the way, amid the undeniable grimness there were some remarkably inventive responses to food poverty, such as Jack Monroe's blog, 'A Girl Called Jack',[55] in which a young single parent living on the breadline wrote and spoke about her struggles to eat nutritiously on a miniscule budget and also suggested recipes to help others make their money stretch a bit further. However, such was the hypersensitive politically charged nature of food poverty by 2013 (fuelled in part by the media lambasting people struggling financially for supposedly misspending or mismanaging what they did have and gorging on expensive ready meals[56]) that even Monroe came in for flak for daring to put herself 'out there' and to speak up for poorer people. Some on the Left accused her of glorifying food poverty[57, 58] while on the Right she ended up being (absurdly) lauded by austerity pushers as an example of how all the poor had to do was learn to cook and be virtuous like their counterparts in the past.[59] In November 2013 she was smeared in a breathtakingly inaccurate rant by *Daily Mail* right-wing columnist Richard Littlejohn, who tried to paint her as a 'benefits skiver'.[60] True to form, Monroe challenged Littlejohn's abuse head on, taking each of his misinformed points and debunking them.[61]

Jack Monroe did what a hundred formal reports couldn't – tell it like it was, first hand from the front line. But if her blog was an unusual response to austerity and poverty it spoke to a rising tide of dissatisfaction and desperation. In late September 2013 reports began appearing confirming that in some parts of the country the police were seeing a rise in the numbers of people stealing food staples. Under the headline 'Austerity Britain: Starving families "stealing meat and cheese" as cuts begin to bite', the *Mirror* newspaper reported starving families 'being forced to shoplift':[62]

> Lancashire Chief Constable Steve Finnigan said: "With regards shoplifting, we are seeing an increase. The offenders

are very often first-time offenders and when you talk to them, they are not doing this to sell stuff on. The stuff they talk about is food stuff. It is very often meat and cheese they are stealing and it is for themselves and their family."

In a Commons debate on food poverty at the end of 2013 (which the Secretary of State Iain Duncan Smith left after just one hour) former Labour Minister Fiona MacTaggart told of how some desperate people in her constituency had been fighting with each other for discounted food in a supermarket. She did so to heckles and taunts and laughter from the government benches.[63]

But while food poverty and food banks may have been among the most conspicuous indignities borne by people in the social and economic tapestry of Austerity UK, it turns out it was merely the tip of the iceberg. In many ways people's suffering remained a largely hidden experience, consisting of juggling shrinking household budgets that were under attack on two separate but related fronts: falling living standards generally and merciless reductions to benefits and public services.

There was no doubt at all after travelling the country and talking to people – and especially those in the most deprived communities – that people felt their suffering simply wasn't registering, that the government was disinclined to alter its path whatever the evidence. This was felt very strongly in St Peter's, Ashton, in central Manchester. As one of the top 5 per cent most deprived wards nationally, the area, despite some investment during the New Labour years, remains plagued by high rates of long-term unemployment and disability. Among a population of approximately 12,000, worklessness stood at 29.2 per cent in 2012, while the rate of child poverty hovered around 37 per cent, compared with a national average of 20.9 per cent for the whole of the UK.[64] People on the ground in Manchester were adamant that without a change of course on cuts – and without an end to food poverty – the consequences for current and future generations would be dire.

Catherine Hollingrake, a local housing worker, described what was being felt:

> "We've got very little income to start with. It's going to be
> a question of are we going to keep warm or are we going to
> feed ourselves? It's just going to be a nightmare."

The strain on living standards Hollingrake was referring to – motored in part by rising household bills, low pay and sparse employment opportunities – was drastically compounded by austerity policies, the composite impact of which have been relentless, brutal – and widespread.

TWO

The big squeeze

Financial insecurity: austerity and the erosion of household income

"We're told by the government that we are living well. I think we are scrimping to – I wouldn't say live – I would say survive, from week to week. I do not want to be living off hand-outs for the rest of my life. I don't want that. There's times and there's weeks where I have to go and borrow money off people and it's so [long pause to choke back tears], so degrading. Do I deserve better? Do other people deserve better? I think they do." ('Dec', 47-year-old man, Marsh Farm estate, Luton)

When government services are cut because of 'profligate spending', it will absolutely not be people at the top end of the income distribution who will be expected to tighten their belts. Rather it will be those who lie in the bottom 40% ... who haven't had a real wage increase since 1971. (Mark Blyth, *Austerity: The history of a dangerous idea*)

It's hard to watch someone you've only just met struggling to hold back tears. It's even harder when it happens three times in the course of a single interview. The sterile formality of the

—

meeting room in the local community centre on the Marsh Farm estate in Luton where the interview took place belied the abject distress 'Dec', a long-time community volunteer and lone parent, exhibited. As someone who obviously prided himself on his community work – and the community itself – Dec was visibly uncomfortable talking about how hard he was finding things.

Echoing interviewees all over the country, Dec explained that he was "doing the best" he could but that money was tighter than it had ever been, while finding the kind of stable, secure work that paid more than the Minimum Wage and gave people a chance of lifting themselves out of poverty was an uphill struggle. And, he said pointedly, if politicians were under any illusions about how much harder austerity was making things, they needed to dispense with them – fast. They needed to rid themselves too, he insisted, of the idea that people who rely on benefits to get by are somehow "playing the system" and living a cushy existence.

Referring to a statement by Iain Duncan Smith, Work and Pensions Secretary and architect of what is universally acknowledged as the biggest shake-up of the UK's welfare state[1,2] since its inception, that he could live off £53 a week if he had to, Dec was incredulous. Duncan Smith's claim, met at the time he uttered it in early 2013 with a media frenzy and hail of criticism including calls for him to put his money where his mouth was, upset thousands. An online petition for him to live on £53 garnered over 475,000 signatures.[3]

As with many other people interviewed, Dec was furious that a Cabinet with 18 out of 29 millionaires in it[4] was telling people 'living on the breadline' that they had plenty. This is what he had to say:

> "I would challenge him. I will make him this promise – if
> he can come along and live on £53 a week for a month I

will give him my dole money back for a year.... Because he's talking bullshite."

He continued:

> "I have to shop around between all the major supermarkets and corner shops and I know that eggs that were £1.39 this time last year are now £2.19 pence....There's no point in a millionaire telling me that I'm doing well by getting a 1% rise ... on my £77 [benefits] that I'm getting. Luxuries? What are luxuries? Out of touch? I'm sure [ministers] are all smoking weed they're that far out."

(A three-year cap on benefit rises was announced in January 2013: 'There will be a three-year cap of 1% – which is below the expected rise in the cost of living – on most working-age benefits and tax credits for three years from 2013/14. Child benefit, housing benefit and universal credit will be capped for two years from 2014/15.'[5])

Further north in Croxteth, the women I interviewed said the situation, even for people in work, was becoming increasingly fragile, and that the government was failing to grasp the impact this was having. This is what one of the women had to say:

> "It's more about despair. I live in Norris Green. And it's social housing. Everybody in Norris Green, whether you're working or not, you're one step away from being in the same boat. It's the majority of people who are on low incomes that [austerity] is affecting. They like to say ... it's the scroungers ... it's the out of workers lying at home with the curtains drawn watching Jeremy Kyle on the television. The majority of people that this is affecting are out there every day working."

In the spring of 2013, at an after-school club in the Southmead estate in Bristol in the west of England, the raucous laughter of toddlers filled the air in what was a very popular free service. Some of the mothers talked about how changes to social security benefits were beginning to really hurt, and how increases in the cost of living were punishing for people already struggling to get by. Southmead is an area with high unemployment and high levels of deprivation, so the women were especially cognisant of managing a tight budget in a climate of unstable work and rising prices for staple goods and utilities. All were pleased that their free after-school club was still around when many other local services were facing the axe, but feared it might not be around much longer, forcing them to pay for childcare. This is how one mother of two described her strategy for making money go further:

> "For some people it's really hard. Doing the shopping you get three packs of meat for a tenner. I do a big shop every two weeks, set out meals. I'll keep the meat for sandwiches and stuff the next day. You've got to because otherwise you ain't got enough money to go out and buy fresh meat every day. It's just too expensive."

Joan Bennett, a retired postal worker who has lived in Southmead since the 1960s, and is a regular attendee at the community centre where the after-school club takes place, talked at length about how hard it was to watch young families struggle:

> "I'm glad I'm not bringing up my children now to be truthful. A lot of the food has gone up in price. But with rent increases every year, council tax increases, water [increasing] every year, gas, electricity? I don't know how young mums manage to budget – probably day by day. But it only needs

a birthday or a new pair of shoes needed and that's gone out the window."

Income and household budgets: why pressure was mounting

In the course of criss-crossing the country for this book, financial woes were paramount. It was almost possible to see the weight it was placing on people's shoulders. When stripped down, the concerns among those at the sharp end were threefold. First, increases in the prices of essential everyday goods meant the pound in people's pockets was not stretching as far as it had done even a couple of years before – whether they were in work or not. One of the main culprits was the cost of fuel and electricity, which had more than doubled (up 234 per cent) since 2000, and had steadily made it harder for poorer people to heat their homes adequately, as did the rise in the cost of food.[6] (Both food and fuel increases were directly linked to the value of the pound plummeting after the bank bailouts of 2008, making imports more expensive.[7])

Second, where work was available, too much of it was part time, low paid, unstable, or came with no guarantee of hours – a phenomenon meticulously documented in the book *Poverty and insecurity: Life in low-pay, no-pay Britain*,[8] which describes the unremitting 'churn' of hundreds of thousands of people from benefits to underpaid, undervalued jobs and back again – often for years. Even when the Minimum Wage was increased in October 2013 in accordance with the Low Pay Commission's recommendations from April in the same year, unions warned that the small increase would do little to ease the burden. General Secretary of the Union of Shop, Distributive and Allied Workers (Usdaw), John Hannett, commented: "Whilst this is a welcome increase of almost 2 per cent, it does not keep pace with inflation, currently 2.7 per cent. There is no doubt that rising bills and low

—

wages mean that life is getting harder for millions of families, with average pay having fallen in 38 out of 39 months since the 2010 General Election."

And third, austerity-driven reforms of social security were defeating even the most diligent low-income household budget managers, not only because they were so severe, introduced at rapid speed and often inadequately administered, but because multiple cuts and caps often affected the same group of people, with grim consequences. It was, for want of a more benign description, a cuts 'clusterfuck' that was tipping hundreds of thousands of people into abject need. For example, a piece of research by the New Policy Institute in 2013 found that around two thirds of households hit by the 'Bedroom Tax' (an extremely controversial financial penalty placed on people in social housing who were deemed to be 'over-occupying' by having more rooms than the government believed they needed) also experienced cuts to Council Tax Benefit, resulting in an average of £16.90 less income per week. In addition, almost two thirds of the 2.6 million families affected by one of the benefit cuts were also expected to see a fall in real terms in other benefits, due to the below-inflation 1 per cent cap in benefit rises.[9]

It was these kinds of cuts – the ones that stripped people with very little money of much-needed regular financial assistance – that were the straw that was fast breaking the collective camel's back. Claims by Coalition ministers that the pain – or 'belt-tightening' as they liked to call it – was absolutely essential simply didn't cut it with those suffering. With each passing month through 2012 and 2013, as yet more austerity policies were introduced – including cuts to vital services by local authorities – there was a noticeable escalation in anxiety among the people interviewed about austerity, as the predictions about the harm the cuts would do over time began to really hit home.

As one community worker in a deprived part of inner-city Belfast put it: "You see the impact [of austerity] on an already vulnerable person and a politician telling them it's going to get worse and they can't imagine that. They can't imagine how anything could be worse than what they are currently experiencing." One resident and welfare worker from the same part of the city summed it up: "If you look at people walking up and down the road they're not living, they're just existing. You can see it in their faces. They are worn out. On the streets it's called survival."

From rural Northumberland to the Home Counties to Glasgow and the Welsh Valleys, whether it was rural villages, inner cities, commuter towns or suburbs, the people interviewed for this book universally spoke of the financial peril of surviving in Austerity UK, and of how drastically their incomes were being squeezed. Terms such as 'breaking point' and 'desperate situation' came up in every location. Frontline community workers spoke of how escalating bills and benefits changes were squeezing household finances to such a degree (to say nothing of the bewildering task of trying to understand the myriad changes) that it meant many people were 'hiding their heads in the sand' and 'living day-to-day' because even to think of how much more they would have to endure might push them over the edge. As Gary Parsons, an interviewee who lived in the inner-city London borough of Tower Hamlets (listed as the third most deprived area in the country), put it:

> "To me people just seem to get poorer and poorer. We get a kick in the teeth every time. It's going to get worse."

At the other end of England in the village of Lynemouth in rural Northumberland, an area that at the end of 2012 had seen its largest local employer – the Alcan aluminium smelting plant – shut down with the loss of over 500 jobs, local resident and credit union worker, Alec Crumplin, reported people buckling under the pressure. He said:

"I am seeing people on a day-to-day basis in dire financial trouble, more and more people who can no longer make ends meet. Not just people on benefits but working people as well, where one little bill is enough to topple them over the edge and leave them in a situation where they've got no hope of being able to survive the rest of the month."

He continues:

"As bills are going up people are finding it harder to pay for their heating. People who were comfortable last year are in dire need of just getting something for the kids for Christmas. People are struggling to pay their rent; they're struggling to pay their mortgage. I know every time I go to the supermarket it's going to cost me a bit more. I dread to think what my gas and electricity bills are going to be after the winter. I know a lad in his 50s who, by the time he's paid his rent, lives in one room. He said he'd be better off in prison because he'd get three meals a day."

On the Easterhouse estate on the outskirts of Glasgow, Pauline Smith, a manager at Connect Community Trust,[10] which provides a range of services to local people including employment and debt advice, pointed out that many people were failing to grasp the full extent of austerity policies – because they didn't dare contemplate it.

"I think they are putting their heads in the sand. We've seen people coming through who are actually accessing food banks now – it's really hitting home that they've not had money for two weeks. How do you live without money for two weeks? So they are ... not realising what the impact is going to be long-term."

(The Easterhouse estate was the same location where, in 2002, Iain Duncan Smith – the minister responsible for many of the austerity policies pushing people into poverty – had his infamous 'epiphany' about how hard it was for people to live in poverty that convinced him (pre-Coalition) to set up his think tank, The Centre for Social Justice, to examine alternative approaches to fighting poverty.[11])

When it came to the *way* in which austerity policies were being introduced and the subsequent impact on household budgets, Pauline Smith had a number of reservations:

> "I just think they're doing way too much way too soon. You can't have a blanket approach for absolutely everything. People's circumstances are very different, y'know?"

Local Easterhouse resident Eddie Andrews, who after volunteering for Connect Community Trust eventually secured employment, suggested part of the reason austerity was wreaking so much havoc was down to the way it was being implemented and its inherent lack of fairness:

> "It's as if they just cast a net out. I think it's populist as well, the way it's going to hammer people [on] benefits for a vote winner. Look at the other issues like tax avoidance that could be done quite quickly."

Meanwhile, in Ladywood, Birmingham, a number of residents anxiously spoke of what the future might hold for families on low incomes and for the most vulnerable people in particular. Many appeared mystified by the way the government was going about its cuts programme. Not only was it all-encompassing and savage, they said, it was also deliberately calibrated to hit those most in need the hardest. One local man, 'Pat', was genuinely perplexed that the government had instituted so many radical

cuts and that ministers had somehow failed to see the potential
for long-term disaster:

> "If you can't help someone, don't add to the burden. They are
> making everything worse and that will have a ripple effect
> through families and it's going to get much, much, worse."

A local woman, 'Annie', added:

> "I can't think straight when the government cuts certain
> things. I don't know how they come to these decisions. I
> don't think they live in the real world. They're cutting benefits
> people need to survive on."

Explaining how hard it was for those affected to come to
terms with the extent of changes to benefits and services when
they could barely manage week-to-week beforehand, another
woman, 'Mina', commented:

> "A lot of people don't think that far ahead. They are told, but
> they are thinking about their next week's shop or their gas bill
> that's coming. It's [survival] on a day-to-day basis. Literally."

Shaking her head in disbelief, a frontline advice worker in
Birmingham who was dealing with people on a daily basis
ominously summed up the perspective of many people thus:
"It's survival. It's like drowning. As long as my head isn't under
water I'm okay."

Martin Holcombe, chief executive of Birmingham
Settlement,[12] a charity that has worked with impoverished
communities across the city for over 100 years, spoke passionately
about how existing entrenched and complex social problems
were being made "much worse" by the combination of cuts
and social security changes:

"I am stunned by the level of desperation and deprivation
that is going on within communities. People have absolutely
no choice here [about cuts]. The most vulnerable people
seem to have no choice. The biggest and immediate [issue]
is obviously welfare reforms, which is impacting massively
around here. People don't necessarily understand how it
works."

Elwyn James, another head of a voluntary sector community
organisation, Arts Factory, in Rhondda, Wales,[13] concurred,
suggesting part of the problem with the government's austerity
drive was that the people it affected most were already battered by
longstanding problems – for example, long-term unemployment
in the case of Rhondda – and therefore scraping by financially
even before cuts. He cautions:

"A lot of the people we work with feel smashed to pieces by
the system. They feel the system is not out there to help them;
it's out there to punish them. They're trying to make decent
lives out of very little. I don't think people are necessarily
aware of the magnitude, the extent of the impact. If you grind
people down over and over – for generations really – they
become incredibly disempowered. People don't want to know
about things they don't think they can have an effect on."

In Northern Ireland, part of the UK with one of the highest
levels of poverty prior to the recession,[14] and predicted to fare
particularly badly in the longer term from welfare changes and
cuts to public sector jobs (the province depends on the public
sector for almost 30 per cent of all employment – proportionately
more than any other part of the UK), austerity was being viewed
by many as nothing short of an outright assault on poorer people.
With high rates of disability, high levels of fuel poverty (most of
the population rely on oil for their heating, which has soared in

price in recent years) and both relative and absolute child poverty expected to increase significantly by 2020, according to the IFS,[15] there was a parlous and powerless anxiety among interviewees.

There was also, however, a clear conviction that the government was exercising a choice to target low-income citizens, that it could have taken another path and didn't, and that consequently the cruelty unleashed was all the more reprehensible for it. Here's what 'Maria McGee', a woman in Cookstown, County Tyrone, had to say:

> "What annoys me is people say 'Oh they're on benefits, they're getting everything'. You try living on that. I would defy anyone to try living on the pittance that there is. Austerity is not working. It isn't working anywhere it's being used. I do not know why anybody with a so-called intelligent mind would attempt to bring austerity in when they can see it isn't working anywhere else.
>
> The only way to fill that pot is through taxes and the only way to get taxes from people is to provide work and to provide work you need to invest. I would stress to anybody who is actually going to be listening to these interviews – you must take a risk right now and say, 'Y'know what, we're not making any more cuts.'"

In the centre of Derry, Northern Ireland's second city, I met Jackie Gallagher, manager of the local Citizens Advice office. She summed up what it was like for her growing group of clients and the desperation they felt about a government that seemingly didn't care or want to fully understand the devastating implications of its own policies. According to Jackie, any suggestion of fairness or equity in the implementation of austerity was farcical. As with many critics of the cuts, she regarded it as a moral issue as much as it was economic or political. She said:

—

"It's got much worse. Debt in Derry is chronic. We've had job loss after job loss after job loss. I think the moral test of any government or of anyone with any humanity is do you look after people in the dawn and twilight of their life and, in between, do you look after the people who are sick, who are lonely and depressed? That ain't happening. People are scared stiff. I can't even park my car in the morning ... without being stopped by at least five people [asking] 'Jackie, what's going to be happening with these cuts?'"

She continued:

"People are demented, they're worried, because all they're hearing is about these cuts and is about these austerity measures. I think really that the Coalition government really should take stock of who they are targeting – really, really seriously. Let the banks off with everything, let the rich get richer, let the poor get poorer, target them, knock them down, kick them when they're down. Please stop that. That's wrong."

Attack on living standards and its victims

Throughout 2012 and 2013, what these interviewees were seeing and feeling on the ground was being documented by an ever-growing body of authoritative reports, both on living standards and on how the bevy of cuts were having an impact as months of austerity morphed into years. An analysis of official data from the ONS published in August 2013 revealed that prices had risen faster than wages in all but one month from May 2010, while pointing out *no other* G7 country saw workers' incomes decline as much as the UK.[16] The charts below illustrate the figures.

Real wages since David Cameron became Prime Minister

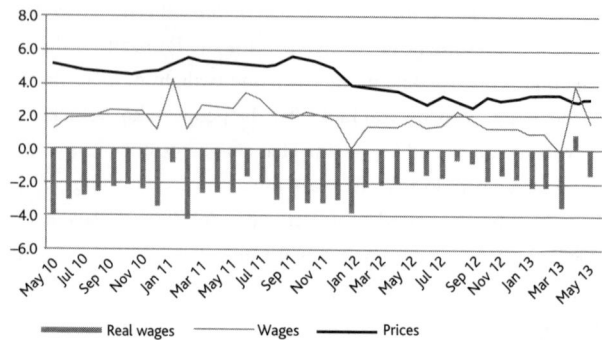

Source: ONS, Labour Market Statistics, 17 July and ONS, Consumer Price Indices, RPI, 16 July 2013

Months of falling real wages

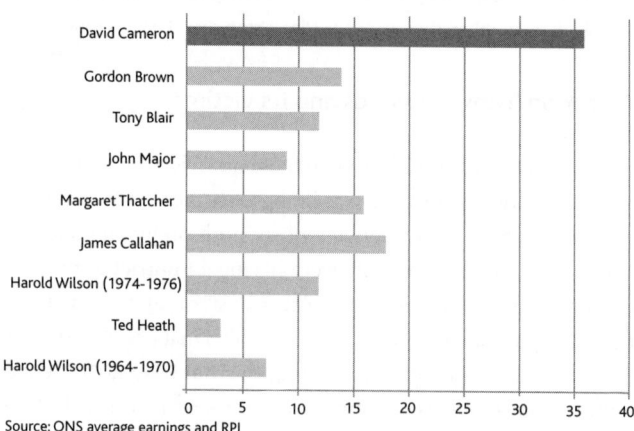

Source: ONS average earnings and RPI

G7 real incomes, % change since Q3, 2010

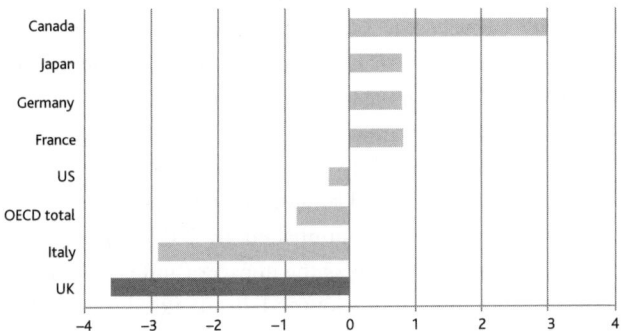

Source: OECD, Labour compensation per unit input, House of Commons Library calculations

Almost since the beginning of the financial crisis, the adverse backdrop to austerity as far as income and earnings were concerned was under the spotlight. It should be said that some elements of this bigger picture, such as wage stagnation and the boom in insecure employment contracts, predated the Great Recession, and while they continued unabated afterwards, weren't necessarily causally linked to austerity.[17] For example, the fact that average earnings shrank by 4.4 per cent in 2012, while FTSE 100 directors' pay leapt by 49 per cent,[18] was symptomatic of a much broader problem around remuneration, and something politicians of all hues failed to act to redress more generally. However, the critical fact was that all of this provided fertile ground for the further undermining of household incomes once cuts were introduced. People were already struggling, so what did it matter if they struggled a bit more?

To a degree this questionable orthodoxy was persuasively challenged by global protests courtesy of the 'Occupy' and 'Uncut' movements following the banking crisis. By directing attention towards the 'super-rich' and the offensive levels of wealth they were syphoning from national economies and hoarding in tax havens[19] (garnering worldwide outrage and excoriation), more of us than ever were made aware of the raging gulf between the very rich and the rest. These trends around wealth disparity – and what the Resolution Foundation identified in its third annual audit of pay in September 2013 as a 'two-tier' workforce[20] that saw the incomes of the wealthier, managerial class soar while everyone else's shrunk – were exacerbated and entrenched by austerity policies.

A report from Oxfam published in 2013 summed up succinctly the 'perfect storm' of the impact of austerity on those whose incomes were already low and shrinking.[21] It concluded:

> The combination in the UK of economic stagnation and public spending cuts is causing substantial hardship to people living in poverty. This amounts to a "Perfect Storm" of falling incomes, rising prices, public service cuts, benefit cuts, a housing crisis, and weak labour rights. By making different political choices, the government can both protect people in poverty and help to stimulate economic recovery in the short term, and set the UK on the way towards economic, social and environmental sustainability in the long term.
>
> The UK is the sixth richest country on earth yet one in five of its people lives in poverty. Before the financial crisis and the economic recession prosperity was not shared. The UK is one of the most unequal rich countries in the world, with the poorest 10th of people receiving only 1% of the total income, while the richest 10th take home 31%.

In the meantime, *Impoverishment of the UK*, a project on poverty and social exclusion funded by the Economic and Social Research Council (ESRC), published a report in March 2013[22] on the magnitude of poverty and privation being experienced across the country. It produced some shocking figures, among which were:

- a quarter of the UK population had an unacceptably low standard of living;
- around 5 million adults were going without essential clothing;
- about 4 million children and adults were not being properly fed;
- approximately 1.5 million children were living in homes that weren't heated properly;
- roughly 14 million people could not afford one or more essential household items.

It concluded:

> These results reflect the situation *before* the majority of proposed benefit changes come into place and *before* benefits payments are revised to increase at less than the level of inflation. The impacts of the current government austerity measures are set to hit hard those whose standard of living is already well below that seen by a majority to be minimal.

Indeed, such was the state of things in 2013 that the IFS predicted that, after years during which child poverty in the UK had been reduced significantly, it would rise substantially, and largely due to the shake-up in the tax and benefits system under austerity.[23] The IFS forecast that a quarter of children in the UK – 3.4 million – would be living in relative poverty by 2020. The projected increase would see the UK falling far short of stated targets to reduce child poverty to 1.3 million by 2020. The report concluded: '... tax and benefit reforms introduced since April 2010 can account for almost all of the increases in child poverty projected over the next few years'.

A startling number of those most affected by austerity were children, especially those already living in or near poverty. If something has a profoundly negative impact on a family it stands to reason that it would place the children in those families in difficult if not distressing circumstances. In November 2013 The Children's Society published alarming findings after it interviewed 2,000 children between the ages of 10 and 17. The study, *Through young eyes*,[24] found that not only were over a quarter of the children interviewed living in cold, damp homes, but that they had a clear perception of how dire their situations were and of the stigma poverty brought with it.

The charity's chief executive, Matthew Reed, said at the time:

> "For millions of children up and down the country, poverty is a grinding reality – and it is getting worse. Many families are facing stark and unacceptable choices, like heat or eat. This is disgraceful in any country, especially in one of the world's richest."

A few months earlier, the Office of the Children's Commissioner flagged up just how serious the impact was on children when it launched a child rights impact assessment examining the combined repercussions of tax benefit reform and reductions in spending on public services from 2010 to 2015.[25] It was an eye-opening report. Its analysis concluded that low-income families with children were losing more as a percentage of net income than those without children, and losing more of their net income proportionally than their wealthier counterparts. Families with children in the poorest 10 per cent of the population were losing most – an average reduction in living standards equivalent to a 22 per cent fall in net income – while for the richest 10 per cent it was just 7 per cent.

Looking at cuts in public services, poorer families were also going to be disproportionately affected, the report concluded, because they tended to use the services being cut more than better-off families. And, just in case the cuts weren't unfair enough, those poorer families who had a child with a disability, were headed by a lone parent or were of Black or Asian origin, suffered even more compared to other groups.

A detailed analysis from the lone-parent charity, Gingerbread, in December 2013 highlighted the dramatic impact of cuts on families headed by one adult. In its report, *Paying the price: Single parents in the age of austerity*,[26] it laid out the degree to which single parents and the children they cared for were struggling more with each passing month, and how this was set to worsen as more reforms and cuts came down the government's austerity conveyor belt. After surveying single parents it found:

- 77 per cent found managing household finances a constant burden;
- 64 per cent were in arrears for at least three months for at least one bill;
- 22 per cent had lost more than £100 a month or more from their monthly income following the reforms introduced in April 2013;
- 64 per cent said they would be worse off in 2015.

The charity's chief executive, Fiona Weir, called what was happening "unprecedented", and pleaded with the government to "think again" about the path it was taking. She told me: "The thing the government doesn't seem to get is that people's reserves are running out. They have stretched and stretched but now there is nothing else they can do."

In July 2013 a report from the Resolution Foundation (a think tank that specialises in the financial stresses on low-to-middle income groups – what became known in common parlance as the 'squeezed middle', or what politicians euphemistically refer to as 'hardworking families') highlighted the fact that the value

—

Poor pay

Real value of the minimum wage

Past and future trends in the National Minimum Wage if it follows Office
for Budget Responsibility projections for wages

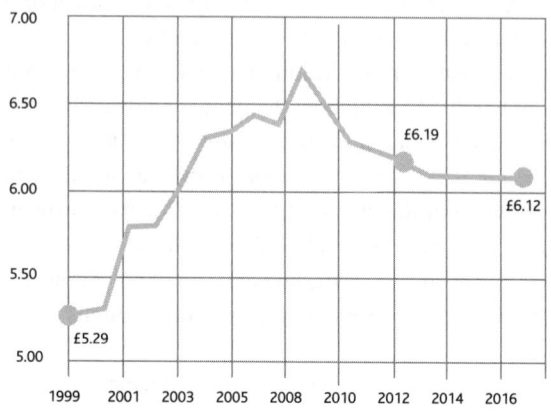

Source: Resolution Foundation

of the National Minimum Wage – a key plank of the previous
government's anti-poverty strategy first introduced in 1998 – had
in fact declined in value over the previous five years as wages
had failed to keep pace with inflation and, significantly, that it
was in danger of being eroded further.[27]

Hitting the most vulnerable hardest

As if that wasn't bad enough for people managing on diminishing
incomes, there were over 300,000 people in the UK earning less
than the statutory National Minimum Wage. In late 2013 it was
revealed that just two firms had been prosecuted for breaching
their legal duty to pay it.[28]

According to Zita Holbourne, joint chair of the anti-cuts
group, BARAC (Black Activists Rising Against Cuts),[29] which
campaigns on how cuts were affecting disproportionately people

from black and minority ethnic backgrounds, the degree to which these groups – already much more likely than their white counterparts to be poor or living on low incomes – were suffering was "absolutely horrendous". Long-term cycles of unemployment, poverty and racism were being exacerbated by austerity, she concluded, while some, including black women and young black men, were dealing with "multiple barriers" such as benefits changes and discrimination. A number of the key planks of austerity including public sector job cuts (black and minority ethnic workers have a higher representation in the public sector compared to the private sector, particularly for women) were hitting people very hard, she told me, and putting increased pressure on household budgets. Around 250,000 of the public sector jobs set to be lost under austerity would be held by people from black and minority ethnic backgrounds, according to Holbourne, who is also a trade unionist.

"Black people are also more likely to be poor so they are more likely to be affected", she explained. "We can expect to see dramatic increases in black unemployment and a consequent increase in the level of child poverty which is already at 50 per cent for African and Caribbean children, whilst Bangladeshi child poverty is above 70 per cent."

As many sceptics had predicted at the beginning of the government's austerity drive, the most vulnerable in society, including poorer people and people with disabilities, single parents, women and many people from black and minority ethnic backgrounds,[30] were indeed hit hardest – something borne out time and again by the experiences of interviewees. While bankers lined their bespoke suit pockets with bonuses and enjoyed another financial boost courtesy of the Treasury when people earning above £150,000 a year cashed in from a reduction in the top rate of income tax from 50 per cent to 45 per cent as of April 2013, people in or on the verge of poverty were losing tax credits, facing cuts to housing benefits alongside higher rents, watching local services disappear and being denied crisis funds in emergencies. (In early 2014 David Cameron refused to rule out a further reduction in the top rate of tax for high earners from 45% to 40% when questioned by MPs in Parliament.[31]) By autumn 2013 almost half a million people in England were estimated to be in Council Tax arrears, with court orders arriving on the doorsteps from councils, according to Labour.[32] The government claimed official statistics showed a different picture, but others countered that around 3 million of the poorest households across the country were set to see Council Tax rises due to changes in Council Tax Benefit.[33] (In June 2013, the Chancellor, George Osborne, announced that Council Tax would be frozen for a further two years, until 2016. However, by November 2013, nearly a third of councils had decided to raise it, rejecting the government funds available to councils that froze it.[34])

In December 2013 a Freedom of Information (FOI) request by the campaign group False Economy found those councils that had passed on the government's cuts to Council Tax Benefits had seen the number of households threatened with bankruptcy, repossession and possibly prison for arrears increase at double the rate for councils that had not implemented them. In local authorities that made no cuts to the benefit, there was a 15 per cent increase in the number of liability orders issued by magistrates' courts for non-payment of Council Tax compared to the previous year (evidence in itself that financial difficulties were spreading). However, the figure jumped to 30 per cent in local authorities that passed on the cut.[35]

Universal Credit and the assault on social security benefits

On top of the multiple hits people's incomes were taking, there was one major reform on the horizon that many critics argued that, when fully introduced, would destabilise people even further. This was the centrepiece of the government's social security reform agenda: Universal Credit.[36] Its planned introduction was one of the gravest concerns interviewees for this book brought up because when introduced it would constitute the biggest shake-up in decades of how social security benefits were administered. In 2013 it still felt like an unknown entity (in part because of its complexity and in part because its introduction was much slower than anticipated). However, many of the people I spoke to believed the radical shake-up would not meet the government's stated objectives for it – incentivise people into work – and that the mechanics of distributing the new benefit would propel people whose incomes were already stretched to breaking point into greater financial chaos.

Citizens Advice workers told me of people queuing in a panic to understand what it would mean for them alongside all the other benefits changes being introduced, while debt advisers in community organisations said they were being inundated with enquiries about it.

An extraordinarily complex, ambitious and transformative adjustment to how benefits would be distributed, Universal Credit was conceived as a way to simplify the system by replacing tax credits and six existing separate means-tested benefits – Jobseeker's Allowance, Employment and Support Allowance (ESA), Income Support, Working Tax Credit, Child Tax Credit and Housing Benefit – and merging them into one monthly payment. For the first time, Housing Benefit would be paid to the recipient, who would then be expected to pay their landlord rather than the government directly paying landlords. Among the primary concerns was the shift to a single monthly payment. Worries were raised that faced with the prospect of one larger lump sum, people who tended to organise their household budgets from week to week (usually because they had so little) would find managing their finances much harder and more would turn to payday lenders as funds dried up towards the end of the month. In addition, the introduction of online accounts for recipients to manage their benefit was a major cause of stress because of a lack of computer literacy and access to the internet among poorer people.

Another concern was the potential impact on women and in particular of the single payment per household rather than per claimant, which campaigners argued could dramatically reduce women's financial independence.[37]

Meanwhile, the small print of the reform was littered with inconsistencies that could leave very vulnerable people worse off. Gavin Kelly, chief executive of the Resolution Foundation, warned at the end of 2013 that a number of 'stealth cuts' buried deep in the small print would hammer the working poor.[38] He wrote: 'The result will be further downward pressure on living standards in an era defined by working poverty.'

The IFS[39] and the charity Gingerbread reported that lone parents would fare worst of all.[40] Fiona Weir of Gingerbread pointed out that, for example, single parents under the age of 25 would receive the same amount of money as a single adult under the age of 25 with no children. "It's quite shocking," Weir told me. "And there is absolutely no logical justification for it."

Universal Credit was pitched by its champion, Iain Duncan Smith, as another string to the 'Make Work Pay' policy bow, with the added goal of simplifying the system and improving back-to-work incentives by ensuring that benefits were reduced – or 'tapered' – at a consistent rate as people returned to work. The result, in theory, would be a staggered loss of benefits when work was secured rather than a sudden loss of support.[41] It was an audacious proposal that was also intended to reduce administration costs in the longer term by having claimants manage their benefit online. The problem? Where to start…. Suffice to say that the policy was plagued by problems and its implementation dogged by criticism and delays.[42] Despite frequent and repeated protestations by the Secretary of State in Parliament and in the media[43] that it would be delivered on time and on budget, what unfolded was a costly bureaucratic fiasco that saw the gigantic IT system that was supposed to facilitate it balloon out of control – the estimated cost rose by 60 per cent, from £396 million to £637 million by autumn 2013.[44]

A damning report from the National Audit Office[45] listed a catalogue of errors, which provoked outrage at the waste of public money. By the end of October 2013 a batch of leaked documents revealed that the IT write-off could reach £120 million,[46] and in November the Public Accounts Committee in Parliament accused the Department for Work and Pensions of squandering public money due to 'shocking' errors and mismanagement.[47] By the end of the year yet more delays were announced,[48] and it was confirmed that the transfer of all claimants to Universal Credit wouldn't make its target for implementation of 2017, with around three quarters of a million people unlikely to be on it by the (already repeatedly moved) deadline. Among the many criticisms levelled at the reform was that the repeated moving of goalposts was enormously destabilising for those who would be affected.[49] By December 2013 only 2,000 claimants, with the least complicated benefits, were on Universal Credit.

The media focused on the political embarrassment of the failure to reach targets and overspend, but whatever happened with implementation setbacks, there remained potentially serious ramifications for people once on it, according to many critics. An evaluation commissioned by JRF and carried out by the University of Portsmouth[50] concluded that the initiative would unintentionally 'trap people in poverty' by incentivising individuals into part-time work rather than full-time employment, and by imposing yet more income-sucking sanctions. The policy had been designed with a plethora of sanctions for non-compliance – what was generally referred to in policy wonk-speak as 'conditionality' – and which the Child

Poverty Action Group (CPAG) argued would throttle people in need once again:'The need for more conditionality comes across as a "moral crusade", rather than being evidence based,' the organisation concluded.[51] The National Housing Federation meanwhile warned that direct payments to tenants could trigger unprecedented levels of arrears[52] as well as lead to increased collection costs.[53] There were also concerns that evictions would surge due to unpaid rent.[54] The shift from weekly or fortnightly payments to monthly was identified as a particular concern and something that could push more people directly into debt.[55]

As the chief executive of one voluntary organisation told me:

> "It has reached a point where people simply say:'Here we go again, why don't you just come and bash us some more?'"

"We are talking about really vulnerable people who can't budget themselves and they are going to go suddenly to having a month's money", community worker, Sharon, in Liverpool, explained of the potential impact on household incomes for those being shifted on to the new regime. "Immediately they are getting put into a more vulnerable position through no fault of their own but they will get blamed." Pointing out that if the choice for a mother was between food and paying rent, another woman in Glasgow suggested it was a "no brainer". She said: "People with children – what do you do? Pay your rent or buy them shoes? If [the money] is in your bank account you'll use it."

Benefits reform and the absence of fairness

What Universal Credit and reforms more widely signified was a glaring injustice or, as one interviewee in London put it to me, "a war against the poor". Even those who might have conceded there was a case for improving the benefits system rejected what was being done as biased against those in need of a leg up in life. The themes of social justice and fairness came up all over the country. Speaking at a conference on the impact of austerity at the University of Bradford in September 2013, Labour peer and long time anti-poverty campaigner, Ruth Lister, articulated what many people felt when she accused the government of "paying lip service" to social justice and fairness "while pursuing a strategy that will skew the distribution of income and wealth even further in favour of the better off and is already hurting many of those reliant on benefits and public services to get by".

Indeed, the first signs of exactly how unfair and ferocious the austerity drive would be was apparent right from the Coalition's opening salvo. The first Emergency Budget in June 2010, a month after the election, pushed through some spectacularly inequitable measures.[56] It increased VAT, a regressive tax disproportionately affecting the poor if ever there was one, from 17.5 per cent to 20 per cent, instituted a two-year pay freeze for public sector workers and confirmed that welfare cuts to a tune of £11 billion by 2014/15 would be ushered in, with many government departments to have their budgets slashed by a third. (It pledged to 'ring-fence' spending on the NHS, but the large-scale privatisation of parts of the health service, together with figures showing budget cuts in real terms for primary care and harsh cuts in mental health, proved to upend those promises three years into the austerity programme.[57])

For people reliant on benefits either wholly or partially, the early austerity news was particularly miserable as, among other things, the fact that benefits increases would now be linked to the lower measure of inflation, the Consumer Price Index (CPI), meant that future benefits would progressively lose value. A month prior to the Emergency Budget in May 2010, when the Coalition produced its *Programme for government*,[58] full of the glow of his newly minted power, the new Prime Minister, David Cameron, had optimistically and misleadingly declared:

—

"Difficult decisions will have to be taken in the months and years ahead, but we will ensure that fairness is at the heart of those decision so that all those most in need are protected."

Yet, just a few weeks later, when austerity had barely got off the starting blocks, the IFS published its assessment of the government's Emergency Budget and roundly rebuffed the Prime Minister's claim. It concluded that the UK faced 'the longest, deepest sustained period of cuts to public services spending at least since World War II'. Its then Director, Robert Chote, commented:

"The Budget looks less progressive – indeed somewhat regressive – when you take out the effect of measures that were inherited from the previous government and when you look further into the future than 2013. [The cuts] are likely to hit poorer households significantly harder than richer households."

(Chancellor George Osborne subsequently appointed Robert Chote Director of the Office for Budget Responsibility.)

Suffice to say, the cuts momentum from those early first steps in June 2010 was unrelenting and, in just three years, amounted to a wholly manufactured devastation of those most in need. If all the government had needed was some time to prove that social security changes were indeed 'fair', as they claimed, this was categorically proven not the case by year three of austerity. Any assertion that they were fair or equitable – or indeed that they did in fact tackle the government's favourite straw man, so-called 'benefits cheats' – came from either those within the Coalition or partisans. There was some evidence of public support for benefits cuts as the government ratcheted up the rhetoric against people in receipt of benefits and (frankly) hyped the degree to which fraud was a drain on the system.

For example, the *London Evening Standard* and others reported on a survey that found nine out of ten residents in the capital supported the benefits cap of £26,000,[59] with many believing it should be lower.[60] Introduced in April 2013, it capped benefits at £500 per week for couples and single parents and £350 per week for single adults. It was designed in part to return 'fairness to the benefits system', as well as to encourage people back into work by stopping the 'sky-high claims that make it impossible for people to move into work'. (Duncan Smith's claims in July 2013 that the benefits cap was encouraging people into work were 'unsupported by the official statistics', according to the UK Statistics Authority.[61])

Meanwhile, research by the Trades Union Congress (TUC) found that hardened attitudes to people who claimed benefits were based largely on ignorance about how much people were actually able to claim (for example, by assuming wrongly that Housing Benefit was paid to claimants – who were raking in taxpayers' cash – rather than to landlords) as well as a misguided idea of levels of fraud.[62] It concluded:

> Voters least able to give accurate answers about benefits are the most likely to back the government's policy on cutting benefits. The poll shows that once people learn that the benefit up-rating cap will hit workers in low-paid jobs, support moves away from the government, with 40 per cent overall opposing the cap on low-paid worker benefits and only 30 per cent backing them.

The then General Secretary of the TUC commented:

> "It is not surprising that voters want to get tough on welfare. They think the system is much more generous than it is in reality, is riddled with fraud and is heavily skewed towards helping the unemployed, who they think are far more likely

to stay on the dole than is actually the case. Indeed, if what
the average voter thinks was true, I'd want tough action too."

In March 2013, Margaret Hodge MP, former Labour minister
and chair of the Public Accounts Committee, a parliamentary
body that holds government to account on expenditure and
described in 2013 as 'the unofficial opposition' by *Guardian*
columnist Simon Jenkins, reached the extraordinary conclusion
that the Coalition "did not fully understand" the impact of
its own spending cuts. She added that it was: "... focusing on
short-term priorities rather than the longer term view". But it
didn't matter where the criticism came from or how convincing
it was – to quote the queen of attacks on the poor, Margaret
Thatcher, the government "was not for turning".

By autumn 2013 over £20 billion had already been slashed
from public spending, including but not limited to:

- cuts in tax credits, including Childcare Tax Credit, seriously
  diminishing the incomes of the 'working poor' in particular;
- a freezing and then means-testing of Child Benefit, affecting
  millions of families nationally;
- a total household benefit cap of £26,000 – regardless of the
  number of children;
- drastic cuts to disability-related benefits;
- restrictions on the annual increases to benefits for most
  people below pensionable age (to just 1 per cent per year for
  three years regardless of the rate of inflation), a change that
  substantially reduces the real value of benefits over time.

Take as just one example what happened with the Working Tax
Credit – this was something hundreds of thousands of families
who fell into the category of 'working poor' had benefited from
since its introduction in April 2003.[63] The changes that came
into effect in April 2012 (the revisions meant the number of

hours work needed to qualify for the credit was increased from 16 to 24) were roundly criticised as a heartless and thoroughly misguided attack on low-income families by raising the bar to entry. Referring to the harshness of the changes, the chief executive of CPAG, Alison Garnham, said at the time:

> "This will pull the rug from under the feet of hundreds of thousands of families desperately trying to make ends meet. It's shocking how many children in some places are going to be hit by this change and it is inevitable that many will be thrown into poverty. Just imagine how hard it will be on low pay, with low hours and with kids to take care of when suddenly up to £70 a week gets taken away."

According to a report from JRF and the New Policy Institute, *Monitoring poverty and social exclusion 2012*,[64] even before the Welfare Reform Bill became law in April 2013 – unleashing an enormous volley of additional benefits changes – there was formidable evidence that people were worse off. It found that (excluding pensioners) in-work poverty by 2012 outstripped workless poverty (6.1 million in-work households in poverty as opposed to 5.1 million workless households), while the number of working-age adults without children living in poverty had risen markedly (7 per cent in 1981 versus 20 per cent in 2011/12). Against this backdrop, it concluded, austerity was making matters worse:

> The welfare cuts so far are likely to hit low-income households more than once, through changes to both income-related and housing benefits. Changes to disability benefit could mean low-income disabled people being hit even harder.

Meanwhile, in August 2013, another report from JRF, this time with CPAG,[65] reported that the value of Child Benefit and Child Tax Credit – something low-income and lone-parent families in particular relied on – *relative to the costs of raising a child* – had decreased over the previous year. Katie Schmuecker, Policy and Research Manager at JRF, concluded:

> Flatlining wages, cuts to benefits and tax credits, and the rising cost of essentials [are] creating a growing gap between income and needs. The next election is likely to be the first since the 1930s where living standards are lower than the last poll.

In spring 2013 a report from the Family & Parenting Institute following an Ipsos MORI poll picked up on what the charity called 'hidden austerity effects', such as emotional fragility brought on by financial strains. The poll found that 85 per cent of parents surveyed felt families were worse off financially over the 12 months to April 2013, while three in five parents had experienced increased levels of stress.[66]

Anand Shukla, the charity's chief executive, called the research (yes, that term again) "a wake-up call". She said:

> "This research is a wake-up call, reminding us that we can't afford to rely on the resilience of families indefinitely. Despite their best efforts to adapt to austerity, we see that family life, good parenting and childcare become uphill struggles when financial strains build up. The lack of economic growth coupled with significant expenditure cuts are imposing a high cost for families in Britain, storing up a troubling long-term legacy, affecting both this and future generations."

A double whammy for the poorest: Education Maintenance Allowance and the 'Bedroom Tax'

As if all of the sweeping, 'cost-saving' ventures targeting benefits and tax credits weren't inflicting enough damage, there were other more pernicious components within the austerity arsenal taking aim at the poorest (and which, incidentally, provoked some of the most prominent protests). These were things the government arguably had initially regarded as 'easy targets', including cuts to legal aid that effectively barred many people from recourse to the law when they needed it most. One of the most indefensible of these 'easy' targets turned out to be something called the Education Maintenance Allowance, or EMA, a small grant introduced under the previous government providing financial assistance to encourage young people from less well-off families to stay in education. It was abolished at the very beginning of the cuts process.[67]

The Coalition met with considerable opposition to the move from educators and campaigners, first, because the scheme had been judged to be successful,[68] but also because the total sums involved were paltry in the grand scheme of government coffers. There was simply no compelling reason why one of the few policy initiatives in recent times specifically designed to give poorer children a leg up by incentivising them to stay in education should have been dumped. By getting rid of it, the government saved £500 million per year.[69] The families whose young people received it lost £1,260 a year – a considerable amount of money for a family with not much to begin with.

As Zita Holbourne of BARAC pointed out: "The EMA was a genuine way of helping young people from the poorest families. It was utterly disgraceful that it was abolished."

But if EMA was a prime example of just how unfair and merciless the government was prepared to be and how far it would go to satiate its appetite for cuts then nothing compares with what became known as the 'Bedroom Tax'. From the moment it was introduced, it pushed those people already most affected by cuts towards a financial abyss. It's fair to say that this policy – what the government referred to as 'the removal of the spare room subsidy', even though there was no such thing as a subsidy before ministers arbitrarily decided there was – prompted some of the most profuse condemnation and outrage of the austerity era. It was brought up in every single location I visited, and quickly became an emblematic symbol of the government's cuts programme, provoking a blend of bafflement and fury from social housing tenants as diverse as army veterans, people with disabilities, 'empty nesters' and young parents. The 'Bedroom Tax' was so feared and despised that it triggered numerous protests and demonstrations (often led by people with disabilities) all around the UK, including outside and inside Parliament.[70]

The policy, which came into force in April 2013, introduced financial penalties for anyone of working age living in rented social housing who was in receipt of Housing Benefit and deemed to be 'over-occupying' – according to a set of criteria set out, of course, by the government, with the policy planning equivalent of scribbling on a napkin. The new rules meant that each single adult or couple should occupy one room while two children under 16 of the same gender were expected to share a bedroom and two siblings under 10 of different sexes must share. Some exceptions were introduced in response to vigorous protestations from among others, disability activists.[71] These included when an overnight carer was needed, for foster carers, some serving members of the armed forces and in the case of some people with disabilities and families with children with disabilities who could not share a room with a sibling. Nevertheless, even the exceptions had to meet a set of strict criteria, and the hundreds of thousands who continued to fall foul of the policy were pushed just that bit closer to the financial edge.[72] Some two thirds of those affected (420,000) had a disability – even after exemptions had been put in place,[73] while

—

victims of domestic abuse were also being adversely affected,[74] as were carers, with estimates that 70 per cent were negatively affected and being forced to cut back on essentials to survive.[75]

The 'Bedroom Tax' meant that a substantial proportion of tenants' benefits would be withdrawn (14 per cent for one 'extra' room and 25 per cent for two, ranging on average, according to the Scottish Federation of Housing Associations, from £34 to as much as £140 a month) if they did not move to a smaller property, either in the social or private sector.[76] Approximately 660,000 people were estimated to be affected[77] (a third of all existing working-age Housing Benefit claimants in the social sector, the majority of whom had one 'extra' bedroom and many of whom were already living in poverty). As the policy rolled out, reports of those forced to leave the homes they had cared for and the communities they had put down roots in were released almost weekly.[78] To make matters worse, the areas people were leaving behind often then saw the community scarred as larger properties were left vacant because smaller families couldn't afford to live in them.[79]

The government's astoundingly simplistic justification for the policy was that (in addition to supposedly saving money by clawing back Housing Benefit subsidies) unacceptable numbers of people were living in properties too big for their requirements when there were families on waiting lists who needed larger properties.[80] They were, in effect, 'over-occupying' these homes, all the while having their rent subsidised by those wonderful 'hardworking' taxpayers. So – the logic purported – wasn't it only right to do something about this unfair distribution of housing?

Even if, on the face of it, it was sensible to resolve a situation in which, for example, one person could be living in a four-bedroom house while there was a family of four on a waiting list, it was patently clear immediately that the 'Bedroom Tax' was spectacularly ill-thought-through and clearly the wrong response to a broader housing crisis. For a start, it didn't address

—

the most fundamental of housing issues – supply. It was, in effect, presenting already cash-strapped tenants with an appalling Hobson's choice – that is to say, no choice at all – when investing in social housing would have been the rational answer to the housing supply issue. But of course it wasn't about housing – it was part of a much wider strategy to undermine the welfare state and the people who needed it most.

Two of the biggest practical criticisms levelled at the policy were being flagged up from long before it officially rolled out. Namely, that there was a huge shortage of social housing properties generally, but in particular, an acute scarcity of smaller properties for those with 'extra' rooms to move into[81] (the social housing sector traditionally tended to build family homes of three bedrooms or more), and that rents were often so high in the private sector that tenants couldn't afford them.[82] Instead, thousands of people who were already just about scraping by and who depended on Housing Benefit chose (or, arguably, had no choice) to stay put. The resulting squeeze on their household income further aggravated the 'heat or eat' culture that had already swept across poorer parts of the country.[83] At times the policy's cruelly farcical side appeared to know no bounds. For instance, in many cases people with disabilities whose homes had been specially adapted for their needs – often at great expense – were being declared to be 'over-occupying' with the risk of having to move to smaller, 'non-adapted' properties.[84]

It wasn't just tenants and campaigners challenging the policy either. Housing associations also warned that it would lead to greater hardship for tenants, while predicting a loss of income for social landlords as more people who took the financial hit rather than move ended up in arrears. The result? Housing providers would have less income to invest in new properties or to maintain existing ones.[85] By the end of 2013, a number of housing associations were reporting one of the more perverse consequences of the policy – that three-bedroom properties were facing demolition in some areas because they couldn't find tenants who could meet the cost of renting them.[86] Even a housing association boss who was generally in favour of the government's overall austerity policies declared the 'Bedroom Tax' "inexcusably stupid". In an open letter in November 2013 to Iain Duncan Smith and Lord Freud, Mick Kent, Head of Bromford Homes, which manages around 27,000 homes in central England, laid out his quarrel with the policy, echoing those of many campaigners.[87] He wrote:

> Well, it feels right that taxpayers should not be subsidising people to live in homes that are bigger than they need but the way the 'Bedroom Tax' has been implemented has clearly been unfair to many people. Most of the people who need a spare room due to disability will probably eventually be covered by the extra discretionary money made available to local councils but the government has failed to recognise that the children of divided families need a place to stay with each parent or that teenagers need space for study without a younger sibling sharing their room. And failing to understand that not all bedrooms can accommodate two people is inexcusably stupid.

The sorts of questions people were raising at a grassroots level as I conducted interviews mirrored those being raised by campaign groups and social housing providers. Questions such as: why don't they just build more homes? What if there were no available properties to move tenants to? What if the only thing to be done was move out and away from friends, family and support networks? What if a single parent lived in a property but needed a spare room for when their children came to stay?

Helen Gilmore, a 57-year-old widow from Glasgow, had had two strokes that left her with difficulties processing numbers and concentrating. It made form-filling difficult, which in turn made it harder for her to navigate the benefits system. When told in late 2012 she would have to pay the 'Bedroom Tax' as of April 2013, she was left in a state of abject distress, fretting about how she would pay. She didn't wish to leave her two-bedroom home because she was ill and her support network was nearby. Plus, she needed the room for a carer. After months of waiting and appealing she was eventually exempted, but says the stress of the whole thing was at times "unbearable". She told me:

> "I've got a lot of health issues and I need the spare room for carers coming in and out. Even if I could move there's only 34 one-bedroom houses [in the area]. We are told to pay the charge through no fault of our own. The [housing association] landlords don't have the [housing] stock for us to move into. A lot of people just don't have that [spare] money because their [other] benefits are being cut anyway."

Sheila Sweeny, a community worker in Liverpool, talked of how whole communities were being damaged by the policy:

> "The housing associations are not renting to small families. In one street there's six empty properties. In another street there's eight empty. The housing associations are losing money because they are not taking the rent and the other daft thing is you can [go to] private landlord and [have to pay more] rent. The other cruel thing is they can't now use the courts because of the legal aid has gone. I think almost immediately we are going to see rent arrears and we are going to see evictions."

In Manchester, Helen Bradbury, a housing association tenant and advocate for tenants' rights, explained the fear she and others felt at the instability the 'Bedroom Tax' was bringing and about and "the absolute failure" of the policy to recognise that properties are not just places to live, but homes. She said:

> "People are scared. There's a lot of social housing around here, a lot of poverty, a lot of single parents, a lot of vulnerable people who are finding it difficult to see how the changes are going to affect them. The government [is] talking about housing mobility – about people moving to different properties. What they don't consider is this isn't a property. This is my home. It's where I raised my children, it's where I've got the support network that I need. I don't just want to up sticks and move to another property because I've got a spare bedroom."

And then there was Cath Hollingrake, who worked for a social landlord in the North West. She said that 50 per cent of the homes in the organisation's high-rise properties were now classified as 'under-occupied':

> "People are really worried. We've got a lot of single parents so they'll be affected. We've got a lot of dads who have access to the children and in the past we've allowed them to live in two-bedroom properties ... so they could actually provide a room for the children and now they are going to be penalised for that."

A long-time community nurse in Bristol, 'Wendy Rogers', told me of how the 'Bedroom Tax' had been a source of confusion as well as stress for the vulnerable people she treated around the city. It was "impossible" to see how it could be justified by anything other than ideology, she said.

> "There's a lot of evidence that this policy is going to cost as much as it's going to save because of the knock-on effect

of homelessness, temporary housing, demand for local authorities to provide support and services. The original idea of [public housing] was that people had some long-term security in a home that they could bring their family up in. What's happening now is that it's starting to feel like people who live in council or housing association properties are being put in a different class – as if they don't deserve that level of security."

'Susan', in Ladywood in Birmingham, articulated the sentiment of many people:

"Did they really do their research on this? I'd love to meet the person who came up with the Bedroom Tax. What kind of idiot came up with it?"

What I was finding was reflected in a veritable deluge of studies and reports on the fallout of the policy.[88] At times the absurdity of the policy was simply unfathomable. For example, the charity Shelter in Wales reported on a woman who was waiting for her children to be returned from care who, had she downsized as instructed, would have had nowhere to put them.[89] Then there was the story of a lone parent who was sole carer for her autistic 20-year-old son but was told she'd have to pay £82 a month from her meagre income for the room his respite carer stayed overnight in. There was no exemption within the policy for carers who filled this role for children with disabilities.[90]

Opposition to the 'Bedroom Tax' was fierce and multifaceted and ranged from petitions[91] to pre-planned protests at party conferences,[92] to online discussions[93] to incredulous members of the public railing against ministers who tried to defend it on the radio. When Lord Freud attempted to justify the policy on a BBC Radio 5 Live call-in show he was berated by listeners furious that someone with two multi-million-pound, multi-

—

room properties could dare to claim it was necessary to penalise people who lived in social housing.[94] There were also numerous legal challenges made by individuals affected and supported by organisations such as CPAG and the human rights organisation, Liberty. There were challenges revolving around potential human rights breaches and even about what size of a room constituted 'a bedroom'.[95] At the time of writing, many cases were ongoing.

The political sensitivity of the policy was revealed in September 2013, when United Nations (UN) special housing investigator Raquel Rolnik, on a visit to the UK, said that the "shocking" 'Bedroom Tax' should be axed, unleashing a media and political storm.[96] Tory chair Grant Shapps rounded on the UN representative, calling her comments "an absolute disgrace",[97] and wrote a letter to the UN General Secretary Ban Ki-moon calling for an investigation (the UN responded, saying Rolnik had broken no rules[98]), while one Tory MP called her "a loopy Brazilian leftie" on Twitter.[99] And true to form, the tabloids had a field day fulminating with unfiltered sanctimony that someone from outside the UK dared to criticise a UK policy. In one of the many extraordinary reactions, the *Daily Mail* ran a piece accusing the 'Marxist' Ms Rolnik of 'dabbling in witchcraft' and animal sacrifice.[100]

By the end of 2013 the policy had been in place for half a year and, whatever the twitchy remonstrations from its defenders, the human cost was piling up. Deputy Prime Minister Nick Clegg reacted by launching a review but, with any conclusions not likely until the autumn of 2014, and no commitment from him to eradicate it, the move was dismissed by critics as too little too late.[101]

The Labour Party, meanwhile, pledged to abolish the 'Bedroom Tax' if elected to power in 2015.[102] (It wasn't lost on many campaigners that it was a Labour government that had introduced the equivalent of the 'Bedroom Tax' for the private rented sector, and many accused the party of hypocrisy as a result).[103] Many of its MPs were singularly outspoken about the policy, and in November the Party held an 'Opposition Day' debate on scrapping it (they lost).[104] Liberal Democrat MPs who had failed to vote for axing the policy were 'outed' on Twitter, while social media and blogs reported on events as the day unfolded. And what a day it was. In many ways the debate crystallised for opponents not just of the 'Bedroom Tax', but of the entire inglorious stockpile of policies that constituted austerity, the contempt the government appeared to have towards its most vulnerable citizens.[105] For starters, Work and Pensions Secretary Iain Duncan Smith didn't even turn up to the debate[106] (he was in Paris instead at an international summit on youth unemployment), while numerous Conservative MPs displayed zero empathy when it was pointed out time and again how the policy was devastating the lives of thousands.

For someone unfamiliar with the antics of MPs as they taunt and prod across the House of Commons floor, the behaviour of advocates of the 'Bedroom Tax' during the debate would have been shocking. There was open mockery and even laughter from the government benches as tales of the trauma and financial hardship caused to families were recited. One Tory MP, Bob Stewart, was spotted apparently napping while the litany of carnage was being discussed.[107]

One after another Conservative MP spoke up, with implausible and frequently ill-informed defences of the policy. However, if there was one comment that encapsulated the ignominious spirit of the debate and of the entire 'Bedroom Tax' debacle (while also vying for the accolade of most memorably dismissive of the austerity era) it has to be one from Anne Main, Conservative MP for St Albans.[108] She said:

> "Unicorns do not exist, fairies do not exist and a Bedroom
> Tax does not exist. It does not matter how often opposition

members [of Parliament] say it – a Bedroom Tax does not exist."

The MP may have hoped to amuse her colleagues by indulging in some creative pedantic semantics about whether what was under discussion was a tax or a charge or a benefits cut, or something else entirely, but her statement was so much more than that. It was symptomatic of a ruling party that, as many on the Labour benches and protesting outside the chamber[109] were pointing out, was "out of touch", wedded to a rigid right-wing dogma, and steadfastly refusing to so much as acknowledge the pain its policies were foisting on the poor, never mind accept that the whole sorry adventure was utterly unnecessary.

The government was right about one thing though: the upshot of the stockpile of cuts and reforms was most definitely the 'tough times' their austerity policies were intended to unleash. One of the most unsavoury and destructive repercussions of these deliberately callous 'tough times' was the menacing spectre of personal debt – something that served to augment the UK's austerian trajectory towards a pre-welfare state incarnation into a country of 'haves and have nothing'.

THREE

Welcome to 'Wongaland'

The rise of personal debt: austerity and the predatory lender

It has become clear that payday lenders are not just profiting from poverty; they are adding to it. (Rowena Davis, journalist and Labour Party councillor in South London, writing in Carl Packman's 2012 book *Loan sharks: The rise and rise of payday lending*)

"The sense of panic is getting stronger practically on an hourly basis, never mind a daily basis. And we don't see the situation getting any better." (David Martin, debt adviser, Glasgow)

Payday lending and the exploitation of the poor

In the summer of 2013 the head of the Church of England, Archbishop of Canterbury Justin Welby, took a highly irregular and controversial step. Welby, a former financier who sits on the Parliamentary Commission on Banking Standards, and who has been an energetic opponent of predatory and high-interest lenders for some time, met with the head of the UK's biggest 'payday' loan company, Wonga. At the meeting he told the company's chief executive, Errol Damelin, in no uncertain terms that it was his intention to put them out of business.

Recalling the meeting for BBC News the Archbishop commented: "I said to him quite bluntly that 'we're not in the business of trying to legislate you out of existence; we're trying to compete you out of existence'".[1] His goal, the Archbishop said, was to create a church-run credit union to rival the £2 billion payday loan industry and to bolster existing credit unions across the country that lend money to less well-off people responsibly – and at far lower rates of interest than the likes of Wonga.

It was a move that generated reams of press coverage and sparked vigorous debate about the nature of payday lending,[2] an industry renowned for interest rates as high as 6,000 per cent APR (credit unions typically lend at less than 30 per cent), almost instant delivery of credit to people's bank accounts without the kinds of suitability checks administered by mainstream lenders, and a willingness to hand over cash to people with little or no means to pay it back. To many longstanding critics the industry's activities amounted to little more than exploitation of poor and vulnerable people – and successive governments had done nowhere near enough to curb it. And, while the Archbishop's highly unusual intervention would lose some of its lustre when it emerged that the church's own pension scheme had indirect investments in Wonga,[3] and he had to concede his alternative would take a long time to set up,[4] the point was nevertheless made.

Calls for greater regulation of these expensive, easy-access loans grew louder throughout 2013 as austerity tightened its grip and financial hardship grew. The government was widely criticised for inaction, and in April 2013 it announced an investment of £36 million in credit unions.[5] Then, in July, ministers hosted a meeting with payday loan firms to discuss growing concerns, but ruled out any option to cap interest rates.[6] Finally, the pressure on the government became irresistible. At the end of November

2013 the Chancellor surprised many commentators when he announced during a BBC radio interview that the government intended to introduce a 'cap' on payday loans.

All the while, those who had been advocating for change for a long time, such as Martin Lewis, founder of the website moneysavingexpert.com, and the national advice network Citizens Advice, were drumming home the damaging effects such loans were having in a climate of cuts. Writing in the *Daily Telegraph*, Lewis argued that while Welby's involvement in the debate was 'laudable', it had actually let the government off the hook by volunteering to step in and help when actually what was needed first was tighter regulation.[7] In what was, in effect, an open letter to the Archbishop, Lewis wrote:

> Wonga and other 6,000pc APR loans are the crack-cocaine of the money-lending world – recent studies even suggest some people are now payday loan addicts. And while I'm a fan of credit unions and cheer Bishop Welby inviting them into churches, that's unlikely to scratch this 21st century problem's surface. Many payday loan customers are as likely to visit a church as the Archbishop is to win Olympic gymnastics gold.

He continued:

> These loans are about speed and ease.... As one of the few places where there's not been a crackdown, the UK's a crock of gold for payday lenders. That's why they fill our high streets … we do need tight controls on this industry. Competition from the Church is not enough. Costs should be capped, ads banned from kids' TV, the application process slowed, and mandatory credit checks enforced. Those of us who've campaigned on this for years have recently built up pressure on a government reticent about acting – and I worry your

much reported intervention risks letting politicians off the hook.

Payday lenders defended their industry on numerous occasions, with some backers calling criticism 'financial snobbery',[8] but as criticisms of the loans came thick and fast, there was particularly vocal outcry about the practice of 'rolling over' loans – where firms encouraged borrowers to extend the life of an existing debt rather then pay it off quickly, thereby increasing the total amount customers had to pay back as further interest accrued.[9] One piece of research by Citizens Advice found seven out of ten people were put under pressure to extend their loan.[10] Indeed, in July 2013, the Office of Fair Trading (OFT) trained its own spotlight on what had by then become a lightning-rod issue for anti-austerity activists when it wrote to 50 payday loan companies after an investigation revealed concerns that they were engaging in problematic activities, including rolling over.[11] Fifteen firms quickly exited the market before the deadline by which they would have to respond and, in August, the regulator referred the entire industry to the Competition Commission.

Meanwhile, following its own research, Citizens Advice – which, among other indictments of the industry, found numerous instances of harassment by industry staff and that loans were in some instances being given to people while they were drunk – launched a campaign urging people who had been mistreated by payday lenders to report their experiences to the OFT. By September 2013 the organisation was warning that four million people were forecast to take out payday loans over the following six months – this was on top of a 10-fold increase in the previous four years.[12] Its chief executive, Gillian Guy, said:

> "Citizens Advice sees people day in day out who have been left in absolutely desperate situations by irresponsible lenders.

Saddled with years worth of debts, many people are left feeling completely powerless."

In an effort to stem the stream of people getting into greater financial difficulty by turning to payday lenders, some local councils even took the extraordinary action of barring access to payday loan sites on council-supplied computer terminals – in libraries, for example. One group of councils in Yorkshire embarked on the strategy in late 2013, ensuring that anyone trying to log on to a payday site was automatically redirected to alternative services offering debt advice, such as Citizens Advice.[13]

And there were signs too that the wider population was cottoning on to the insidious nature of payday lending, and how people accruing more debt due to benefits cuts were being snared into borrowing more. In August 2013 a YouGov poll found that 89 per cent of people in the UK believed payday lenders 'take advantage of the vulnerable' and 88 per cent felt they 'encouraged people to get into more debt'. It also found that 90 per cent of the public was in favour of limits being applied on the amount payday firms could lend to individuals. The findings clearly demonstrated the degree to which outrage had grown at what was once seen as a relatively marginal issue affecting a small quarter of society.[14]

In late summer 2013, when Wonga announced record annual profits of £62.5 million – up by a third on the previous year and representing loans totalling £1.2 billion to over one million borrowers – there were yet more calls for government to legislate to rein them in. When the figures were released, Labour MP, Stella Creasy, a long-time campaigner on high-interest loans targeted at poorer people, said the surge in profits should be "of great concern" to the whole country. She went on: "What that says about families who are struggling financially, what it says about the kind of regulation we currently have in the UK and the things we need to do to make sure people in Britain can borrow affordably – Wonga might be celebrating today [but] I am very, very concerned about what this might mean for people in my community and across the country who are paying the price for their profits."

Those in the payday loan business argued that they were merely meeting a rising demand and responding to, as Wonga's chief executive put it to ITV News, a "tech-savvy" public wanting a more convenient kind of service: "This is not about people on breadlines being desperate …", he told the interviewer, "this is about us serving customers who want to take a loan and know they can pay it back in three days." However, when the company's accounts were published, the disclosure of how much debt Wonga was having to write off – as *The Guardian* reported: "it wrote off £96 million and made a £126 million provision for customers defaulting in 2012, double the levels of 2011" – made it apparent that many of the people taking out loans were not able to repay them.[15] According to Citizens Advice, three out of every four people had problems paying back their loan.[16]

Untenable debt: the exponential pressures on household income

It was clear that the ascension of companies such as Wonga since 2010 (Wonga alone was three times the size of the 390-strong credit union market in 2012[17]) was directly related to falling incomes and cuts to benefits. It wasn't just the availability of payday loans that was driving growth and profits – it was the ballooning need among hundreds of thousands of people. As with food banks, personal debt had become a totem of the torturous battle by households to make ends meet in an atmosphere of severe austerity. And – no need to point out the horrible irony here, but I will – if the boom in the UK and elsewhere pre-crisis had been fuelled by spiralling personal debt handed out like candy by irresponsible banks, it turns out the bust was exacerbated by a new tranche of reckless lending, although this time courtesy of a different cabal of financial operators.

And if in the past people had largely used payday loan avenues for, say, emergencies or 'big spend' times of year such as Christmas, as evidenced in numerous reports tracking their use,[18] once austerity had kicked in people were increasingly turning to them for cash to purchase essentials such as food or clothing for their children. Richard Lloyd, Executive Director of Which?, the consumer rights group, told the *Mirror* newspaper that the problem with payday loans and other forms of high-interest borrowing was intimately linked to more people seeking credit for basic purchases. He also added that much more needed to be done to regulate the industry in order to protect vulnerable citizens.[19] He explained:

> "People are increasingly turning to high cost credit just to pay for essentials or repay other debts, so it is vital that the government and regulators continue to get tougher on irresponsible lenders."

Many campaigners were singling out high-interest lenders for protest. The People's Assembly, a coalition of anti-austerity activists, was among those advocating for action on what it called 'legal loan sharks'.[20] When announcing a public protest in early autumn 2013, the organisation stated bluntly:

> This government is responsible for the biggest drop in living standards for over a generation. Wages are falling and thousands face precarious work with the rise of zero hours contracts. This is forcing people into the hands of legal loan sharks who are targeting the poorest in society, charging outrageous interest rates and pushing people further into poverty.

Debt for survival, not luxuries, had become a part of everyday existence for people on low incomes facing rising bills and slashed benefits. As Debbie in Croxteth pointed out:

> "I'm in more debt than I've ever been. I'm feeling the pinch now even though I'm working. Sometimes I think I'd be better off not working. Obviously I'd never do that. I've got debt on my head because I'm trying to maintain a standard of living. And it's not a high standard of living I can assure you."

In South Tyneside, Lynne Middleward told me how tough her life had been since losing her job and surviving on benefits. After three years out of work she was desperate, and in order to avoid plunging into debt she couldn't handle, she was eking out an existence as best she could. If it wasn't for a local women's centre, Middleward said, her situation would be unbearable. Describing the near-destitution she experienced, Lynne told me:

> "I've got no TV. I had to cancel my TV licence. I've got no fridge running, I'm not using the heating at all yet. To me it just looks so gloomy. I've done my best. I've got two degrees. I'm so lonely. I'm afraid to put the light on at night because of the cost of energy. It makes me very angry but there's not the support out there. I'm just so stuck."

Again, as with the reasons for turning to food banks, the fact that multiple cuts were hitting the same homes and the same vulnerable groups played a pivotal role in stoking debt concerns. For example, according to Carers UK, people with disabilities and carers were particularly badly affected. Research by the charity found that carers were being pushed into debt as a direct result of the 'Bedroom Tax', because the £25 million Discretionary Fund set up by the government to help affected disabled tenants was being denied to nine out of ten carers who applied for ongoing assistance.[21] Also, in common with the use of food banks, rising utility bills and their bedfellow fuel poverty had a role to play in escalating debt. According to the charity Barnardo's, the average amount that people were in debt to energy companies rose exponentially in the second half of the last decade, and by 2011, just when a multitude of austerity policies was being rolled out, the average debt was £320 for gas and electricity, up from £170 six years earlier. According to analysis by Citizens Advice in early 2013, 28 per cent of people approaching the organisation for advice related to energy also had utility-related debt problems.[22]

Fuel poverty had been a problem for the poorest in society for a number of years and, as the recession and austerity took hold, campaigners including Citizens Advice warned that unless something was done by government to address it, the problem would worsen. Many low-income families don't have access to a bank account – and thus can't access the savings brought by direct debits – so the cost of energy for poorer people tends to be higher, and they have traditionally been disproportionately affected by energy price hikes.[23] According to Citizens Advice, by the end of 2013 household utility bills would have risen by 37 per cent in just three years. In November 2013 its chief executive, Gillian Guy, warned:

> "People have been hit with price hikes of 37 per cent over three years while energy firms continue to make bumper profits. This has sent household budgets into disarray as people struggle to afford to heat their home. Consumers need assurance that the big public debate on energy will result in bills that are affordable now and in the future."

Meanwhile the consumer group Which? reported that worries about energy prices were at their highest since it began tracking the issue, with six out of ten people saying they didn't

—

trust energy firms – making it the least trusted of all consumer industry sectors.[24]

By the end of 2013 energy bills were at the top of the political agenda. As figures emerged that over 30,000 people had died needlessly in the winter of 2012,[25] and debate raged about price hikes in gas and electricity while energy company profits soared by 75 per cent in 2013,[26] the main political parties locked horns over whose policies would help consumers. The government pledged to knock £50 off the annual average fuel bill by altering the 'Green Levy', while the Labour Leader, Ed Miliband, accused the government of a 'smoke and mirrors' approach to the issue and reiterated his promise to freeze electricity bills for 20 months if Labour won the election in 2015.[27]

Adding further controversy to an almost gladiatorial spectacle, it also emerged that with the passage of the Energy Bill into law the government intended to change the definition of fuel poverty – thereby automatically 'officially' reducing the number of people deemed to be living in it.[28] Instead of the old definition of fuel poverty as those households that need to spend more than 10 per cent of their income on fuel 'to maintain an adequate level of warmth', the Energy Bill was scheduled to change this to those households that needed to spend more than the average to keep warm. The result? In an instant the numbers supposedly living in fuel poverty in England would plummet from 3.2 million to 2.4 million. Chair of the parliamentary Environmental Audit Committee, Joan Walley, MP, said the government was "shifting the goalposts on fuel poverty so that official statistics record far fewer households as fuel-poor".

Another contributor to the debt problems of the poorest households was the government's removal of the emergency loans that had previously helped to tide people over – and keep them out of the hands of the payday and high-interest lenders. In April 2013 the government abolished the Social Fund's primary planks: Community Care Grants (non-repayable grants to help people to live independently in the community, or to ease exceptional pressures on families) and Crisis Loans, both of which were administered by Jobcentre Plus. They were replaced by Local Welfare Assistance schemes (in the name of increased 'localism', a policy trope lauded by the Tories) to be delivered by councils in England and the devolved government of Wales and Scotland. (The situation was different in Northern Ireland, where at the time of writing, the Welfare Reform Bill had not yet come into law. The Welfare Reform Bill for Northern Ireland proposed changes to the Social Fund, which would come into force in Spring 2014, with a similar impact to those in the other UK nations.[29]) According to a report by The Children's Society, *Nowhere to turn? Changes to emergency support*, the replacement schemes were mainly shifting to a 'benefits in kind' grants system, such as vouchers or offering loans that were no longer interest-free.[30] The charity raised alarm bells about the changes, warning that children and the most vulnerable families would end up suffering further. Dr Sam Royston, poverty and early years policy adviser at the charity, contended:

> "The Children's Society is concerned that the loss of this crucial form of interest-free credit will mean that families turn to high-interest lenders instead. This comes at the worst possible time. A recent Which? survey found that one million households are using payday loans each month – including four in ten using them for essentials like food and fuel."

There was another facet to the household debt problem. Referring to the issue in the context of the bigger economic picture, economist Ann Pettifor told the BBC's Today Programme in August 2013 how it was artificially underpinning recovery and masking ongoing problems.[31] She said: "I think it's artificial and can't be sustained." She added: "At a fundamental level it's quite dangerous because household debt is still 153 per cent of GDP.

There's nothing seriously underpinning this recovery, and that's why it's Alice in Wongaland, the confidence fairy is out there."

In October 2013 figures from the Bank of England revealed that household debt in the UK had reached a record high of £1.43 trillion. In the same month the Money Advice Service reported that only a fraction of the nine million people in serious debt were getting help.[32] Some parts of the country such as the North East of England had disproportionately high levels of personal debt and insolvencies, raising concerns that, since the region was also one of the hardest hit by cuts, even greater problems lay ahead.[33] Meanwhile, data released by the Bank of England revealed that people were increasingly turning to high-cost consumer loans such as credit cards and personal loans to maintain their standard of living – an annual rise of 3.5 per cent and the largest since 2008.[34] And then there was the related and often terrifying problem of bailiffs descending on people's homes to enforce debt payments. One report from the Money Advice Trust concluded that councils in England and Wales were deploying bailiffs 'excessively' to recoup debts, while Citizens Advice found there had been a 38 per cent increase in the number of complaints against private bailiffs between 2008 and 2013.[35]

In November 2013 an alarming report from The Centre for Social Justice (the think tank Iain Duncan Smith founded, no less) found that personal debt in the UK was spiralling – reaching £1.4 trillion – and that 'problem debt' was a scourge for many families. The think tank warned that poorer people were bearing the brunt, and that those at the lower end of the income scale were paying more than a quarter of their income in debt payments. The report, *Maxed out*,[36] also found that approximately 5,000 people a year were being made homeless as a result of mortgage arrears. Payday lenders, pawnbrokers and home-collected credit providers between them lent almost

£5 billion in high-cost credit in 2012 – up from £2.9 billion in 2009, it found.

Even when there was some good news about personal debt, it usually came caveat-loaded. For example, *The financial capability of the UK*, published by the Money Advice Service in late summer 2013, concluded that, as money became tighter, many people were developing 'positive money habits' to keep some control of ever-more precarious personal financial situations. However, it also found huge numbers of people struggling to keep up with bills – up from 35 per cent in 2006 to 52 per cent in 2013. And this wasn't just the poorer segments of the population. It also found that a fifth of people had experienced 'a large drop in income' since 2010, and that 42 per cent of people would 'have to think' about how to cover an unexpected bill of as little at £300.[37] Concerns about how people would cope going into 2014 were raised once again when in the autumn of 2013 it was projected that average fuel bills would rise to a record £1,500 a year, with one consumer organisation calling the proposed price hikes "horrifying".[38]

Debt: the view from the front line

The key question, of course, is what all of this has really meant for people at the sharp end. What did people think and feel about the debt they were accumulating during austerity in order merely to survive? And what about the people and agencies picking up the pieces? Perhaps unsurprisingly, debt was a touchstone issue all over the country. There was acute awareness that a large number of households were scrimping by *only because* of access to unsecured debt. In many cases, the interest rates were neither understood nor even considered in the decision to borrow, because the need was simply too great. What tended to happen, judging from the debt advisers I interviewed, was that when a crisis point was finally reached, more people were desperately reaching out to community organisations and debt advisers for help – themselves often struggling to offer a full service because of funding cuts.

In Lynemouth, Northumberland, Alec Crumplin described a rapidly worsening situation where debt was becoming the only way for many people to stay afloat – especially in a community where the jobs that were available tended to be Minimum Wage or part time. Extortionate interest rates were, he said, trapping people in intractable debt cycles:

> "The payday loans are absolutely rife, so are the likes of Provident and the other doorstep companies and they are taking people down because they are not careful about who they actually lend to or how much they're prepared to lend. At present some of the payday loan companies are over 4,000 per cent. Somebody borrowing £200 suddenly finds out a year later when they are still paying it off at £20 a week they are still nowhere near having paid it off."

According to Crumplin, the credit unions were able to help a lot of people but, he added: "unfortunately unless we've got the money coming in from savers – who aren't around any more – it becomes harder and harder".

In Glasgow David Martin, a debt adviser, referred to a marked mushrooming of people reaching out with debt problems – and not just people who were struggling before austerity:

> "What we are seeing is an increase in people who may not be on benefits but are also experiencing debt problems. So even the people who are out working we are now seeing an increase in those types of people coming to see us. Basically they are struggling with the amount of money they have to pay out for food and heating and stuff. The current economic climate even seems to be affecting people in full-

time employment. Admittedly, Minimum Wage full-time employment, but we are definitely seeing an increase, which makes us think that the problem is a lot worse. People that were able to cope before ... are really starting to feel the pinch."

He added:

"The demand for our services is getting incredible. We could double the number of staff we have and we would still not be able to see everyone who comes to see us. The sense of panic is getting stronger practically on an hourly basis never mind a daily basis. And we don't see the situation getting any better."

Jackie Gallagher at Citizens Advice in Derry suggested in early 2013 that the full scale of the problem with debt had yet to be fully realised because so many people were ignoring demands for payments due to stress. She predicted that by 2014 things would be beyond crisis point. In addition, she said, there was no way to know how much further people would fall into debt due to rent and other arrears once things like the benefits cap and Universal Credit came into force.

"What we're seeing now is bills dropping on the mat. Nobody wants to see the postman coming because they're worried, they're in debt [and] they're hiding it. Their marriages are breaking up, they're taking anti-depressants to try and cope with it."

In Hull, one local Citizens Advice senior debt adviser suggested the biggest problems with debt for the most vulnerable – such as lone parents – would not even begin to be fully apparent until many months after the introduction of policies such as

---

the 'Bedroom Tax', which, in percentage terms, would decimate incomes and lead to debts spiralling out of control. She said:

> "If you run up a debt with the Council Tax, £60, £80 – and that doesn't take long when you have no money – the first thing you're going to get is a liability order which is then going to cost you £80. The next thing a couple of weeks later if you haven't paid is it's passed to the bailiffs.[39] The bailiffs will then add on approximately another £50 to that just by the fact that they've taken over the case and dropped a note through the door. They will then come back and try to gain access to the property to levy on goods which will be another £100–£200.
>
> From April we will find it increasingly difficult to help people maintain their essential expenditure. Rents will go up, rent arrears will go up … people will then start facing repossession with nowhere to go."

Just a few minutes' walk away from the noisy traffic speeding by on an overpass near Bromley-by-Bow tube station in the East End of London, nestled among densely packed streets and housing estates, are the leafy surroundings of the Bromley-by-Bow Centre, a local not-for-profit community centre. In the cafe people sit around drinking coffee and chatting. It looks and feels like a welcoming space – and it is. However, the reason the centre was so busy in the spring of 2013 was because of debt. Over the previous few months the centre had seen its debt advice service swamped by people with acute debt problems and, according to one worker at the centre, Amanda Hopewell, demand was expected to keep on rising as more cuts kicked in.

Since Bromley-by-Bow is in one of the most deprived boroughs in the country, Tower Hamlets, the centre had always had a steady flow of locals coming through the doors taking advantage of services such as employment advice and money management classes. But by 2013, Hopewell pointed out, the nature and urgency of enquiries had altered dramatically.

"Recently with cuts what's massively changing is the demand we've got for the advice service", she explained. "[Debt] is starting to be something that everyone is talking about."

To make matters worse, Hopewell said, the centre was forced to cut the number of advisers by half because the local council – which was under its own financial strains due to austerity – had cut its funding for the debt service just as demand was spiralling upwards. Hopewell explained:

> "It's a massive cut. It makes it difficult. A lot of volunteers are helping out at the moment. Y'just don't understand how they can justify making any of the cuts when they know people will always need us. If they're going to make cuts to the benefits then they can't make the cuts to welfare centres that are there to support people."

Gathered in the cafe, some of the remaining staff manning the debt advice service spoke animatedly to me about the growing financial difficulties of clients old and new, and how this was stretching resources to the limit. They talked of the "frightening" accumulation of debt as a result of benefits cuts that were leaving hundreds of clients confronting indebtedness. Many just didn't know how to cope. They couldn't see a way out.

"People are getting themselves into financial hardship and struggling, getting themselves into debt, and that's when they turn to us to access our services to get them back on track", one adviser said of the constituency of people increasingly relying on the service.

Referring to how much harder it was becoming to deal with demand, another told me: "We do monitoring every quarter and if I look at the whole report ... you can see that for the last two years clients who have been in debt has increased twice as much". "It's a huge problem" another interjected: "I felt really angry when we got the bad news that our main funding from the council had been cut by more than 75 per cent – the council gets the report every year and they can see that demand has increased. There is a queue at 8.30 every morning on our doorstep."

Another debt adviser warned that the scale of the truth was startling. "I just think there's going to be a crisis. I don't know how they are going to cope … dealing with the burden of debts."

The dangerous side of debt

While payday lenders often played a huge part in turning a difficult debt predicament into a ruinous one, and while people turned in droves to debt advisers wherever they could locate them, there were additional serious debt-related issues to contend with for many people, according to many interviewees. Around the country grassroots advisers and community workers talked about how, as people's options for getting their hands on money dwindled, many looked to riskier sources of income to plug the gaps. In most of the areas I travelled to people raised the issue of the proliferation of doorstep lenders and loan sharks operating in local communities already laid low by cuts. Not only were thousands of vulnerable people taking on expensive legal loans, it seemed, some were taking on illegal and dangerous ones.

When the TUC embarked on its 'Austerity Tour' of the UK in 2013 to amass frontline insights on the impact of austerity, it found that illegal loan sharks were an ominous presence in communities across the UK.[40] When the tour visited Newcastle in the North East of England, its report *Drowning in debt* concluded:

> If you find yourself in trouble financially there's always cash available to you. The problem is that it's very rarely the right option to take. Loan sharks operating in local communities

are on the increase. The CAB [Citizens Advice Bureaux] are seeing this right across the city but have focused particularly on Byker where they're currently finding a lot of cases. It's a guy on a street corner who makes it their business to know everyone in the community.

It went on:

They know when you get your pay or benefits in, how your circumstances might be changing and when you're likely to be short. A quick deal with them and one of their mates pops round in a car with an envelope of cash. They operate outside the law, and anonymously, so it's hard to track them down and for groups like the CAB to talk to them about cases, and as a borrower you can't afford to fall foul of them as their huge interest rates are backed up by the threat of violence.

The TUC's findings were widely reflected in news reports about predatory loan sharks operating in deprived areas,[41] and in a number of the more deprived communities visited for this book. Billy Hutchinson, a neighbourhood renewal worker at Epic, a community organisation in one of the most deprived parts of Belfast in Northern Ireland, the Shankill, spoke pointedly on the issue. According to Hutchinson, despite the stigma attached to debt, cuts and benefits changes were pushing many people in the area he lives and works in towards the kind of loans they would not otherwise contemplate, while at the same time mounting pressures were becoming too much for some to bear:

"We had a woman who lives in the flats with two children and under [the benefits changes] she's going to lose £2,000. So what's going to happen is she's going to be even deeper in poverty. People don't know how to cope with this other than to turn to people who are actually giving [high-interest] loans. So [there are] big, big problems…. It's going to get worse."

The links between cuts, debt and personal pressures were there for anyone to see, Hutchinson said:

"We are talking about people being able to pay rent, people being able to clothe and feed their children. People are very proud and don't want to [rely on hand-outs]… People have been living in poverty; the difficulty now is it's getting worse….What I can see in my community where I work and I've people are coming up to me and saying what are we going to do? People are choosing whether to put a coat over their bed or turn the heating on. We are going to find people dead….All they're hearing is austerity cuts and that's the reality."

Tom Roberts, Director at Epic, and David Colvin, a local resident, agreed, saying people were being preyed on precisely because they were vulnerable, and that many were left stranded with few options. Roberts said:

"You have unscrupulous people who are profiting from people's situations. I see examples of it on this road here. People can't afford to fill their [heating] tanks with oil so they buy these small [containers] at exorbitant prices. Then you have the loan sharks. People are desperate and they have nowhere else to turn for money. They're going to these people and then they are getting into trouble if they can't pay back the money."

As many interviewees pointed out, the warp speed at which vulnerable people or those on low incomes were being engulfed by debt was astonishing, with the long-term effects on financial and indeed psychological wellbeing yet to be fully determined. But if debt was wearing people down, then the extraordinary pressure brought to bear by the government's much-touted 'welfare-to-work' reforms represented a colossal slap in the face to the hundreds of thousands all over the UK battling to survive austerity. It is to this, and the wider implications of worklessness, that we now turn.

FOUR

Work maketh the person

Demonisation of the jobless: austerity and the myth of the skiver

"I find the language of 'skivers versus strivers' particularly offensive when it comes to single parents, who are already working around the clock to care for their children. Such rhetoric drains confidence and self-esteem from those who desperately want, as I did, to get back into the job market.... Meanwhile the government mantra that work is the best route out of poverty is ringing increasingly hollow, with nearly 1 in 3 children whose single parent works part time still growing up in poverty." (J.K. Rowling, author and president of the charity, Gingerbread)

Having softened up their audience with a press campaign of tales of 'scroungers' and fraudsters, the Tories couldn't have been clearer about their purpose: to turn the low paid against the unemployed. (Commentator Seumas Milne writing in *The Guardian* in January 2013)

Cunning narrative behind the cuts

When author J.K. Rowling speaks, people listen. The creator of Harry Potter and former unemployed single mother is one of those rare individuals who went on to accumulate great wealth after having lived on the bread line, yet never lost sight of her previous status, using her own experience to highlight the ongoing difficulties of others by speaking out. In September 2013 Rowling harnessed her fame and her platform as president of Gingerbread,[1] a charity that campaigns for the rights of lone parents, to launch a stinging riposte to what had turned out to be one of the most contentious issues associated with austerity: the propagation of the idea – the myth – that a person who isn't in work is not just jobless, but worthless.

With understated eloquence Rowling was able to get straight to the heart of the matter. Referring to a disparaging comment by the welfare minister and former investment banker, Lord Freud, suggesting those on benefits needed to take more risks to remove themselves from welfare dependency (the minister said, "people who are poor should be prepared to take the biggest risks – they've got least to lose".[2]) Rowling responded that such statements spoke "to a profound disconnect with people struggling to keep their heads above water".

That the government (and mainstream politicians generally) were guilty of a kind of 'profound disconnect' was a sentiment shared by people at the sharp end of austerity all over the UK. Everywhere I went terms such as "they live on another planet" and "they have no idea what it's really like" were used by people genuinely baffled by why so much vitriol was being levelled at them while they were trying to find a job. The notion of unemployment as a 'lifestyle choice', as the Chancellor George Osborne was so fond of referring to it, was laughable to the interviewees. And, they asked, when it was an international banking crisis and unprecedented recession that had wreaked havoc on the economy, how was it the fault of people who were out of work that they couldn't get a job? Were they merely convenient scapegoats for a failed system?

The pillorying of people who were claiming benefits was also a concern expressed by staff at voluntary organisations. In most instances I didn't even have to ask a question about the 'striver versus skiver' debate. The despair and anger about it came pouring out before there was a chance to. Most expressed consternation that anyone, never mind elected politicians, could so wilfully label their own citizens as idle, and almost all spoke of how (already vulnerable) people's morale was being erased in the face of ratcheted-up rhetoric that painted them as useless.

Chief executive of Birmingham Settlement, Martin Holcombe, talked about people being "demolished" by the combination of cuts and condemnatory rhetoric, saying that it would be folly to underestimate the real-life impact of relentless, unjustified public vilification.

"There's a real issue around the fact that people have very, very low self-esteem. They are constantly being put down. They are constantly demonised", Holcombe told me. "They are seen by many in the media and many in the elite classes as scroungers and [as] people who don't contribute. There are always going to be one or two instances of people who work the system but the overwhelming, vast majority of people we see have no choice about where they are. That constant bashing and demonising is really depressing for people."

"For a lot of people", he added despondently, "they start to see that as what they actually are. It's easier to slip into this role you're being portrayed as. And then where do you go from that?"

In Hull, an area with a longstanding dearth of job opportunities,[3] Martin Davis, a community area manager at the Goodwin Development Trust, spoke of how, despite people "doing their very best" to find work – and volunteering in ever-greater numbers to improve their prospects – there were over 50 individuals chasing every vacancy. The situation was only made worse, he suggested, by the media unfairly painting its jobseekers as 'feckless'.

> "We are just like any other big city [yet] we get bad press. We get certain television stations telling us we are the worst place to live ... that we have the worst local economy. It grinds people down. Times are hard enough as it is [so people] don't need that sort of publicity."

Meanwhile, in Leeds, 'Anne Jones' was desperately looking for work when I spoke to her. Along with a small cohort of others in a similar position she was involved with a project called Dole Animators, an unusual initiative that used animation voiced over by jobseekers to bring a message to the government about what it was really like to look for work in a climate of castigation. The project evolved from academic research undertaken by the University of Leeds that tracked the effects of welfare changes on jobseekers from the beginning of austerity. Jones and other participants all stressed how important it was in helping them "not feel alone" against the constant demonisation they were facing.[4]

A middle-aged lone parent, Anne was retraining as a teaching assistant in an effort to find secure, stable work that would allow her to support her daughter. She was convinced that the "daily struggle" of jobseekers appeared to be beyond the comprehension of those in power. Jobs were so scarce, she said, that even though she'd worked hard to acquire new qualifications, her lack of experience was hindering her chances. As a result she found herself, dispiritingly, being told by jobcentre staff that she should jettison her goal and become a care worker instead, because that's the kind of (low-paid, low-skilled) job that was available.

Sounding exasperated, she said: "Does that mean I can't compete? I have the same qualifications. Am I not good enough? I don't understand."

Anne said having to contend with a bombardment of negativity from jobcentre staff and the wider accusations from politicians and the media that being out of work was tantamount to being a skiver made the process of looking for work unbearable. "I have ended up on anti-depressants", she explained. "Everything is too much. I would love nothing more than standing on my own two feet and not having to go to that job centre to sign on, [yet] someone is telling me I am getting something for free. I really hate it. People are willing to look for jobs but if you push and push and make them feel low ... you will not get the results. The pressure is too much. [Politicians] live on another planet – I don't know which one. They don't know the reality of it."

There can't have been a person living under austerity in the UK who was unaware of the brazenly toxic mantra 'skiver versus striver' – or shirker, or scrounger – all of which were unashamedly bandied about by politicians and pundits to denigrate unemployed people. The epithet was ubiquitous, it was barbed and it somehow managed to become cemented within public discourse almost from the outset of the government's cuts programme.[5] From the get-go in Austerity UK, open season was unofficially declared on people who were out of work or on benefits. It didn't matter whether you were ill, had a disability, whether you were a carer, lone parent or indeed someone made redundant due to the government's swingeing cuts to public sector jobs – you were a target for the opprobrium of every opportunistic politician with a nasty sound bite to peddle and every newspaper with an axe to grind.

As Owen Jones put it in his 2011 book, *Chavs: The demonization of the working class*,[6] the notion of jobless people as feckless, indolent leeches hoovering up taxes paid by that convenient chimera politicians loved referring to – 'hardworking families' – was already in motion prior to May 2010. In fact, as Jones pointed out, being unemployed had increasingly been conflated with cheating the system during the previous Labour government. He wrote: 'Extreme examples of "benefits fraudsters" are hunted down with relish by the tabloids, and are passed off, not as isolated examples, but as representative of an endemic and far bigger problem. The "scrounger" has become the public face of the unemployed in Britain.'

In the months following the publication of Jones' book, the denigration of the unemployed escalated. As austerity bit ever harder, 'skivers' would become not just a fantastical whipping boy for advocates of benefits reform – the skiver was deemed to *represent* the majority of unemployed people. People who were out of work became the outcasts of the austerity age. Tabloid headlines gleefully reported any fresh government crackdown on people claiming out-of-work benefits. There were too many examples to list here, but suffice to say that within months of the election in 2010 the tone had been set. Try a Google search for 'benefit scroungers' and a very long list of articles will pop up, such as one in August 2010 when *The Sun* launched a campaign calling on readers to help the paper 'beat the cheats' who, it posited, were ripping off the state in zombie-like droves thanks to an 'out-of-control handouts culture'.[7] (There was rarely a mention, needless to say, of the millions of pounds being saved by the Treasury every year due to benefits – ranging from pension credit to Jobseeker's Allowance – going unclaimed, or indeed of the individuals and corporations enthusiastically avoiding paying taxes.[8]) A typical article in the *Daily Mail* a year-and-a-half later referring to the government's plans to reassess people 'on the sick' declared: 'The only way is easy street: How Essex town of Brentwood is skiving capital of Britain.'[9]

Even if you were in work, but happened to be in the public sector, there were plenty of (as Patrick Butler in *The Guardian* called them) 'nasty, gratuitous and casually vicious' articles around spreading falsehoods about civil servants as (again pointed out by Butler) 'lazy, wasteful and inefficient', and therefore deserving the loss of hundreds of thousands of jobs.[10]

And on and on it went. From newsrooms to parliamentary benches to the average high street, the skivers were invoked as to blame for an 'out-of-control welfare bill' and were apparently guilty of rampant 'benefit dependency'. So how did the concept of the skiver become so entrenched over the course of just a few years that the people I interviewed consistently ranked it as one of the most adverse and 'soul-destroying' characteristics of austerity in the UK? Back in 2012 at the Conservative Party Conference, George Osborne made a speech that hit a nerve.[11] In it he finessed a plethora of previous attacks by Tories and the press[12] against "the benefits culture" and the people who supposedly partook of it. Just in case after two years of austerity the country hadn't quite grasped the skiver narrative and its analogous trumped-up polarising of people in and out of work, he made what would become an infamous declaration: "Where is the fairness, we ask, for the shift-worker, leaving home in the dark hours of the early morning, who looks up at the closed blinds of their next door neighbour sleeping off a life on benefits?"

The speech was among the most emblematic of numerous attempts to paint people who were out of work as undeserving layabouts and, following these incendiary remarks, anti-poverty and anti-cuts campaigners made their indignation heard.[13] One was Ruth Lister. Countering the contrived notion of people lounging around in taxpayer-funded luxury while others valiantly marched out to work (to say nothing of the fact that the people behind Osborne's fictional blinds were just as likely to be shift workers themselves, exhausted by the same low-paid jobs their mythical counterparts were supposedly on their way to), Lister was unequivocal. Speaking to a conference in Bradford in Autumn 2013 she concluded: "This has encouraged the framing of the [welfare] debate in the loathsome terms of 'skivers' vs 'strivers' in which striving is synonymous with paid work and skiving with out of work benefit receipt – apart from anything else totally ignoring the extent to which many people on low incomes are constantly moving in and out of work."

Like Rowling and Lister, the people I interviewed were keenly sensitive to the proliferation of pejorative language to demean anyone who was out of work and/or living in poverty. It permeated almost every conversation precisely because it was such a powerfully blunt narrative, but also because it was seen as integral to the ideological architecture propping up a stream of 'back-to-work' policies, benefits reforms and cuts.

In Croxteth, the women interviewed were stridently opposed to the noxious implications of labelling people as shirkers, pointing out that the maligning of whole swaths of people as 'spongers' was as alienating as it was insulting. Not only were the working poor among those most affected by cuts and increasingly being flung into poverty, the women said, but the skiver narrative was actually hurting people battling to, as one said, "pull themselves back up" and get back to any kind of job.

This is what Debbie concluded:

> "You know, they are sitting down there [in Downing Street] saying they're just lazy Scousers; they won't work. I'd rather work every hour that God sends in a week than have to go and tell my children there's nothing in for tea."

Referring to the 2012 Osborne Conference speech, this was what Sharon had to say:

> "They like to say, oh, it's the scroungers and the out of workers lying at home with the curtains shut watching Jeremy Kyle on the television. The majority of people this is affecting are out there every day working."

As for Jamie Gates from East Sussex who, due to his mental health difficulties, had been out of work for multiple periods of time, the deliberate deployment of negative references to people without employment was nothing more than a tactic to validate benefits changes. It was, he said, putting enormous stress on already vulnerable people. "I can't strictly work. I can do voluntary work; it's the pressure I can't take. What upsets me quite a lot is that if you're on benefits you're [labelled as] lazy ... you're a scrounger. It's not actually true. I'm using it as a safety net. I want to go back to some kind of employment."

Also in East Sussex, Rachel Hesterbanks, an employment adviser who had years of experience dealing with claimants, was unwavering in her view that the berating of people on benefits as if they were one homogeneous mass of cheats was risible. As a frontline worker, Hesterbanks insisted that seeing desperate people come through the doors for help – often people who'd held down well-paid, secure jobs for years prior to the recession – was a far cry from the image presented in the press or by politicians. The actions of a tiny minority were, she said, being transposed on to a populace in genuine need. This is what she had to say:

> "Fair enough, there are a tiny, minimal amount of individuals who know the system and play it. And don't get me wrong, I have met those individuals. We all know them. We've been at this job long enough. You can pretty much tell straight away which ones are sincerely there and sincerely require support and those who really don't care."

On Marsh Farm in Luton, the scorn of politicians and the more cynical corners of the press was something 'Dec' was intimately familiar with. He talked about how, like many people, he had moved from benefits to part-time employment and back, and about how destabilising it could be. But, he stressed, sometimes worse than the process itself was the stigmatising rhetoric from "out-of-touch" politicians who made people like him feel like "second-class citizens". For Dec, the whole employment ecosystem was predicated on contempt for people in need of benefits, and felt as if it were designed to be humiliating and destructive.

> "There's people that are suicidal. There's people with mental health issues – and if they didn't have mental issues before, they have them now because they are being so degraded. They are being so run down in life. I'm not saying I want a life of luxury. I don't want a life of luxury. Do you know what I want? A life. [Pauses to choke back tears] A life. It's just so degrading to be honest. I know I don't know it all. I'm not a million pound adviser to David Cameron. If I was I'd tell him he's an asshole and he's doing it wrong. And I'd tell all the rest of them that unless you really understand what's going on … get out there, get advisers that have lived it."

According to Martin Holcombe at Birmingham Settlement, the situation for many vulnerable people was worsened by a sense of powerlessness. He argued that people felt unable to challenge either the welfare policies and cuts or the dominant discourse surrounding it: "People are being wiped away. The vulnerable people seem to have no voice. They have no mechanism to feed back."

An unholy partnership: the media and austerity politics

Holcombe's conclusions were perhaps unsurprising bearing in mind the seemingly unstoppable success of the skiver mantra. Indeed, the pincer-like choreography of politics and media was nothing if not impressive. Take what was happening by 2013. In February of that year, almost three years after austerity began, *The*

Sun newspaper ran what by then had become a familiar 'benefits scrounger' story.[14] Above a picture of a young mother of two sitting with her children on the floor of her council property – flat screen TV as backdrop, laptop open in front of her, and one child clutching a games console – was the headline: 'I'm the mother of all scroungers'. As was the way with such stories, there were self-incriminating quotes. 'What was the point of getting a crummy job on minimum wage?', the young mother was reported as saying. 'I was 16, had income support, child tax credits and my housing paid for.'

A couple of months later the Prime Minister wrote an article for the same paper (the UK's best-selling tabloid was running a campaign with the loaded moniker, 'Britain's bonkers benefits' at the time) about his reasoning for reforming the welfare state.[15] He went through the government's standard litany of justifications, including that benefits had "trapped too many people" and had become a "lifestyle choice". The situation was, he said, "causing resentment". As well as omitting the obvious fact of there not being adequate employment opportunities in much of the country,[16] there was no mention of the possibility that the jaundiced views towards people who were out of work or claiming benefits was actually intensified by a wholesale misrepresentation thanks to the routine wheeling out of extremely rare and sensational cases, and regular instances of ministers citing increases in the total welfare bill as if it were down to people playing they system. (It wasn't. The bill was going up because pension payments were rising and Housing Benefit payments were more costly as rents soared.[17]) What the Prime Minister also steered away from in his article was any acknowledgement of the ever-harsher language employed by ministers (himself included) in relation to people who were out of work, or how this was having an impact on those who were struggling.

Among the most shocking and flagrant attempts to disparage people in receipt of benefits was one from the Chancellor in early 2013. While being interviewed on ITV News[18] he made what must be one of the most ludicrous segues in television history: he linked the killing of six children in Derby through the deliberate arson of their family home by their parents with supposed flaws in the welfare state. Osborne was quickly branded "sick, sick, sick" by the Labour opposition for taking the exceptional case of Mick Philpott and his criminality and using it to insinuate that the welfare state was somehow responsible for causing him to kill. (Mick and Mairead Philpott, and their friend Paul Mosley, were found guilty of manslaughter after killing Mairead's six children in a deliberate act of arson of the family home in May 2012. Mick had already gained notoriety through media appearances, including on the Jeremy Kyle show, as an extreme example of a benefits scrounger.[19])

This is what the Chancellor had said: "I think there is a question for government and for society about the welfare state and the taxpayers who subsidise lifestyles like this and that debate needs to be had."

It was a brazen and incredible suggestion that, perhaps not surprisingly, came the day after the *Daily Mail* ran a controversial front page with the headline 'Vile product of Welfare UK' in reference to Philpott that itself had sparked a flurry of outrage. It also came as ministers (and some newspapers) were calling for a cap on Child Benefit (on top of those already introduced for higher earners), and for the benefit to be paid only for the first two children in any family.[20] Shadow Chancellor, Ed Balls, responded to the Chancellor's assertions about criminality with undisguised indignation, accusing him of demeaning his office and calling it "the cynical act of a desperate chancellor". However, the disgust provoked by Osborne's statement did not appear to dent the resolve of the government one jot. The next day, in fact, the Prime Minister himself came to the defence of his Chancellor.[21]

He said: "I think what George Osborne said was absolutely right.... But what the Chancellor went on to say was that we should ask some wider questions about our welfare system, how much it costs and the signals that it sends." Reiterating the mantra that divided so-called 'hardworking' people from everyone else, he added: "And we do want to make clear that welfare is there to help people who work hard, it shouldn't be there as a sort of lifestyle choice, and that's entirely legitimate."

But if the Chancellor and indeed the Prime Minister's questionable comments were extreme, they were far from unique. Analysis by *The Guardian* published in April 2013 of the previous year's worth of government communications found that it was increasingly using value-laden and pejorative language when discussing benefits and welfare.[22] Reiterating what poverty charities were warning – that such language led to the stigmatisation of people who were living in poverty or out of work – the analysis revealed that an examination of Department for Work and Pensions speeches and press notices connected to benefits showed a 'significantly increased' use of terms such as 'dependency','entrenched' and 'addiction' when compared with the end of the Labour government. In 25 speeches by Work and Pensions ministers on welfare over the 12 months studied, 'dependency' was mentioned 38 times.[23] The article reported:

> [Iain] Duncan Smith appears to be the most frequent user of value-laden terminology, regularly including terms such as 'entrenched and intergenerational worklessness and welfare dependency' in his speeches.

Referring to the culpability of the media in shaping the narrative it went on: 'Analysis of language in the media a similar picture. In the past year, the term "benefit cheat" was used 442 times in national newspapers, an increase of almost two-thirds on the 12 months before the coalition took power.'

Responding to *The Guardian* report, Helen Barnard, policy manager at JRF, said the bombardment of negativity was having a direct impact on the ground:

> "It sets up this idea that there are poor people and people on benefits and then everybody else, and never the twain shall meet. When you look at the research, it's very much the opposite. The majority of people in the UK will experience poverty at least once in their lifetime."

Tim Nichols, of CPAG, concurred, saying his organisation believed government rhetoric on the issue was having a discernable effect on those claiming benefits:

> "It's without doubt got worse. It is very much linked to the fact they've got a major programme of cuts to social security under way, and are seeking a narrative to justify this. It's becoming increasingly hard for us to find people in poverty or receiving benefits who are happy to speak about their situation in the media. They fear the effect of this stigmatisation if they put themselves in the spotlight – how it might affect them and their children. They really are scared."

Targeting vulnerable citizens

As Rowling had pointed out, lone parents (especially if they were young and on benefits) had long been the poster girls of 'shirkerdom' and on the receiving end of denigrating press coverage.[24] However, perhaps one of the most shocking developments as the skiver narrative took hold and changes to social security began to have a disproportionate impact on certain segments of the population was how people with disabilities were affected by the amplification of the skiver narrative. In August 2012, Disability Rights UK, an alliance of disability organisations, published a report that pulled together some of the evidence of how people with disabilities were being affected by cynical and disparaging press coverage.[25] It made for alarming reading. The organisation concluded that not only did people with disabilities feel discriminated against by press coverage, but that it was contributing to a startling rise in disability hate crime, some of which was believed to be connected to the ubiquity of slurs against benefits recipients.[26] A survey of people with disabilities found that most believed the situation was being worsened because "the government is sometimes behind negative portrayals of disabled people in order to justify cuts in essential support".

According to the survey:

- 94 per cent felt media portrayal of people with disabilities was unfair;
- 76 per cent said negative coverage was 'significantly' increasing;
- 91 per cent said there was a link between disability hate crime/abuse and how people with disabilities were portrayed in the media.

The Sun and *Daily Mail* were the papers mentioned most often as printing scorn-filled stories. Respondents to the survey highlighted how the application of the term 'scroungers' was offensive and extremely distressing, including for people with 'invisible' disabilities who had no immediate way of signalling their situation. They also talked of being made to feel "like an outcast" and being too "scared to go out". Others said it contributed to depression and even to suicidal feelings.

A large proportion of respondents to the study – 77.5 per cent – believed there to be a causal link between negative coverage and the rise in discrimination and hostility towards people with disabilities. Here is what some had to say on rhetoric, coverage, and the fallout:

> "We are an easy target for newspapers and other news media that support current government attacks on the welfare system trying to scare people into seeing mainly as a drain on resources."

> "I've been yelled at, sworn at and insulted, crutches kicked."

> "Personally experienced verbal abuse in the street, after ... articles calling disabled claimants scroungers. I was followed by a group of youths in the street and called 'A scrounging disabled bastard'."

> "A relative, using her mobility vehicle in a supermarket, was sworn at and called a 'fat scrounging cow' and heckled to 'get a fucking job'."

> "Colleagues at work [have been] making derogatory comments about disabled people based on stories they read."

Other research came out with equally disturbing results. *Bad news for disabled people: How the newspapers are reporting disability*, a piece of research conducted by the Strathclyde Centre for Disability Research and Inclusion London in 2012,[27] reported an increasing number of articles depicting people with disabilities as 'a burden' as well as greater use of pejorative language that labelled people with disabilities as 'undeserving'. In addition, it found that articles focusing on disability benefit led some people to believe fraud was as high as 70 per cent. (The government's own figure puts total benefit fraud at 0.7 per cent.[28]) A year earlier in May 2011, research by the disability charity Scope found more than half of people with disabilities (56 per cent) had experienced aggression or violence from strangers.[29]

However, just in case anyone thought the government and certain quarters of the media were entirely accountable for the spread of the toxic skiver narrative, it is worth remembering that there were those in opposition who, either in their hesitancy to challenge it or by making their own contributions, actively compounded the problem (to say nothing of the Liberal Democrats in the Coalition government who were accused of colluding with the Conservatives by virtue of being in government with them and appeasing them in key parliamentary votes – with the occasional exception).[30] Take the comment from (then) Shadow Work and Pensions Secretary Liam Byrne in an interview with the *New Statesman* in November 2012. While in one breath accusing the government of crossing 'the threshold of decency' by 'conjuring up' vulnerable groups to 'kick the crap out of', he then went on to repeat the same mantra as his political foes:[31]

> "It's not Britain's shirkers who are having to pay the cost of failure, it's Britain's strivers. The Tories are screwing Britain's strivers."

In a 2011 speech at the Labour Party Conference,[32] Byrne talked of how Labour needed to respond to comments on the doorstep from voters who thought the Party "stood up too much for shirkers not workers". He added: "We have to deal with that if we want to get re-elected." And he ran into trouble again on the issue when challenged on the BBC's Daily Politics programme in January 2013 about his repeated use of such language[33] (although on this occasion he seemed to squirm a bit at having it pointed out).

What is clear is that the ground was laid for the rise of the skiver under the previous Labour government. As some commentators have pointed out,[34] terms such as 'feral youth' and 'chavs' became common parlance prior to the Coalition, and were clearly employed to demonise particular sections of society that were easily identified and targeted. But, as Zoe Williams wrote in *The Guardian* at the height of the skiver debate in 2013, Labour in opposition were complicit in shoring up the concept of shirkers.[35] Even when opposition politicians like Byrne and Labour Leader, Ed Miliband, weren't directly using the word skiver, she remarked, the *very fact* that they used its antithesis so freely – the fabricated 'striver' – implied the elevation of one group of 'worthy' citizens at the expense of another.[36] She said:

> Why does Ed Miliband now use 'striver' as though it were an acceptable way to describe someone, by a stranger's groundless estimation of how hard they are hypothetically trying?…
> The skiver, in opposition parlance, is always unmentioned, yet he lurks; Labour won't tolerate him either, this feckless bogeyman of Westminster's devising.

Echoing Martin Holcombe in Birmingham, Williams and many others, including academics, campaigners and even some tabloids such as the *Daily Mirror*, pointed out that cynical terminology was being appropriated by the very people it was targeted at – perhaps because they were just so wearied by it. Again, Williams:

> The point is that it has seeped so far, so fast, into the national consciousness as a meaningful idea that the very people vilified by it – the people who know they are unemployed by circumstance and not by choice – feel their lives judged against its fictional benchmarks.

Ruth Patrick, the academic who was leading the Dole Animators project for the University of Leeds, told me her years of research had demonstrated this pattern clearly. One of the reasons, she surmised, was that people at the sharp end who logically should be at the forefront of discussions about welfare reform were instead sidelined.[37] She concluded:

> Talking to disability benefit claimants, young jobseekers and single parents between 2011 and 2013, it is striking how many have begun to internalise and tacitly accept a discourse that pits hard-working 'strivers' against 'shirkers', undermining and demoralising those relying on benefits for all or most of their income. [Yet] most out-of-work benefit claimants do want to work, where this is a realistic aspiration, and are stopped not by laziness or an absent work ethic but by structural barriers such as the absence of jobs....

In the 2012 book, *Poverty and insecurity*,[38] outlining their research on working life in Britain, Tracy Shildrick and her co-authors noted that despite their findings clearly demonstrating that people were much more likely to express 'enduring commitment to work' and to move in and out of multiple low-paid jobs rather than opt for so-called benefits dependency, the idea of skivers took root. It was, they concluded, 'repeated as fact and ... too little challenged'. The authors queried the claim that an overgenerous benefits system was creating dependency, arguing instead that unemployed people tended to see claiming benefits as a 'sometimes necessary but mostly a costly series of obstacles, delays and loss of income' that was shrouded in a stigma they did not wish to have directed at them. As the authors wrote, their research was 'a corrective to the prejudicial modern-day myth-making so beloved of tabloid editors, social commentators and politicians' about welfare dependency.

With both academic work on the subject of stigma and the voices of those most affected largely outweighed by extreme cases of alleged benefits fraud within mainstream media coverage, it was left up to anti-poverty campaigners and charities to lead the challenge to the skiver narrative as austerity's tentacles spread wider. Many, such as disability rights activists, persistently called out those who were promulgating the dependency agenda. They became especially vocal in the run-up to and following the Welfare Reform Bill becoming law in April 2013 (as indeed did many MPs in Parliament), when the rhetoric around scroungers was intensifying. Alison Garnham, chief executive of CPAG, was at the forefront of highlighting the financial impact of austerity on families. Launching a campaign in September 2013, 'People Like Us', with an open letter to the leaders of the three main political parties, Garnham called on politicians to cease "promoting inaccurate, offensive and misleading stereotypes".[39]

She said:

> "The shocking truth about 'Benefits Britain' is that people receiving benefits are just like us. Perfectly ordinary UK families rely on benefits and tax credits to provide an income to live on or to top up low pay, but our political debate lets them down. Politicians seem very happy to talk about fraud and reinforce dangerously misleading stereotypes about people not wanting to work but seem to go missing when it comes to doing something about the benefits system letting down ordinary people who have to rely on it when they lose their jobs, have a disability or become ill or are in low paid work."

If populist propaganda around shirkers was reinforcing a forceful dependency mantra, it was one that was also tapping into a specific mindset: the public's ignorance of the social security system. In July 2013 a survey by Ipsos MORI for the Royal Statistical Society and King's College London[40] revealed a huge level of misunderstanding by the UK public about what would be saved by the public purse as a result of the Coalition's austerity drive, indicating that the overriding media message about excessive benefits spending and overindulged fraudulent benefits claimants had proved extremely persuasive. The public was spectacularly misinformed as to which benefits changes would save most cash. Twice as many respondents thought the £26,000 benefit cap would save the most as those who picked eradicating Child Benefit for wealthier households. In fact, the benefits cap came with an estimated annual saving of £290 million, compared with £1.7 billion per year for Child Benefit. And that wasn't all. A third of those surveyed believed the government paid out far more in Jobseeker's Allowance than on pensions, when the truth was that state pension payments outstripped Jobseeker's Allowance (just 3 per cent of the total benefits bill) by a ratio of 15:1 (£74.2 billion versus £4.9 billion). The chart below shows how government spending was carved up.

Welfare spending 2011–2012

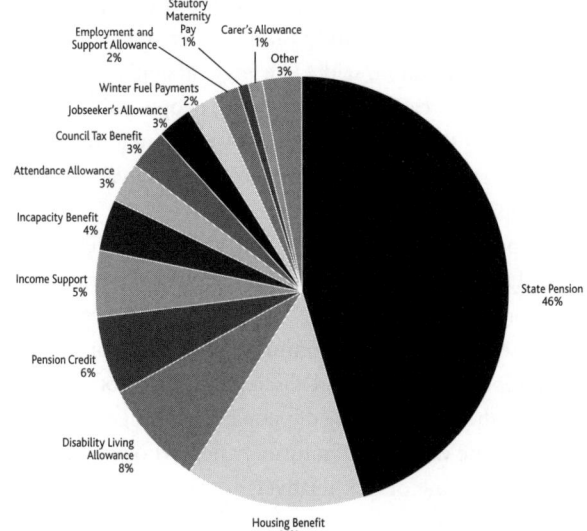

Source: http://grayee.blogspot.co.uk/2013/04/uk-welfare-spending-2011-12-fact-not.html

These misconceptions were convenient for ministers who, as *The Guardian* reported in December 2013, 'have an annoying tendency to lump together the money spent on pensions and the money spent on benefits to alarm people with the huge overall sum to bolster the case for cuts – when there is no question of cutting pensions'.[41] In fact, as *The Guardian* highlighted, the degree to which ministers were blatantly playing with statistics to suit their mantra of 'welfarism' sapping the taxpayer of their hard-earned cash was deliberately deceptive and calculated to reinforce its overall skiver agenda. Time and again ministers – including the Prime Minister[42] – recited the figure that "one pound in every three spent by the government goes on welfare", ignoring the fact that the figure includes pensions and not just out-of-work benefits.

The Ipsos report, meanwhile, also found that the public believed levels of fraud perpetrated by people in receipt of benefits were far higher than in reality. Writing in *The Huffington Post UK*, Bobby Duffy, managing director of the Ipsos MORI Social Research Institute and visiting senior research fellow at King's College London, said: 'The biggest single error in our survey is on the scale of benefit fraud; people think that out of every £100 spent on benefits, £24 is claimed fraudulently, when the best government estimate is that it's actually only around 70p.'[43]

In the spring of 2013, nef, along with the Tax Justice Network, published a fascinating evaluation of the wider skiver debate. Its publication, *Mythbusters: Strivers versus skivers*,[44] was a vigorous rebuff to some of the most common misconceptions. One by one the report unpicked and discredited many of the claims that fuelled the mass labelling of people as scroungers, including highlighting the vast army of informal carers who often left work to look after ageing or sick relatives.

It concluded:

> A great many people who are not in paid employment
> nonetheless do valuable – unpaid – work, caring for others,
> bringing up children and looking after their families, homes
> and neighbourhoods. The formal economy would grind to
> a halt without it. The division between strivers and skivers
> is a false one. Increasingly, people are forced to shuttle
> between spells of unemployment and short-term, low-paid
> insecure jobs.

It went on:

> All but a tiny minority of jobless people are out of work
> because they are disabled, have caring responsibilities or
> simply cannot find a job. Much more of the social security
> budget is used to subsidise low wages than to support
> jobseekers....

Significantly, it wasn't just activists, established charities and
think tanks countering the skiver narrative. Those directly
affected took advantage of social media to get their point across.
In one of the most impressive and fearless first-person blogs
that emerged after the onset of austerity, 'Diary of a Benefit
Scrounger',[45] Sue Marsh, who set up the blog to raise awareness
of living with a chronic illness, proved particularly adept at
confronting untruths and misrepresentations about people who
didn't work. In both her blog, and subsequently in mainstream
newspapers, she helped make sure a spotlight remained on
the issue of demonisation. Here's what she had to say in one
comment piece published in July 2012 in *The Guardian* after
the *Daily Mail* made a link between criminal activity and people
claiming sickness and disability benefits:[46]

—

> Stooping to new lows in the defamation of those with long-term illnesses or disabilities, the *Daily Mail* ran an article over the weekend claiming that 'a quarter of those claiming sickness benefits have a criminal record'. Chris Grayling, the Conservative employment minister, called it a 'truly alarming discovery'. Only it wasn't alarming at all. It was the same as the figure for criminal records among the general working age population: the UK has around 38.4 million people of working age and, according to the Police Crime Database, 9.2 million of them have criminal records.

In one of her Diary posts, Marsh also took the opposition to task for appearing to endorse the skiver spiel. Responding to the Labour Leader, Ed Miliband's, pledge in 2011 to deal with the so-called 'take what you can culture', this is what she wrote:

> Please be very, very careful what you say and how you say it. Millions of sick and disabled people will be listening to every word. Will you throw us in the pot with the scroungers?

In her newspaper column, blogger Jack Monroe also challenged the ritualistic labelling of poorer people and those who were out of work as benefits cheats. In one, she deftly asked why, when 165,000 higher earners had kept claiming Child Benefit to which they were no longer entitled after means-tested changes to the benefit, this group wasn't demonised.[47]

'When is benefit fraud not benefit fraud?', Monroe wondered. 'When it's committed by "hardworking" people, of course. It's hard to imagine these stragglers, if they don't stump up the money they owe, being called benefit fraudsters. When you think of someone "scrounging off the state", it probably doesn't call to mind the people on more than £50k, does it? While certain tabloid newspapers are busy demonising those that are out of work, or even the working poor, based on their appearance, weight, or number of children they have, nobody seems keen to point the finger at the "hardworking people".'

Another interesting, equally compelling blog was written by a teenager, Amy Feltham.[48] When she posted on the mental health charity Young Minds' website under the banner 'Don't judge those on benefits', she garnered the biggest response the site had ever had. Amy told readers about her mental and physical health problems, noting that, despite having done various kinds of work, when she became ill she had no choice but to rely on out-of-work benefits to get by:

> I know society doesn't accept me. To be honest, I don't accept myself. I claim Employment and Support Allowance and Disability Living Allowance, amounting to about £221.80 a week. I wish I didn't need it. But the truth is, without this money, I could not survive. In my every day life, I am made to feel an outcast, unwanted and alone. The more I feel hated by society, the more I hate myself. I don't think society knows this, the way they make us benefit claimants feel behind closed doors. Maybe we are guilty of not talking about it enough, but maybe society is also guilty of not being ready to listen. What I am saying is, please don't put us all in one box. We are doing our best. So please, try not to judge us.

'Poverty porn' and the age of austerity

As part of her blog, Amy drew attention to another aspect of the demonisation of people in receipt of benefits – what became known as 'poverty porn'. For a while in 2012 and 2013 it was difficult to turn on the television without a pseudo-documentary following hapless 'povs' around their homes, observing them eat badly and flop in front of their gigantic televisions. As with the striver narrative being played out in the press, it was suddenly acceptable to mock people living on the poverty line – but this time under the auspices of documentaries and on television as if they were pure spectacle. It was a well-worn trope by 2013 that poor people couldn't possibly be that poor if they owned a television or a mobile phone, but one that was increasingly being challenged by some parts of the press. For example, *The Guardian* exposed the extortionate interest rates charged by some companies selling such goods who actively targeted people without access to other cheaper, credit.[49]

This was what Amy had to say after watching one BBC programme, 'Nick and Margaret – we all pay your benefits':

> The programme sent taxpayers to live with long term benefit claimants to see what their lives are like, and whether they think people are getting enough, or maybe too much, money. As I watched, I saw the taxpayers describe what they expected to find; namely lazy people (with flashy phones and flat screen TVs) who did not want to work. This was not a perspective new to me.

A growing 'austerity nostalgia' lexicon had evolved too, artificially harping back to eras when being poor supposedly entailed some kind of noble destitution. Long-time television reviewer (and not a journalist who writes on social policy), Andrew Collins was one of many critics who questioned the poverty porn trend. Writing for *The Guardian*, he said: 'Perhaps poverty doesn't lend itself to being squeezed into existing formats. But who's going to commission a dry, informative, comparative documentary about the welfare state, poverty or immigration when an am-dram reconstruction might make the vulnerable blub on cue?'[50]

A blog on JRF's website in the summer of 2013 pondered how broadcasters could justify commissioning programmes that 'pitted deserving against undeserving poor' and what might be done about it.[51] It read: 'From JRF's research on the portrayal of poverty issues in the media, we know that the media is partial, and that people in poverty themselves feel victimised, stigmatised and objectified.[52] How can campaigners attempt to shift public attitudes, when the media is dominated by such programmes?'

The unsavoury vilification of those who were out of work or poor reached a kind of crescendo in the autumn of 2013 during the Conservative Party Conference in Manchester, when the venue was draped in the new slogan: 'For hardworking people':[53] politicians were once more vying for the title of who could bash the unemployed most incontrovertibly.[54] It was announced amid great fanfare (and with more than a hint of déjà vu) by Iain Duncan Smith that 'the something for nothing culture' would come to an end thanks to government plans to force approximately 200,000 long-term unemployed benefit claimants to either undertake community work in exchange for benefits, attend a jobcentre every day or go on a full-time intensive programme.[55] (It would mean that those who have not found work after two years on the existing Work Programme, where contractors are paid a fee to get people into a job, will face a new scheme called Help to Work. To continue to qualify for Jobseeker's Allowance they will have three options: work placements, such as cleaning up litter; daily visits to a jobcentre; or taking part in compulsory training, for example, to improve their literacy.[56] And, just to make sure those 'skivers-in-training', young people, weren't let off easy, David Cameron also inserted a pledge to remove most benefits[57] for under-25s if elected in 2015.[58])

The responses from the right-wing tabloids were dutifully strident, a typical one being a headline in *The Sun* – 'Earn or learn (Because we won't give you any more of our cash to burn)'.[59] Equally swift, however, were the rebuttals from those arguing that the announcements represented yet another opportunity to demonise jobless people and to kick them while they were down. Citizens Advice responded by calling the moves 'a groundhog day' response that was doing nothing but punishing the long-term unemployed for 'circumstances beyond their control'.[60] In *The Huffington Post*, writer and commentator John Wight accused the government in no uncertain terms of 'hounding' the unemployed.[61] He wrote: 'Adding another layer of indignity onto the indignity already suffered by the most demonised, dehumanised and near-criminalised demographic in the country – the unemployed – can only be described as an obscenity.'

Changing attitudes to poverty and joblessness

Negative attitudes around the welfare state had been bubbling for years before austerity, with independent studies illustrating a longer-term pattern. Back in 1983 the *Breadline Britain report*[62] found a high degree of sympathy with people who were in poverty or out of work. In fact, 57 per cent felt the government was doing too little to 'help those who lack those things you have said are necessities', while 63 per cent wanted to see higher taxes for the rich. Even as recently as 1990 – the year Margaret Thatcher was ousted from office – an updated Breadline Britain survey[63] found that sympathies were strong. However, in the two decades following, while the public continued to regard inequality between rich and poor as unacceptably high, there was a hardening of attitudes. The 2009 British Social Attitudes Survey showed a significant decrease in support for social security benefits and redistributive policies generally.[64]

Over half of respondents believed benefits were too high and preventing people finding work. The one real blip in the new norm was in the 2013 edition[65] that suggested an easing of the hostility towards unemployed and poor people. Anti-poverty campaigners welcomed this as evidence of a public tiring of the relentless demonisation, but, with other reports echoing the pattern of hardening attitudes,[66] whether this was a statistical one-off remains to be seen.[67]

For many people affected by austerity and by the dubious rhetoric in which it was so often couched, any challenge to this demonisation was welcome. Just weeks after the party conference season ended, an alliance of over 70 leading UK charities launched a new campaign, Who Benefits?, aimed at combating the growing hostility in society, the media and among politicians by giving a platform to people to share their experiences of how benefits had provided a security net – not a route to long-term dependency.[68]

Long-time resident on Marsh Farm, Glenn Jenkins, suggested it was "vital" that individuals and communities pull together in order to challenge the dominant narrative wherever possible. Jenkins argued that "the frustration that people feel through being consigned to skintness on a daily basis" needed to be recognised, and that the dignity of individuals and communities should be protected from routine character assassination.

> "It cracks you up when people say 'oh they want a life on benefits!' Well they've never tried it and wouldn't try it for a week never mind a year. The poor and the disaffected and the weak and the people who can't defend themselves, they're all fair game. There's something vicious about it."

Perhaps one of the most erudite broadsides against the repeated maligning of people who were out of work came from a writer who, like Rowling, showed solidarity with the less fortunate. Before his death in early 2013 the author Iain Banks offered this searing yet succinct appraisal of the situation:

> "Your society's broken, so who should we blame? Should we blame the rich, powerful people who caused it? No, let's blame the people with no power and no money and these immigrants who don't even have the vote – yeah, it must be their fucking fault."[69]

FIVE

All work and no pay

Work and wages: austerity and the jobs crisis

"I've been in recruitment for over 30 years helping people into employment and I'm finding that this is the worst time I've ever experienced for jobseekers because of the lack of jobs. I feel that people are panicking. And they're not panicking [just] about finding a job, they're panicking about keeping the jobcentre and DWP happy." (Lynette McKechnie, employment support worker, Glasgow)

"I suffer from anxiety, depression, I worry all the time. My weight's low, I'm only 6 stone 10. I feel like there's no light at the end of the tunnel. After three years I'm still struggling." (Lynne Middleward, unemployed woman, South Tyneside)

The problem with employment

If you had been on the same journey I was on around Austerity UK during 2012 and 2013, one thing would have been abundantly clear: work – or the lack of it – was a major problem. You would have encountered a country in the throes of a jobs crisis where citizens were expected to grapple with a dramatically changing employment landscape typified by high and entrenched unemployment in many parts of the country and an increasingly low-wage economy – all against a backdrop of the drastic roll-out of punitive 'back-to-work' reforms. If you asked someone about their experience of being unemployed and looking for work, they would more than likely have told you that it was painstakingly hard, frequently fruitless and fraught with barriers.

People everywhere I went spoke of the vast array of hurdles to finding suitable employment, including the invidious spread of the skiver narrative that appeared to have seeped into the entire jobseeking system, from ministers down to the staff at jobcentres.

And people also told me that following the election in May 2010, initiatives aimed at forcing those without work into jobs (however illusory the prospective work might be) had taken previous endeavours under New Labour to address 'worklessness' to a whole new, merciless level.[1] If those who bought wholesale into the skiver narrative were tempted to dismiss claims about how harsh conditions were, the evidence proved they were wrong. The reality in fact was that many people were being pushed to the edge because jobs weren't available or the pay and/or hours were so low they would still leave them in poverty. Everywhere I went, there was a vivid 'reality gap' between what were promoted by government as the merits of back-to-work strategies and how these were experienced on the ground. The mechanics of finding or keeping work in Austerity UK, according to those caught up in it (and not just jobseekers, but the advisers trying to assist them), was an onerous and frequently debasing trial with no end. As one unemployed man, 'Fred', gathered with a group of other residents of Ladywood in Birmingham put it, talking about dealing with jobcentres:

> "It's regimental. It's literally a piece of paper and they won't divert from that. When it comes down to it – you're a number."

Another, 'John', added: "Sometimes they speak to you as if you shouldn't be there. It's dehumanising."

'Susan' interjected: "They just want to hit their targets. They're not sympathetic. They are just trying to keep their own jobs. It's about ticking a box."

The perception of a hostile employment climate both in and outside the jobcentre was certainly the case in the village of Lynemouth. Set between what was once thriving mining country and the coast of rural Northumberland, residents in Lynemouth and surrounding districts had been bracing themselves for the closure of the Rio Tinto Alcan aluminium smelting plant that, up until the end of 2012, had employed hundreds of people. They were anxious about where replacement jobs on the scale of Alcan would come from. With unemployment already high across the region, a shortage of skilled or well-paid work opportunities, large numbers of low-income households and high rates of child poverty, there were well-founded worries about what lay ahead. Forty-year-old Craig Thompson, who was employed at the giant Alcan plant for 15 years until May 2012, had worked his way up to team leader before being made redundant. The loss of so many jobs on such a large scale was having a profound impact across a community where skilled work was scarce to begin with, he said.

"It's not just the employees [at Alcan], it's all the businesses that feed off it", he pointed out. "It affects thousands and thousands of people in this area. The impact is huge." As he watched former colleagues "getting really down" who were unable to find alternative work, Thompson began researching the possibility of setting up his own business, and sought out training courses so he could build on his existing skills. He had just set up as a self-employed caravan engineer when I spoke to him.

"I had a well paid job. Try finding a job in this area that pays that kind of money [now]. They just don't exist. There is the odd job [that's] good, well paid but there's literally thousands of applicants for every job. The prospects up here – there's just nothing", he said of why he went down the start-up route. "[I'm] speaking to lads [who are] applying for dozens of jobs every week and getting nothing. They're good lads and they are wanting to work; there's just nothing for them."

As someone who had worked since leaving school, coming into contact with a jobcentre for the first time was, he says, a "humiliating" and frustrating experience. The encounter left him feeling like the system was more interested in him 'ticking boxes' than in helping him take advantage of his entrepreneurial goals.

"There's a stigma with being unemployed. I'd never been unemployed before so I didn't know anything about the jobcentre. Its absolutely soul destroying when you go there. They make you feel like rubbish." While setting up his business (he paid for the training courses from savings), the Department for Work and Pensions' stipulations that he continually apply for work merely placed more obstacles in his way, Thompson explained. "They knew I was doing courses to set a business up but they still wanted to know: 'What jobs have you applied for?'. I said I haven't applied for any jobs. I'm training. And they said, 'Well we'll take your money off you' [so] I just signed off. I got no help off them."

He continued:

> "It was unbelievable the way they treat ya. Speaking to friends of mine who are in contact with the jobcentre, they are at the end of their tether. They are all [grafters] and they are being put into that class of people where they're not. Because of where we were working a lot of the lads have big mortgages and now they've got no money coming in. Any job they can get isn't going to pay their mortgage and it means they are relying on the state for benefits. It's crazy."

Thompson said he was especially worried about what lay in store for the next generation. "I've got two sons and, to be fair, there's nothing round here for them. I can't even imagine trying to buy a house with the wages employers are paying."

'Emma Hope' from Bishop Auckland, a 37-year-old former mental health professional in the NHS and a lone parent, was another person navigating the harsh jobs market. After escaping an abusive relationship, she and her daughter spent time in a refuge and, with the help of support workers, she was trying to get back on her feet. She was determined to support herself and her daughter, but said finding work or retraining assistance from the jobcentre was proving impossible. It was hard enough adjusting to the trauma of violence, she explained, but finding work was proving to be another obstacle in her way:

> "I've worked every day of my adult life. I've never claimed benefits before so it's been a massive culture shock for me. I've lost everything. I've lost my home. I want to work. I'm constantly looking for work. I would do anything. Just because I came from a really good job that was really well paid doesn't mean I won't go and clean toilets. They're expecting people to go out and get these jobs and saying there are jobs out there and they'll retrain but there aren't the jobs out there. What do they want them to do?"

In South Tyneside, Lynne Middleward thought she was doing the right thing by studying for a degree in criminology in her mid-30s (she graduated with a First in 2010), but had been unemployed for three years when I spoke to her towards the end of 2013. Lynne had been hoping to get a job with the police, but a 20 per cent cut in police funding had seen dramatic reductions in jobs.[2] To say she was doing all she could to find work wouldn't do her efforts justice. The process of searching for work in a high unemployment area was driving her to despair:

"I've been on Jobseeker's Allowance for three years and I'm finding it really difficult to get back into the labour market. I can't find a job. I'm applying for at least three jobs a week and I don't hear back from anybody. I don't even get letters. Over the last three years I've just had two interviews. I've been applying for waitressing; I've been applying for administration. I was applying for care [work]. I just apply for anything. I'm so capable but I hear from nobody."

Talking about the knock-on effects of trying to manage on benefits while looking for work, she went on:

"When I've got to sign on I've got to walk one hour and twenty minutes there and back. If I bussed it, it would cost me £3.80 when I've only got £10.80 a week for food. It would have to come out of that. Because I'm on Jobseeker's Allowance I've got to do [Universal] Job Search so twice a week I've got to go to the library and I've got to walk an hour there and an hour back. It's very distressing, it's very degrading.... I suffer from anxiety, depression, I worry all the time. My weight's low, I'm only 6 stone 10. I feel like there's no light at the end of the tunnel. After three years I'm still struggling.

"If there was a job for me to go to tomorrow I would. My GP believes if that if I had a job I'd have better self-esteem. I'd have something to get up for in the morning."

(The Coalition's Universal Jobmatch was introduced in November 2012, an online job search system designed to monitor Jobseeker's Allowance claimants' online job search activity to confirm that they were complying with the requirement to do a minimum of three job-searching activities per week. Registration with Universal Jobmatch can be made mandatory for receipt of benefit, and sanctions applied if the jobseeker does not comply.)

So what exactly were the broader circumstances in which jobseekers were expected to find work? And why was it so tough? From the moment the Coalition came to power it was made clear that getting people off benefits and into work would be at the centre of the austerity enterprise. If public spending was to be brought 'under control', ministers declared, then not only would hundreds of thousands of supposedly unnecessary public sector jobs[3] have to be culled, but social security bills would have to be drastically reduced by, among other things, 'incentivising' people into work. Put simply, they insisted that as well as slashing the benefits bill, the goal was to get those people who the government believed were 'dependent' on state support – especially the long-term unemployed and people 'on the sick' – back into work, thereby magically transforming them into those mythical 'hardworking' taxpayers.

As I travelled from location to location a set of discrete work-related themes emerged that mirrored many of the 'red flags' that campaigners had been raising as the government's austerity agenda was coming into force. These flags fell into four broad (but connected) categories. First was the scarcity of employment opportunities in many areas, and for specific clusters of the population such as young people, all of which resulted in fierce competition for any vacancies that were advertised. Second was the *type* of work available. The trend towards the casualisation of the jobs market and resulting job insecurity, the increase of 'zero-hour' contracts and the rise of part-time work and 'under-employment', all ensured that even when a slight recovery did begin in late 2013, it was not, as it was after previous recessions, a jobs-based one that generated substantial full-time employment.

Third was the entrenchment of low pay coupled with wage rises falling far short of inflation, a combination that meant it was a struggle for many people in work to get by even when in receipt of supplementary benefits and tax credits. The fourth area (and one that was sold by the government as part of its austerity 'efficiencies' but was actually a Tory ideological article of faith) was the radical redrafting of 'back-to-work' policies. These reforms included a slew of contentious alterations, not least of which was the introduction of unprecedented savage sanctions – that deleteriously (some would say disastrously) affected mainly (but by no means exclusively) the long-term unemployed, young people, lone parents and those who were sick and disabled.

The big picture on jobs

First, however, the wider employment picture during austerity. One of the earliest, biggest and most unnecessary blows to the employment market after the Coalition government came to power was a deliberate decimation of public sector jobs. One of the many incredible things about this move (on top of the ideological motive and the sheer numbers involved) was that it came so soon after the 2008 crisis and the subsequent contraction of the private sector. At the time of writing the latest quarterly public sector jobs report from ONS, for the second quarter of 2013,[4] revealed ongoing reductions in the number of public sector workers three years on from the 2010 election. It reported an overall fall of 8 per cent between the second quarter of 2013 and the same quarter in 2009, bringing the total number of people in the UK employed in the public sector to 5.7 million (on a headcount basis). (The largest public sector workforce was in the NHS – more than a quarter of the total public sector pay roll – and this experienced a small decline [0.7 per cent on a headcount basis] between the second quarters of 2012 and 2013. Many critics, including the TUC, argued that because the NHS and education had been shielded to a degree from job cuts, other areas such as social care were unfairly and unsustainably targeted.)

Wales, Scotland and Northern Ireland had long had a higher proportion of their workforces employed by the public sector than England, and were harder hit as a result. In the second quarter 2013 report, Northern Ireland had the highest proportion of public sector employees in the UK (27.6 per cent) followed by Wales (25.2) and Scotland (23.0). But parts of England were badly affected by job cuts too, and these tended to be the regions with longstanding high unemployment levels that had also been worst hit by other austerity policies, such as cuts to local government budgets. In addition, many of the public sector jobs being lost were full-time.

According to research published by the GMB union in October 2013, around 600,000 public sector jobs had been eliminated across the nation since the Coalition came to power, with between 200,000 and 400,000 further job losses predicted by 2015 as additional cuts were scheduled to come into force. The union's research concluded that the regions that had seen the biggest cut in public sector employment since May 2010 were also those most reliant on it: the greatest job cuts were in the South West (13.9 per cent), followed by the North East (13.8 per cent), where 22.4 per cent of jobs had been in the public sector, the West Midlands (11.5 per cent) and the North West (11.4 per cent), where 20.4 per cent of jobs had been in the public sector. And there were more cuts to come.[5]

The South East and London were both least dependent on public sector employment and had also seen the biggest growth in private sector employment overall since 2009, according to ONS figures, leading many commentators to conclude (correctly) that any jobs recovery was deeply skewed in favour of the south. (The total number of people employed in the private sector across the UK in the second quarter of 2013 was 24.2 million – four out of five working people – up 380,000 on the same quarter a year earlier.)

There were also clear gender and 'race' disparities in the impact of job losses. Women and people from black and minority ethnic backgrounds were particularly badly affected by job losses in the public sector, as they have traditionally been better represented within it. For example, figures collated by *The Guardian* from ONS data in July 2013 showed that, at that time, twice as many jobs held by women (253,600) as men (104,700) had been lost in the public sector,[6] while Black Activists Rising Against the Cuts stressed the disproportionate degree to which people from black and minority ethnic backgrounds were losing out.[7, 8]

GMB national officer, Brian Strutton, offered a stark warning about what the loss of such jobs would mean in areas that were already reeling:

> "Our feedback from the current round of council budget reviews for next year [suggest] accelerating cutbacks. As a result, many communities in some of the most deprived regions will find their local economy in tatters."

So what about general employment? On the surface the ONS labour market report published in October 2013 held some good news and there were indications of some kind of corner being turned in terms of job creation by the private sector. The top line statistics (covering the months June–August) showed that the UK's overall unemployment rate had fallen (albeit slightly), by 40,000 on a year earlier, by 0.2 to 7.7 per cent.[9] Meanwhile, the numbers of people in employment reached a high of 29.87 million, up 155,000 on a year earlier (although significantly the ONS cautioned that rises in the number of people in employment were outstripped by population increases over the same period). Ministers seized on the report as verification of recovery, but, as with previous reports throughout the post-recession period, a mere scratch of the statistical surface disclosed a more complex and less upbeat picture. First, as the report pointed out, the jobs market was still behind where it was before the crash:

> The percentage of people aged 16–64 who were in work for June–August 2013 (the employment rate) was 71.7%, which is lower than before the 2008–09 downturn.

Second, it reported that while there had been a welcome increase in full-time jobs (up by 148,000 on the year before), there were still vast numbers of people who wanted but couldn't find stable, full-time work so were employed part time or were self-employed. Indeed, a large proportion of the people who had secured part-time work, according to the ONS, would have preferred to be in full-time roles had these been available. The report concluded:

> For June–August 2013 there were 1.45 million part-time employees and self-employed people who were working part-time because they could not find a full-time job, the highest figure since records began in 1992.

The *Monitoring poverty and social exclusion 2012* report from JRF and the New Policy Institute[10] had shown that two years into austerity there was a persistent and worrying trend toward the normalisation of less secure, part-time work. Not only was part-time employment the only option for many, but so too was the 'churn' in and out of part-time and low-paid work. It concluded:

> The underemployment increase since 2009 is primarily due to a rise of 500,000 in the number of people working part time but wanting full-time work. Unemployment has remained quite static in the last three

years because employees' willingness to take fewer hours keeps it from rising.

In addition – and crucially, bearing in mind the government's back-to-work strategy – was the fact that both long-term and youth unemployment remained stubbornly high, despite ministers' claims that these were areas of special focus. The number of people out of work for more than 12 months went up by 3,000 year on year to 900,000 in the second quarter of 2013, according to the ONS October report. Some 467,000 people had been out of work for two years or more – up 23,000 from a year earlier.[11]

When it came to young people, the report offered absolutely nothing in the way of solace. The situation for this group was as entrenched as it was wretched, with the long-term unemployment rate running at a record high of 21 per cent and which without substantial and sustained growth was unlikely to reduce dramatically in the near future. It granted young people the dubious accolade of being among those groups bearing most of the brunt during austerity. And even those in work had been steadily seeing their incomes erode. According to the IFS, between 2008 and 2012 the incomes of people in their 20s fell by 12 per cent.[12] Although there was a slight quarter-on-quarter reduction in youth unemployment in the October report, the enduring level was still hovering just below the one million mark at 948,000 and, at nearly 20 per cent, a substantial increase on the 13.6 per cent rate in December 2007.[13]

Commenting on the trends, chief economist at the Chartered Institute for Personnel Development (CIPD), Mark Beatson, said there was an "urgent need" to address youth and long-term unemployment.[14, 15] He said:

> "Youth unemployment remains stubbornly high, and long-term unemployment has only just begun to fall, so there

is a real need to step up efforts to ensure our young and long-term unemployed aren't left out of the labour market recovery."

And, claiming that the overall situation still constituted a genuine jobs crisis, this is what the TUC General Secretary, Frances O'Grady, had to say:

"Young people are being excluded from the recovery as youth joblessness remains close to a million. There is also a record number of underemployed workers who aren't able to find full-time work. We need more high quality jobs and proper pay rises if this recovery is to begin to feel real for hard-working people."

In the midst of all of this, while failing to acknowledge the role voluntary austerity had played in fashioning such a dire situation, government initiatives supposedly aimed at improving prospects for young people were spectacular failures. The Youth Employment Bill introduced in 2011 to 'establish a programme to provide training and employment opportunities for unemployed young people between the ages of 16 and 25' failed to complete its passage through the House and was not passed into law. In April 2012 the government introduced 'a £1 billion Youth Contract … to help young unemployed people get a job', which aimed to 'provide nearly half a million new opportunities for 18 to 24 year olds, including apprenticeships and voluntary work experience placements'. But by 2013 the scheme was in disarray.[16] The wage subsidy scheme that Clegg promised would create 160,000 jobs delivered just 2.6 per cent of that total in its first year.[17]

Yet, by August 2013, Labour was attacking the scheme as there was no evidence that jobs were permanent rather than temporary. 'Young workers may be losing their jobs shortly after companies are handed a £2,000 subsidy for hiring them under the coalition's flagship Youth Contract.'[18] Youth unemployment in the UK may not have been quite at the apocalyptic levels of Greece, but it was a serious indictment of a government that for all intents and purposes had abandoned its young people.[19]

(For a chronological list of youth training and work policies, Keele University provides a valuable resource.[20])

In many ways, 29-year-old David Marr, from South Lanarkshire in Scotland, encapsulated a number of the problems younger people were facing at the sharp end of the jobs market. A work ethic was central to how Marr saw himself. The idea of a life on benefits horrified him. "My late father always said to me that if you don't earn money yourself then stuff that gets given to you really has no value", he told me, explaining his attitude to social security. What mattered, he added, was whether the government was investing in jobs creation or making it harder for young people to make the leap from benefits to reliable work:

> "I grew up around cars. I'd love to get into that [but] I'm looking for bar work and stuff. If I were to walk out tomorrow and someone was to walk up to me and go 'I understand you're looking for work; I need a cleaner' I'm not the kind of guy to turn round and say 'no'. I would take it in an instant. I would prefer to be out working."

It was evident listening to Marr that while he would take whatever job was going, nothing would have made him happier than finding a job that paid enough to live on and that gave him a chance at reclaiming his self-respect. He understood – but was exhausted by – the vagaries of the 'churn' between low-paid jobs and benefits. Marr had been homeless on a few occasions in between various low-paid jobs. He had grown up and lived in one of the most impoverished parts of Lanarkshire,

Cambuslang and Rutherglen, and so his battle to find work was especially tough.

According to Jane Churchill, Assistant Director at Healthy n Happy Development Trust, a local voluntary organisation that runs projects to bolster the employment prospects and wellbeing of people in all age groups, Marr's was a typically disturbing story in an already deeply deprived area hit hard by recessions in the early 1980s and 1990s, and made even worse by the downturn in 2008. Gearing up for years of benefits cuts set to amplify longstanding difficulties was "very destabilising", she said. Youngsters like Marr were thwarted from multiple directions, Churchill told me, saying many were "falling foul" of drug abuse, low educational attainment and, in the longer term, poor health outcomes.

For Marr one of the most disheartening aspects of looking for work amidst this backdrop was the knowledge of how few opportunities there were, and also how difficult it was to chase the ones that were there (never mind feel any reassurance that, once found, work would be permanent).

"The last company I worked for decided I was surplus to requirements", he explained. "I wasn't best pleased when they said I was being laid off. I've done the occasional voluntary job but beyond that.... Too many companies are shutting down or downsizing."

Making matters worse, he added, was that his council flat had two bedrooms and soon he'd be stuck with a £14-a-week bill for 'under-occupancy' which would strip away what little cash he had to travel to job interviews further afield, or be forced to leave his home. "I'm kind of in a catch-22. I rely on public transport [to get to interviews]."

It was a similar story for Warren Pewtner in Rhondda, Wales. The 22-year-old was on a government training scheme with Arts Factory, a local voluntary organisation, where he had acquired skills including data inputting with an in-house online books enterprise, and was proud of his achievements. He didn't want to give up hope of finding a "proper" job, he told me, but it was clear he was despondent at having to depend on his brother for a place to live (his older brother subsidised his rent payments), and surviving on under £10 a day, with few prospects of full-time work.

"You'd be lucky if you got a job anywhere really", he said of the local area's jobs situation. "I think the benefits are crap. I'm working 40 hours for £50. I just think why do I bother? I'm sick of the dole it's doing my head in." Speaking about how he coped he added: "I just do what I can and take every day as it comes. I don't know where I would be [without my brother to help]. I don't even like to think about it. He won't see me go without but I can't live off him forever."

Declining wages and job insecurity

As if finding a job in the first place wasn't already hard enough in Austerity UK, there was the chronic – and growing – problem of low wages to contend with. At times it was as if wages were in terminal decline. One report in August 2013 from the House of Commons Library found that declines in real wages in the UK were among the most severe in Europe.[21] The October ONS report revealed that wages were rising by a pitiful 0.7 per cent while inflation was running four times higher (2.7 per cent in August and excluding anticipated jumps in energy prices on the horizon). Public sector pay was particularly weak – actually down on average 1.6 per cent in the year to August (despite a plethora of reports in the media claiming that public sector workers were actually doing better[22]). Reporting on the figures, this is what *The Guardian*'s economics editor, Larry Elliott, had to say:

> If the labour market was really strong, earnings would be going up not down.... Seen from this perspective, the labour

market looks less robust. Indeed, it is more like a galley ship in which the wage slaves are strapped to oars and exhorted to work harder for less. Real pay has been falling for the past five years and the average weekly wage is now, according to the Resolution Foundation, at its lowest level for a decade ... there is a disconnect between official figures showing strong growth and the experience of most Britons seeing the real value of their pay fall year after year. For them, a recovery without rising living standards is no recovery at all.[23]

Or, as 'Alexis' in Ladywood, Birmingham, succinctly put it: "Why do [the government] encourage employers to pay their employees such low wages that they always have to be getting family tax credits or whatever to back it up? I'm saying you are cutting and cutting and people are working and they still can't afford to live on what you are paying them."

And just in case all of this wasn't worrying enough, there was evidence too of widespread contravention of the Minimum Wage legislation. In one high-profile instance in the autumn of 2013 it was revealed that 120 care providers were to be investigated by HM Revenue & Customs (HMRC) after the Low Pay Commission reported that drastic cuts by local councils to the amount they contracted care firms for was leading to many breaking the law and paying staff (in a sector already notorious for poor pay and conditions) below the statutory minimum.[24] This was on top of other reports from academics that more than 200,000 care workers may have been being paid less than the Minimum Wage.[25]

By November 2013 the situation with earnings was top of the political agenda. Labour's Ed Miliband had made living standards his battle cry in the run-up to the 2015 general election, while a new tranche of figures revealed that one fifth of employees – 5.2 million people in the UK – were earning below the 'Living Wage' – up 400,000 in a year. (The 'Living

Wage' is a voluntary rate of pay regarded as the minimum to meet the cost of living in the UK.[26] Over 400 firms had signed up to the Living Wage by the end of 2013, up from 78 a year earlier, and the Conservative mayor of London, Boris Johnson, was an advocate.) A report from the international accounting firm, KPMG, reported that two thirds of 18- to 21-year-olds were paid less than the Living Wage in 2013 (£8.80 in London and £7.65 elsewhere at the time of writing). It also found that women and part-time workers were disproportionately stuck on low pay. Over a quarter (27 per cent) of women were earning less than the recommended minimum compared to 16 per cent of men. The report found that 43 per cent of part-time earners were below the benchmark, compared with 12 per cent of full-timers. When it came to regional distribution, the areas most affected by austerity were those where the Living Wage was least likely to be paid: Northern Ireland had the highest proportion of workers paid less than the Living Wage – 26 per cent – closely followed by Wales at 23 per cent.[27]

As the months of austerity unfolded there were numerous reports telling the same story – in areas of high unemployment all over the country the battle to find secure, full-time, adequately paid employment becoming ever harder.[28] Even London and the South East, despite lower rates of joblessness generally, had areas of extreme deprivation and pockets of high unemployment. London, amidst all its great and ostentatious wealth, contained some of the most impoverished communities in the UK.[29] But if wages were one critical part of the equation, then job insecurity was another.

This is how Sharon in Croxteth described living in the shadow of job insecurity:

> "Everybody – whether you're working or not in Norris Green – you're one step away from being in the same boat. I'm lucky at the minute, I'm working full time. [But] my job

could finish at the end of March. My husband works on the building side. He is literally on a week-by-week contract. So we're one step away from being ... [pauses for breath]. And I wouldn't call us scroungers, we've always worked...."

Nowhere was the insecurity of employment in Austerity UK embodied more starkly than in the phenomenon of 'zero-hour' contracts. Hidden in plain sight all over the UK in the early years of austerity was an expanding army of workers who, desperate to be in work rather than on benefits, were grafting in jobs on these employment agreements. The contracts involved a variety of incarnations, but essentially boiled down to a wholesale erosion of what once would have been regarded as basic workers' entitlements: the right to know what hours you were going to work in a week, the right to know what you could expect to be paid and the allied rights to sick pay and holiday pay. Not only were there fewer guarantees for employees under these contracts, but also some reports published in 2013 found that people subject to them earned much less that those signed up to more conventional arrangements with greater protections. One report by the Resolution Foundation found that those on zero-hour contracts earned on average 40 per cent less.[30]

This is how *The Guardian* summed the contracts up just as they were coming to the wider public's attention:[31]

> The worker can end up with zero pay at the end of the week because the employer does not need to guarantee any hours of work. When the workers do work, they must receive at least the national minimum wage but an employer is not obliged to offer sick leave or holiday pay. In some industries, workers on zero-hours contracts will agree to work according to weekly or monthly rotas. In other sectors, especially retail, workers may be summoned to work at a few hours' notice.

It went on:

> If a worker succeeds in grabbing lots of hours on a regular
> basis, they may eventually qualify for sick pay and holiday. But
> workers can simply be told to take a month's unpaid holiday,
> most likely during fallow business periods, and the potential
> for a longer-term relationship is broken.

In August 2013 the ONS confirmed it would be revisiting the way it calculated the official number of workers on zero-hour contracts (for the second time in a matter of months) after acknowledging it had significantly underestimated the total. Some estimates in 2013 put the numbers employed by such contracts at more than one million[32] after it was revealed that some of the country's biggest retailers employed thousands of people on them. The government even acknowledged that 300,000 people in the care sector alone were on them.[33]

By the early summer of 2013 the press was reporting revelation after revelation about the scale of the issue (including that Buckingham Palace employed many staff on such contracts[34]), prompting a cavalcade of condemnation and calls for reform. In May 2013 Business Secretary Vince Cable responded to the torrent of public concern with the announcement that the government would be launching an inquiry into the controversial contracts. However, doubts were still voiced about whether the contracts were in fact here to stay, with Shadow Business Secretary Chukka Ummuna accusing ministers of "having their heads in the sand" and failing to properly investigate.[35] Others claimed the ballooning of the contracts in the name of greater 'flexibility' for employers had actually led to a climate of "permanent uncertainty" and "permanent under-employment".[36]

Employers defended the contracts for offering flexibility[37] to many people such as students who, they argued, preferred not to have designated hours set in stone. However, while that may well have been the case for a few, for others such arrangements were yet another spoke in the wider spiral of insecurity cultivated under austerity. As 'Sharon' in Croxteth put it, summing up such concerns:

> "Lately what employers seem to be doing is nought hour contracts. Nought hour contracts and minimum wage. So even when you are getting jobs, you don't know what hours you're going to work in one week. But because you've got a nought hour contract there's nothing you can do."

The 'back-to-work' revolution and the rise of sanctions

In the midst of this dire combination of factors conspiring to make life harder for millions was the government's ideologically unwavering and – for many people – damaging attempts to shift people from the unemployment rolls into work. Under the Coalition government, back-to-work schemes metastasised into an all-embracing credo of 'all stick with no carrot' and 'one size fits all' system that somehow managed to ignore many of the realities of people on the ground, such as, for instance, the availability of jobs for people to move into.

With daunting speed and emboldened by the compliance of the Liberal Democrats in government, the Coalition concocted a complex web of policies and initiatives in order to get people into work. To bolster its arguments for reform, the government repeatedly propounded the idea of a 'culture of worklessness', implying that unemployment was passed down the generations. However, research by JRF categorically debunked this myth, finding that 'even two generations of complete worklessness in the same family was very rare', and that there was no evidence of 'a culture of worklessness'.[38]

The first official indications of what was on the horizon came on 27 May 2010 when the new Secretary of State for Work and Pensions, Iain Duncan Smith, laid out his stall for a 'root and branch' reform including how to get people supposedly 'parked' on benefits back to work.[39] The minister pledged to replace the back-to-work schemes introduced under New Labour with a new, more effective single scheme, and in June 2011 the Work Programme was introduced. A government flagship initiative, and one that the minister placed at the core of his reforms, it was heralded as a new way to – as Tracy Shildrick in *Poverty and insecurity* put it – 'activate' people for work, purporting to offer additional support and coaching to get them into 'sustained' employment.[40] On the face of it, it is difficult to disagree with the idea of finding long-term, sustainable employment for people who have been out of work for a while and want a job. As Shildrick and her co-authors clearly demonstrated (and as interviews for this book bore out), people wanted to work.

However, from the start the Work Programme was plagued by a catalogue of criticisms for being ill conceived and mismanaged. Some criticisms were to do with the huge cost of implementation.[41] Others, such as those from the National Council for Voluntary Organisations (NCVO), focused on the fact that large private companies winning the contracts were not subcontracting work to smaller community organisations that had years of local experience in employment assistance – and despite the government having predicted that contracts would be won by small organisations.[42]

Most objections focused, however, on the inherent flaws in the objectives of the programme and the large number of problems with its implementation. A significant amount of criticism was directed at what economist and former Bank of England Monetary Policy Committee member, David Blanchflower, called 'crackpot' ideas that, he argued, were not adequately piloted or evaluated.[43] Running through the entire enterprise was the dubious assumption that people were unemployed through their own fault, and that all they needed was to be 'nudged' to find work. It was as if there were a cognitive dissonance between objective reality and what ministers thought (or wanted to think) was happening. Numerous critics argued that there was not enough focus on the 'churn' of people from one insecure job to another, leading to many people experiencing frequent short periods of unemployment. In effect, ministers were ignoring the fact that the available jobs were low paid and often insecure – ergo *not* sustainable as the policy intended. Based as it was on such a deluded premise, it wasn't surprising that it proved to be ineffective at meeting its own targets. A report from the National Audit Office in January 2012, just six months after it was launched,[44] warned that the programme was 'over-optimistic' about its targets for getting people into work. This indeed proved to be the case when a number of reports throughout 2012 and 2013 found it to be seriously lacking, with contractors failing to meet many of their targets – some by a long way – and in particular, those for 'hard-to-place' clients such as people who had been out of work for many years.

In February 2013 the Public Accounts Committee issued a damning indictment reporting that the scheme had managed to get just 3.6 per cent of claimants into sustained employment.[45] Two years after its introduction, the multi-billion pound programme was lambasted for 'being worse than doing nothing'.[46] The Work Programme was also criticised for failing to find jobs for key target groups such as homeless people, people with substance misuse problems, the long-term unemployed and people with disabilities, with some analysts concluding that the outcomes were woeful.[47] It was condemned for producing 'unintended consequences' borne of 'perverse incentives', whereby firms neglected harder-to-place clients because they were paid by results (the number of people they got into work), and so it made financial sense for the contractors to focus on those individuals who did not have complex needs.[48] The government challenged its detractors (of course), countering that it was still 'early days' (a term that somehow seemed to have gained astonishing elasticity) and that significant numbers of people had indeed been helped into work.

Needless to say critics were largely underwhelmed by the government's protestations. This is what David Blanchflower had to say:[49]

> The Coalition's ill-designed Work Programme doesn't work. To this point, studies show it has negative rates of return. Participants' chances of getting a job are lowered by signing up for the WP. They would have had a better chance of finding a job if they hadn't gone on the program.

If the Work Programme was at the centre of the government's back-to-work reforms, then it was surrounded by a veritable constellation of related and equally controversial initiatives – and all possessing a punitive sting in the tail. As Sharon Wright[50] pointed out in research for CPAG, the primary difference between what Labour had done before and what the Coalition was doing was a single-minded goal to reduce benefits payments, underpinned by an unprecedented regime of punitive sanctions. Summing up how these reforms sat within the wider austerity agenda, Wright put it like this:

> Receiving financial support from the state when unemployed or unable to work (because of ill health, disability or caring commitments) is harder now than at any time in the last 60 years. Driven by unequivocal cost-cutting and an ideological drive to tackle 'welfare dependency', eligibility criteria for a range of benefits have been tightened, and claiming benefits is more conditional on actively seeking work – backed by harsh penalties for non-compliance. Furthermore, benefits

are paid at low (often inadequate) rates, which are set to devalue over time.

The greater 'conditionality' Wright referred to incorporated compulsory initiatives such as the mandatory work activity scheme where Jobcentre Plus advisers referred claimants to a compulsory four-week work placement, but among the most condemned initiatives was Workfare, where people on Jobseeker's Allowance were forced under the threat of losing benefits to take part in 'work experience', much of which consisted of low-level jobs that, claimants protested, offered no useful experience at all. The scheme was roundly denounced by critics[51] as nothing short of 'slave labour' that shored up corporations by supplying guaranteed cheap labour while undermining legitimate, paid jobs.

Those who challenged the value of the 'back-to-work' schemes were accused of being 'job snobs', such as Cait Reilly, who gained prominence for objecting to being forced under a 'sector-based work academy' to take a work placement at the discount store, Poundland, to stack shelves rather than continue voluntary work in a museum. She (and others, including the TUC) claimed that such work, below the legal Minimum Wage, was 'forced labour'. The Court of Appeal agreed with her claim that the work schemes, including the Community Action Programme, which required the long-term unemployed to work unpaid for six months, were legally flawed.[52] Under pressure from campaigners, including the grassroots group Boycott Workfare, a number of companies and organisations that had signed up to Workfare withdrew from the programme.[53]

Boycott Workfare[54] summed it up thus:

> Workfare profits the rich by providing free labour, whilst threatening the poor by taking away welfare rights if people refuse to work without a living wage. Many of [the] sanctions

are as a result of workfare, and many are being handed out for the pettiest of reasons.

But even as victories against the government's reforms were being won, additional programmes including Help to Work (yet to be introduced at the time of writing) were being announced that would impose even greater conditionality, including requiring long-term unemployed people to 'work for their benefits'.[55] Mike Moulding of the Green Party in Wigan encapsulated much of the wider criticism when he took to his blog railing against the changes. He wrote:

> I have dubbed it as 'Legalised Slave Labour' because many long-term unemployed only receive just over £70.00 per week in Jobseeker's Allowance and the government says they intend to make these people work 30 hours plus for this meagre amount. Therefore, after years of stigmatisation and no jobs guarantee, the only thing this wretched Tory-led government propped up by the Liberal Hypocrite Party is guaranteeing is 'Community Service' basically criminalising the unemployed.

Increased conditionality and sanctions were at the forefront of people's minds all over the country during 2012 and 2013, and were among the things causing people most distress.

When I visited the vibrant Normanton Road in Derby, people appeared to be going about their daily business. As with much of what was occurring in Austerity UK, just a small scratch of the surface, and another picture emerged: people worriedly looking for work and fretting about being sanctioned. At JET (Jobs, Education & Training) Employment Centre, a grassroots charity delivering training and employment support,[56] throngs of people had been turning up all day hoping for advice on everything from writing job applications to locating vacancies, but a clear priority for many was how to traverse a system that sanctioned their benefits if they didn't comply with strict criteria for jobseeking. Many of those attending didn't speak fluent English and were telling advisers about how they were being sanctioned simply because they didn't understand the questions they were being asked. Many were distressed because once sanctioned they couldn't even begin to negotiate the complicated appeals system to have benefits reinstated. According to JET Director, Mohammed Sharief, without additional assistance, the people queuing to use his services were frankly stumped.

Part of the problem, according to Sharief, was that Jobcentre Plus and the people who staffed the service were overstretched and battling to adjust to a raft of speedily introduced complex reforms; translation services, which were already limited, were being scaled back; and demand for advice about benefits changes and sanctions was rising rapidly. Without extra resources the system was creaking under the strain and people were turning wherever they could for help – including to JET. The kind of support JET had offered for a decade or so was being stretched "to the limit", Sharief stressed, as people turned to the organisation, often out of desperation, as other local charitable organisations were running out of funds and closing their doors. Coupled with a backdrop of declining job opportunities, the problems were spiralling, he argued.

> "The people who live in this community suffer high unemployment [and we] have massive deprivation in the area. I am extremely worried."

Ashiq Hussain, a middle-aged man of Pakistani origin, was sitting in JET's premises at a table in what used to be an old dance hall, diligently filling out forms. Visibly frustrated, he told me he had been doing exactly the same thing for weeks on end as he methodically searched for jobs that never materialised in an area where jobs were scarce – especially for a man in his 50s.

"Now we never get job", Ashiq said looking up from his paperwork. "We try everywhere. I can't find the job. We try to every day. It's very hard. Running the family is very hard. I worry every day because I've not got any money. I feel the trouble. Could you tell me what I should do? It's not my fault. If I get a job I'll do the job."

The father of four has lived in Derby for over 30 years. For almost two decades he had stable, full-time, well-paid work at a Pirelli factory before it closed down and he was made redundant. After a spell working in takeaways he found himself once more on the dole. Despite walking from one takeaway to another, sometimes for days at a time, pleading for any kind of work, there was none to be had. By the time he was interviewed in 2013, Hussain had been out of work for a while and was clearly exasperated. Converting a bleak situation into a stark one was the fact that he had been sanctioned. Explaining how having his £112 per week Jobseeker's Allowance abruptly stopped affected him, he said:

> "Six weeks ago they stopped my money. They never pay me anything. I don't know what to do. What do I do for the children? When I go to sign on they say 'you take this form, take that form' or ring into benefit office. But the money is not in my account. So they say take an appeal form. 'You do an appeal as well' [they say]. But I'm already doing the appeals."

The staff at JET were overwhelmed with cases like Hussain's. The number of clients had risen dramatically through 2012 and 2013. Within one 12-month period demand for advice had leapt from around three or four hundred people a month to over three thousand – and a leading reason was sanctions.

"We have clients who come in and they have sanctions applied to them for a month. We have clients who come in and you can tell they are severely stressed and worried about how to make ends meet – particularly if they are getting sanctioned."

In Glasgow it was the same story, according to Lynette McKechnie. Even while some advisers were seeing 'positive' results and successfully coaching and supporting jobseekers – especially the longer-term unemployed or mothers returning to the labour market following long absences, McKechnie told me – their work could be undermined in an instant if a client was sanctioned:

"I've had people who have come in who have been sanctioned. They could be sanctioned for four weeks, they could be sanctioned for 13 weeks, and if it happens a third time they could be sanctioned for up to three years. That's panicking."

Department for Work and Pensions figures show that the application of sanctions were rising steadily throughout the 2000s[57] under New Labour, but that they shot up to unprecedented levels after May 2010, as harsher sanctions regimes were rolled out as appeals soared. A submission by Dr David Webster (honorary senior research fellow in Urban Studies at the University of Glasgow) to the House of Commons Work and Pensions Committee in November 2013 for its inquiry into the role of Jobcentre Plus in reforming the welfare system, was among many highlighting the spiralling deployment of sanctions, including a sharp rise in those for people missing appointments and in those that lasted for extremely long stretches of time.[58] He said: "Contrary to what was claimed by Lord Freud prior to their introduction, three-year sanctions have built up very quickly, with the 700 to date understating the rate now reached."

People were increasingly panicking about the fact that sanctions were being applied with ever greater fervour and for longer periods but, as case after case came to light, there was an almost diabolical aspect to many of them. In some instances, their use was not only callous but farcical. Newspapers were littered with examples and MPs repeatedly raised the issue in Parliament. Some of the most outrageous were pulled together on the websites such as http://stupidsanctions.tumblr.com.

Here are some examples:

> You've signed in on time, been to interviews and applied for work. Your jobcentre adviser suggests you make a two-line change to your CV, which you do, but fail to give the updated CV to the jobcentre (you weren't told you had to). You are sanctioned for four weeks.[59]

> You get a job that starts in two weeks' time. You don't look for work while you are waiting for the job to start. You're sanctioned.[60]

> It's Christmas Day and you don't fill in your job search evidence form to show that you've looked for all the new jobs that are advertised on Christmas Day. You are sanctioned. Merry Christmas.[61]

> You're five minutes late for your appointment, you show the adviser your watch which is running late, but you still get sanctioned for a month.[62]

> You've been unemployed for seven months and are forced onto a Workfare scheme but can't afford to travel to the shop. You offer to work in a different branch you can walk

to but are refused and get sanctioned for not attending your workfare placement.[63]

And so the list goes on[64]....

As an employment adviser at the Newhaven Community Employment Partnership and a carer, Rachel Hesterbanks in East Sussex saw the benefits system and jobseeking processes from different angles. With years of experience behind her as an adviser she was expected to roll with the welfare-to-work changes, but she was deeply concerned by the ruthlessness of what was happening. The application of ever-harsher sanctions was, she said, among the most disturbing developments she had seen in her career. This is how she described what she saw:

> "Because of the change in the benefits situation – and the squeeze is becoming increasingly tighter – [claimants] are becoming increasingly more agitated and angry. People are petrified. Especially because of the new sanctioning rules coming through. Even we as guidance workers are very scared for our clients. How can you punish someone who for instance is taking anti-depressants? I had a lady this week who is diagnosed with paranoid psychosis, she hears voices, takes anti-depressants, she takes pills for the psychosis, she takes pills for the anxiety. She can't remember what her name is let alone that she has an appointment in two weeks' time. But we are supposed to punish her for that?"

She continued: "We as advisers and support workers are angry on [our clients'] behalf. We are looking at these rules and thinking 'that's not fair, you cannot do that to people who are suffering' – especially with depression and anxiety – and an awful lot of people are suffering now who weren't previously."

Explaining that the bureaucracy alone could be overwhelming she told me:

"It's hard enough filling out the form for ESA [Employment and Support Allowance]. It's something like a 36-page form. I myself am a carer so I know. I have to fill out my partner's form every six months. Yeah! I also have to fill out the DLA [Disability Living Allowance] form every three years and that takes me a month. I'm educated, I know how to fill out a form properly and yet it still takes me a month to fill out a DLA form!"

She pointed out that, combined with other austerity-related stresses such as debt, pressures on people to find work 'or else' were profoundly destabilising:

"Pressure has increased. It's like a cooking pot and there has to be some sort of outlet and I think substance misuse, alcohol misuse – all of these things are increasing. It's the most vulnerable who are suffering. The people who really need it don't have the capacity without support to do it. There are good stories and we do help people and they do get jobs otherwise there wouldn't be any point to doing this. We see the positive effect that our involvement in their lives has and that's heartening, but there are so many more and they are just going to keep on coming."

As the months of interviews came and went, and there appeared to be no hope of wage settlements improving or austerity-driven benefits penalties abating, the people I met became more and more angry. For every politician on television talking up the 'rebounding' economy there were thousands wondering what planet they were on. In Luton, 'Dec' summed up how many people interpreted the increasingly ruthless and perverse nature of looking for work in Austerity UK:

"Whatever way you want to add it up if you don't want to apply for [a specific] job they suspend your benefits for four weeks. And if they [do] they get a tick as being good boys! 'You're doing a great job by stopping these people that are already down there and are being kicked day in day out and you've done a great thing by putting another boot in just to push them over the edge that bit more.'"

In North Tyneside, Fiona Swindle, who had a senior management job at Newcastle City Council but had lost her job in the first round of redundancies by the local authority in 2011, articulated how people felt saying they were being worn down and treated "appallingly":

"I've worked all my life. I've applied for about 20 jobs in the last two months and there's not a lot of jobs. It feels like hell. It's war on the weakest. It's the strongest in society who don't have a clue about ordinary people's lives, who've never had to make difficult choices between heat and eat, who are making decisions about things that are going to have a catastrophic effect on people who they see as being feckless.

I just don't want to believe that people can be so wedded to their ideology that they really don't care and don't have any empathy for people suffering."

Throughout the government's austerity drive, the evidence that some groups – usually the most vulnerable in society – were suffering more than most and being disproportionately affected by a whole range of reforms mounted month on month. In earlier chapters we examined how whole swaths of people were buckling under multiple pressures, but it is to those who were arguably most affected that we now turn.

SIX

Bearing the brunt

The targeting of people with disabilities: austerity at its worst

Disabled people should not be the scapegoats for the financial mistakes of governments, should not be constantly told that there is no money to support them by millionaire politicians. We will not tolerate further erosion of our living conditions or our human rights, nor will we sit quietly while they try to take our rights away. (Declaration on the website of Disabled People Against Cuts [DPAC])

"From a human rights perspective it's very important to have the principle of equality and non-discrimination, meaning that certain groups should not have a disproportionate impact from cuts." (Magdalena Sepúlveda, UN Special Rapporteur on Extreme Poverty & Human Rights, February 2013)

The reality of disability in Austerity UK

There are those who have argued that austerity was a rational, necessary and inevitable response to the economic crisis and, as we know, these are usually the same people who, despite evidence to the contrary, repeat platitudes like 'we are all in this together'.

When UN Special Rapporteur on Extreme Poverty & Human Rights, Magdalena Sepúlveda, came to the UK to take part in a London School of Economics event, 'Austerity on Trial', in early 2013,[1] not only did she make a resounding argument that austerity was avoidable in the UK or elsewhere, she also declared that we were most certainly not all in it together.

With a unique global perspective on austerity, Sepúlveda underscored that the poor and underprivileged were profoundly affected in the UK and elsewhere, even to the extent of infringing on their human rights. She was at pains to drum home that some groups were treated much more harshly than others by austerity-related policies, with dire consequences for them, their families and their communities. Those groups most likely to be left destitute by cuts to essential benefits, she emphatically concluded, were also those most directly affected by cuts to public services – rendering them vulnerable on several fronts. Whether it was Greece, Spain, Ireland or the UK, the people at the very sharpest end were the same – it was just a matter of degree.

> "If you take a single mother, an older person, a person with disability, there is a reality that their welfare benefits have been cut – but it's not only that. At the same time [government] are reducing the money that goes to the provision of basic social services. People living in poverty depend on social services more than the richest segment of the population. It's this cumulative effect that is having the disproportionate impact on them. The process and the results of these measures are violating the rights of people."

Cuts per se were bad enough, but these were only part of the problem, according to Sepúlveda: it was also the *way* in which some cuts were introduced that produced such devastating outcomes. In the absence of formal and systematic assessments of individual policies or the impacts of multiple policies taken together on specific groups, vulnerable people were disproportionately affected, she declared.

> "If you look at the process you see the austerity measures being designed and implemented really [are] without following a democratic process. There is no consultation, no transparency."

By the time I had completed my journey around the UK, in the autumn of 2013, it was evident that Sepúlveda's observations were right on the nose. There were clusters of people all across the country whose lives were beginning to be made almost unliveable by austerity, and who felt their basic human rights were being eroded. An 18-month, in-depth study by nef on the impact of austerity on specific communities was published at the end of 2012.[2] Its conclusions on disproportionality chimed with Sepúlveda's – and with what people were telling me:

> The burden of reducing Britain's deficit is falling predominantly on people who get vital support from public services and welfare: the unemployed, low-income earners, the very elderly and the young and – perhaps most of all – disabled people.

It is to this last group, disabled people – along with people with serious and long-term health conditions – that this chapter turns its attention. There were disproportionate consequences for other groups, such as the working poor and women, but the sheer ferocity of policies affecting disabled and sick people warrants special attention. The degree to which those who were sick or disabled were caught in austerity's trap was jaw dropping. Perhaps more than anything else in Austerity UK it was this that laid bare the spuriousness of any claim that cuts and reforms to the welfare state were equitable.

Talking to people confronting the daily reality of what was, without doubt, one of the sharpest ends of austerity meant walking away with a sense of how mistreated and harassed people felt. Policies such as the Work Capability Assessment, which determined who of working age qualified for ESA, the out-of-work benefit for sick and disabled adults designed to replace the old Incapacity Benefit, were endorsed by ministers regardless of the serious damage they were inflicting, while a plethora of cuts and other benefits changes lumped indignity on indignity. As Scott Randall, a young man from South Lanarkshire who has cerebral palsy, put it when talking to me about the 'irrational cruelty' of the back-to-work reforms for disabled people:

> "There are people who have got genuine things [wrong] and [officials] turn round and say 'yes, you're fit for work,' and you think how can [they] say that when the person clearly is not fit for work and are suffering?"

Or, as Amy Jones, a 24-year-old from London who also has cerebral palsy (and who was frequently targeted on Twitter when she spoke out about people with disabilities bearing the brunt of austerity, by trolls who accused her of believing she was 'entitled'), said of the erosion of vital social security support:

> "People don't seem to understand the difference disability benefits make to someone's quality of life. They are there to make sure someone in my position is able to have the extra support they need. It's about being able to live independently and with dignity. People think [benefits are] easy to get, as if it's all people defrauding [the system]. Well they have never been easy to get. I have always had to fight for every scrap of help. It's incredibly stressful."

In common with what many people were telling me, she added:

> "I really believe [government policy] is about ideology. They say it's about austerity but that doesn't make sense to me. If so many people lose essential benefits – which is what is happening – then it's going to cost more in the long run. It will cause social isolation and its going to put a burden on the NHS and social services because people will need to turn somewhere for help."

In Northern Ireland, where some of social security reforms and cuts (for example, to the public sector workforce) were scheduled to be implemented later than in other parts of the country, the long-term ramifications of a raft of policies on people with disabilities in particular were top of the agenda for campaigners. (This was in part because so many people in Northern Ireland were disabled [around a quarter], some of which was attributable to a legacy from 'The Troubles' including persistent mental health problems such as post-traumatic stress disorder.) In Belfast, among a group gathered to discuss the impact of austerity, one anti-poverty worker said:

> "The actual development of neo-liberalism and the whole economic system caused this [economic] crisis and yet it's the most vulnerable [being hit] ... and people with disabilities are the ones who are bearing the brunt. I think that's the cruelty of it all."

A disability campaigner summed the situation up thus:

> "I think you cannot underestimate the strength of the word 'fear'. There's a lot of fear within the disability [community]."

The harm and inequity experienced by sick and disabled people was incontrovertible and it was pervasive. As the months passed in 2012 and 2013 it was abundantly clear that the radical upending of the entire social security structure that was causing so many problems for non-disabled people was also the primary culprit behind the suffering of people with disabilities – only often to a much greater degree. And this new political world order did not occur in a vacuum.

Despite decades of progress, when it came to disability rights, existing and entrenched disadvantages remained a challenge – including serious barriers to work due to negative attitudes and ignorance around disability. For example, prior to and following austerity, people with disabilities were more likely to live in poverty and be out of work than the wider population. They were also much more likely to be isolated and have a higher instance of depression.[3] As austerity's grip tightened, evidence mounted of greater financial and related pressures. A study in July 2013 from the disability charity, Scope, reported that people with disabilities were 'turning in desperation' to expensive loans to meet basic needs.[4] It also found that they were three times more likely than the wider population to use doorstep loans, while a fifth had been unable to make the minimum payments on credit cards in the previous 12 months.

One piece of analysis published in early 2013 by the think tank, Demos, which attempted a detailed and rigorous appraisal of the situation that people with disabilities were facing, reached some startling conclusions.[5] Many campaigners had long been calling for a 'cumulative impact assessment' (on the international stage, Sepúlveda was one of them, as was the campaign group 'Wow Petition') to gauge the true impact of cuts and benefits changes but, in the absence of one by government (ministers insisted it was too complex), the Demos study was left to fill in some of the blanks. (It is worth noting that changes to some benefits that affected other groups as well as people with disabilities – such as the freezing of Child Benefit that was set to affect around one million disabled parents – were not included in the analysis, which makes the findings all the more disquieting.) The report's author, Claudia Wood, wrote:

> Our research reveals that disabled people are bearing the brunt of the austerity measures, losing an estimated £28.3 billion by 2017/18. While striking, these calculations will invariably be an underestimate of the true impact of the cuts – as we opted for the most conservative estimates on the more unknown elements of reform.

Commissioned by Scope, the report concluded that up to 3.7 million people with disabilities would be directly affected by a platter of cuts simultaneously with parlous consequences. Among its findings were:

- Thousands of people with disabilities (what the report calls 'the hardest hit of the hardest hit') would be hit all at once by six major welfare cuts before the 2015 general election.
- By 2018 a staggering £28.3 billion would be chopped from disabled support budgets and benefits.
- A host of changes to benefits, including Disability Living Allowance (DLA), ESA, Housing Benefit and the 'Bedroom Tax', were hitting the same group of people with disabilities over and over again.
- Around 120,000 people faced the 'triple whammy' of losing a number of core disability benefits including ESA and DLA, while 99,000 would see cuts to four benefits at once.

Launching the report in March 2013, chief executive of Scope, Richard Hawkes, concluded:

"At the moment there's no place for disabled people in the Chancellor's aspiration nation. In 2013 disabled people are already struggling to pay the bills. Living costs are spiralling. Income is flat-lining. We know many are getting in debt, just to pay for essentials. What's the government's response? The same group of disabled people face not just one or two cuts to their support, but in some cases three, four, five or even six cuts....At the same time, disabled people who want to live independently, are seeing the support they need to get up, get dressed and get out squeezed due to chronic under-funding of social care. It paints a frightening picture of the financial struggles affecting disabled people in 2013."

Taking on the austerians

Taking all of this into account, it is not difficult to see why people with disabilities were left reeling by the force of austerity when it hit, but – and this is crucial – one of the things that sets this sector of society apart is that they were shouting from the rooftops right from the start about just how destructive the onslaught would be. The Demos report put some concrete evidence behind what thousands of people with disabilities had been predicting from the beginning. At the Conservative Party Conference in the autumn of 2010, when the first tranche of austerity policies had barely made it off the drawing board, there was a group of people demonstrating in the streets outside, warning of the calamitous implications that lay ahead if the cuts everyone was being told to brace themselves for came into force. The people protesting were disabled, they were angry and they were not about to be ignored.

Under the banner 'Cuts Kill' a diverse group of people with disabilities and supporters coalesced around the issue. The demonstration – which gave birth to one of the most outspoken and effective group of campaigners, Disabled People Against

Cuts (DPAC)[6] – would turn out to be a mere taster of what would happen in the following three years, as disabled activists railed against the government's cuts and welfare reforms using every avenue possible.[7]

Suffice to say that as the months of austerity turned into years, people with disabilities were not only bearing the brunt, they were also unquestionably front and centre of an unprecedented insurgency against cuts. They lobbied MPs and ministers, protested in the streets – even blocking the traffic in central London by chaining wheelchairs together[8] – and accused the government of 'bullying' and turning back the clock on decades of hard-fought-for disability rights that were supposed to guarantee disabled people's right to live as equal members of society, with independence and dignity. One of those at the helm of campaigning was former Paralympian and longstanding outspoken advocate for disability rights, Baroness Tanni Grey-Thompson. She warned that if they weren't stopped in their tracks, the government's policies would take disability rights back decades: 'What we don't want is for Britain to be turned back to the Sixties and Seventies, when disabled people were locked up because that was cheaper and easier', she wrote in *The Times*.[9]

Other campaigners were also making their mark. Blogs including Sue Marsh's and the Orwell Prize short-listed 'Benefit Scrounging Scum – Life in a broken bureaucracy with a bendy and borked body' by young campaigner, Kaliya Franklin,[10] were among many that sprung up, not only articulating the first-hand experiences of people affected, but as dynamic and informed advocacy platforms. Groups such as We are Spartacus[11] (for which Franklin, along with many others, were the driving force), the Wow Petition, which campaigned steadfastly for a 'cumulative impact assessment' of all welfare reforms on people with disabilities,[12] and DPAC emerged to take on the Coalition. These and others drew on networks of local activists all over the country and, along with more established charities, spearheaded campaigns and protests that questioned the government's approach and, in many instances, forensically unpicked individual policies and their ramifications. Social media such as Twitter was also used to great effect, with activists old and new sharing ideas, coordinating activities and challenging policies and erroneous statistics, prejudices and ill-informed reports.

All of these efforts served to highlight what even a few years earlier would have been regarded as inconceivable – that rather than showing adults and children with disabilities the respect they deserved, the government was breaking the most fundamental of social contracts, hell bent as it was on cutting vital benefits and services regardless of vocal objections backed by solid evidence[13] of the misery their policies were foisting on people.

A complex package of discriminatory reforms

In many ways the momentum behind the reaction of people with disabilities and the determination not to accept changes without a fight was incredibly encouraging but – as any campaigner or activist would tell you – even with all of these combined attempts to prevent the worst, as 2014 approached the future was looking very stark indeed.

The volume and complexity of reforms almost beggared belief, and certainly as I travelled around there was as much bewilderment as fury at what was occurring. People with long-term health conditions or disabilities, including those living with mental health problems and older people with age-related illnesses (as well as the people who were advising and supporting them), were – like others affected by austerity – fearful of benefits being cut, changed, delayed or sanctioned, but with bells on. Academic and vociferous campaigner, Simon Duffy, of The Centre for Welfare Reform, encapsulated what many people were saying:[14]

UK Government policy has targeted disabled people for
cuts – that's disabled children, disabled adults, war veterans
and the elderly. Few people understand the severity or the
breadth of the problem.

It would be difficult to find something that summed up the
mood better than the DPAC website, where it says:

Disabled people should not be the scapegoats for the financial
mistakes of governments, should not be constantly told that
there is no money to support them by millionaire politicians.
We will not tolerate further erosion of our living conditions
or our human rights, nor will we sit quietly while they try
to take our rights away.

Reflecting on what had transpired since the first protests of
2010, Linda Burnip of DPAC said poignantly:

"We could not have imagined that three years later we'd
be getting daily emails from disabled people and pregnant
disabled people who were actually starving and being left
without food, money or access to any hardship payments.
We knew but couldn't have possibly imagined that disabled
people would have their benefits stopped for weeks and in
some cases months without any means to support themselves
other than possible prostitution, drug dealing or theft. What
do you do when you are already living on the breadline with
no savings and your only income is taken away? We never
imagined we'd read about children, disabled and non-disabled
being left without food."[15]

She told me:

"I knew it would be bad but did I think [by the end of 2013] I would see [benefits] being taken from disabled people for three months leaving them with no way to feed themselves? The impact of austerity has been massive – and this is on top of barriers that already existed for disabled people. Its not only welfare and benefits but care and support too. Local authorities' funding for care has been slashed. And then anyone who campaigns against it is called an extremist! They say there is no money but if they stopped tax evasion and tax avoidance they wouldn't have to make the cuts."

Burnip was also one of a number of campaigners who stressed that many reforms introduced under the Coalition were made possible by the previous Labour government. For example, the Work Capability Assessment was originally introduced by Labour as part of its own drive to reform social security and the highly criticised French firm hired to carry out the assessments, Atos, was appointed by the previous administration.

The Work Programme

Among the many austerity policies affecting people with disabilities and people with serious health conditions a few areas came up time and again: reforms related to getting people 'back to work', sweeping adjustments to disability-specific benefits and cuts to social care. One of the back-to-work reforms having a detrimental affect (as with non-disabled people) was the Work Programme. The controversial scheme was so woeful at finding work for people with disabilities that, according to critics, the same results could have been achieved if nothing whatsoever had been done – and no money had been wasted paying private companies to implement it.[16, 17]

In October 2013 Liz Sayce, Head of Disability Rights UK, condemned the Work Programme for failing people with disabilities outright after figures published a month earlier found that 93 per cent of people with a disability placed on it were not found sustainable employment – well below official targets.[18] Sayce echoed other critics,[19] claiming that without a more bespoke approach that focused on "better career outcomes" rather than "endless work preparation", money was simply being wasted and unnecessary distress caused. She said:

> "The Work Programme is a non-work programme as far as disabled people are concerned. Britain will only achieve an economic recovery if it is an inclusive recovery – so disabled people can use our talents, confident we can design support that meets our individual needs and aspirations."

The charity's report, *Taking care of Employment Support*,[20] concluded that:

> The Work Programme is projected to cost £3–5bn over five years, yet is not working for a core group: people living with disability or long-term health conditions. It is time to cut out the middleman, releasing the money that is presently being wasted and transferring control of employment support to those who know how it can be used best – disabled people and employers.

Work Capability Assessment

If the Work Programme came in for criticism, this paled in comparison with that levelled at the Work Capability Assessment. It is hard to imagine three words that struck more fear into disabled and sick people as austerity took hold. The system, the ministers responsible for overseeing it and the company originally contracted to administer it came in for some of the most breathtaking condemnation ever levelled at the UK's social security system. It was a test introduced to gauge if someone with an illness or disability was 'fit to work'. If this were deemed to be the case, it would mean they were placed on ESA. The principle that was pushed time and again by the Coalition (as it was indeed when it was originally introduced by Labour) was that the tests would weed out the fake disability claimants from the genuine, thereby reducing the social security bill. The 'test', a computer-based question-and-answer format, was carried out by medically qualified staff hired by the French company, Atos, contracted by government to carry them out. Atos looked at a claimant's ability to carry out certain functions – say, walk for 200 metres or use their hands – and if a candidate was awarded enough 'points', they qualified for ESA.[21] In preparation for work, claimants could then be placed in a Work-Related Activity Group (WRAG) which was set up to acknowledge that people with disabilities who 'qualified' for ESA would need additional assistance beyond that offered to ordinary Jobseeker's Allowance claimants. Those who declared not fit for work were placed in a 'Support Group'. (The rates of ESA are variable, based on levels of National Insurance contributions but, even if the claimant qualifies for the higher contribution-based rate, this will usually reduce after a year to the lower, income-related rate inflicting further financial hardship.[22])

Yet again, here was a policy that was masquerading as being aimed at helping people into work when in fact what transpired was a process that would be exposed as a monumental shambles. Work Capability Assessment brought untold suffering and anxiety to thousands of people, thanks to what could often only be described as its ridiculously cruel application. Stories abounded of people being 'failed' for the most absurd reasons, including those who could barely walk or write a letter being declared 'fit for work'. There were also complaints of the assessment staff being indifferent or dismissive of an individual's condition. Thousands of those being required to take part in an assessment complained of being unduly stressed and humiliated by the process.

Charlotte Walker from London was a professional in the public sector who described herself as "someone who has worked my whole life" before a prolonged episode of incapacitating depression led to her leaving her job in 2012. Recalling her encounter with Work Capability Assessment, she told me staff were rude and unhelpful, even accusing her of "being aggressive" when she asked questions about the nature of the assessment:

> "I was really anxious because I'd heard such bad things. I couldn't understand why [the interview] happened the way it did. They made me put out all my medication on the table – as if I must have been lying about it. It was so embarrassing. I kept talking about how I loved my job but how disabled I had become – how I couldn't function the way I once could. It seemed like everything required an over-simplistic answer. I was asked for example if I could wash and dress myself. I'd say 'it depends, I'm depressed'. When I answered 'it depends' to a few questions she told me 'everybody had good and bad days'. I honestly couldn't believe it. How could she be judging someone with [severe Bi-polar]?"

When the results of her assessment arrived by letter, Walker, who by 2013 was becoming a prominent mental health blogger, said she "couldn't believe" she had been awarded zero points:

> "Just because I said I could meet a friend for a cup of coffee sometimes, apparently was evidence of planning and spontaneity and meant I was fit for work. No matter that some days I couldn't get out of bed! It was like a looking glass world. It's a tick box system that doesn't work. By default it treats people as cheats."

Walker embarked on "a very stressful" appeals process and was eventually put on ESA, but decided the pressure of ongoing assessments was too detrimental to her health so withdrew from benefits and tries to scrape by herself. She refers to herself as "very lucky" after finding small amounts of work as a mental health mentor for a charity.

Jamie Gates from Newhaven, another person with mental health difficulties, had held down lots of different jobs over the years including as a utilities meter reader and a fishmonger – up until the depression he had lived with for years "got on top" of him. He told me that as someone with a 'hidden' and fluctuating disability, he was terrified about being pushed back into work before he was ready by back-to-work 'tests' "not fit for purpose" that assumed that because he was having a good day or a good week he was capable of work. A pernicious blend of cuts to local mental health services and the pressure of possibly being forced to work or face sanctions were only making it harder to manage his depression, he said.

> "With the sort of illness I have, depression and anxiety, it's not a seen illness and I can go for months and I'm perfectly stable and then I'll drop of the edge of a cliff one day, overnight, for no reason at all. The money I get [from benefits] isn't much but it's enough to keep me going. If they start taking that away you find yourself in a position where you've got to go out and force yourself to work, which isn't going to be very good for your health. It's that, y'know, they just think you're malingerers."

In Leeds, 57-year-old Sue Watson was diagnosed with rheumatoid arthritis just months after setting up her own business in 2007. She described going through "18 months of pure hell" as she waited for a drug combination to work that would enable her to keep her business as an aromatherapist. The illness got the better of her, leaving her disabled. She qualified for ESA but after one year was placed in a WRAG, rather than a Support Group, where she should have been. She was told it would take 18 months to appeal and it was only after convincing her MP to get involved that she was able to get the benefits she was entitled to. She told me:

> "I nearly gave up so many times. It had a detrimental effect on my health. Stress can manifest in so many ways it's hard to quantify. I had worked for 37 years before I [became ill]. I hold politicians in utter contempt for doing this [to people]. It seems to me that they have rushed so many policies through without having thought them through."

And it wasn't just those on the receiving end of the policies exposing the system's phenomenal flaws. This is what jobs adviser, Rachel Hesterbanks, in East Sussex had to say:

> "My favourite story out of Work Capability Assessment – and we get a lot – is that a lady actually had a heart attack in the meeting for the WCA and when the guy was taking her blood pressure he realised that this was an onset of a heart attack, phoned an ambulance for her ... put her in an ambulance and then failed her for the Work Capability Assessment and took her off ESA!"

In Liverpool Sheila Sweeny said that the number of families where someone had a disability coming under "enormous pressure" from the Work Capability Assessment was soaring and, she observed, was "absolutely" adding to the feeling that they were being vindictively targeted by reforms.

> "We've seen some horrific stories. A woman who lives down in Norris Green, her daughter, she's 30 and she's [very fragile

and tiny and] in a wheelchair. She makes lots of noises all the time. She had to go and be tested for work! How humiliating is that? It's just awful. You have to go for your [fitness-for-work test] interview and if you can't [get there] easily enough [say because of lack of public transport] but [despite] getting on a bit you are able to walk there then you fail the test. It's these little tricks all the time that are leaving people feeling so alienated."

In Wales, Elwyn James at Arts Factory spoke of some of the more serious cases he had encountered:

"We have a guy who volunteers here with his carer. He was a very able guy but he had a bad accident which left him paralysed and in a wheelchair and with serious brain injuries. Now he is having to go and be reassessed every six months to see if he's capable of work. What's that about? Somebody's making money out of that. A friend of mine was recently called in for an assessment. He had a double lung transplant six months ago. He can barely make it to the front door. Maybe I'm cynical but to me this looks like people making money out of other people's misery. It's nothing to do with saving money. It's about making it."

According to Amber Peachy-Moore, a manager at the Hull and East Riding Citizens Advice Bureau, the scale of awfulness unleashed by Work Capability Assessment was among the most distressing developments she had witnessed in her career – and all the more so because people were made to feel useless for not being in work even when there were no jobs for them to go to:

"There's been a lot of media coverage about the appeals process and people being rejected for ESA. Clients with any range of disabilities or health issues affecting [them] in the most profound ways are told they are fit to work. We are absolutely inundated with people who are saying 'I can barely manage my basic daily life never mind jobseeking … if there was work available perhaps I could do it'. But it's the jobseeking process they're released into if they fail the ESA tests."

She added:

"We recently saw a client who was rejected for ESA and the reasons it gave on his form were that he had been capable of filling out the ESA 50 form [the application form for ESA] and he had been physically able to make it to his medical appointment. Those were the reasons he was given zero points. Because his upper arm movements were suitable to fill out a form and he'd been able to make it no matter how slowly and painfully or at what cost to himself to his health. He was also able to make it from his chair in the appointment room to the appointment office even with a slow limp and a shuffle but because he was able to do those things they assessed that he was able to [work]."

According to Peachy-Moore, one of the biggest frustrations was that prior to Work Capability Assessment it was people's doctors who knew their medical history – not strangers – which meant arbitrary 'reasons' for removal of benefits was less likely.

"It's moved from people's doctors signing them off sick and suggesting 'I know this client, I know what they're about, I've got a long perspective of their health issues and I don't think they are capable of a work environment or a jobseeking environment' to a situation where people are looked at and nothing about their disability is considered other than 'is there a hypothetical job this person may be able to do in a perfect world.' Hull is a city with incredibly low job opportunities at the moment. There are jobs but certainly not jobs for everyone who wants one and a client who is already at a disadvantage with a disability would be almost assured of not getting those jobs. So to say that a client could fill out one form that they can then get a job and be gainfully employed is a complete myth."

This is how she described the hazards created by Work Capability Assessment for people with enduring mental health problems:

"We see a lot of clients with mental health issues who are being put under all these strains regardless of their mental health issues – people who say they can't work due to mental health issues including being suicidal. I've actually seen one case in person and it matched identically another person on a television programme where a suicidal client was asked seriously as part of the medical:

Assessor: 'Are you suicidal?'

Claimant: 'Yes'

Assessor: 'Well then, why haven't you achieved it?'

It's such a horrific, cold perspective. The figures on how many people are dying within weeks or months of having these ESA tests saying they were fit to work [are shocking]. To take people already in financial despair and physical distress and then to put them under unbearable pressure again and again and again while market forces and the papers are saying these people have an easy ride scrounging off the state – I just think it could be catastrophic and the long-term costs of repairing the damage these systems do is going to outweigh any benefits."

This was how Richard Hawkes, chief executive of Scope, summarised the Work Capability Assessment/Atos mess:

> "The government needs to deliver a test that is fit for purpose. Most disabled people want to work but they face significant barriers, such as a lack of skills and experience, confidence and even negative attitudes from some employers. The Work Capability Assessment ignores all this. It's a tick-box test of someone's medical condition."

Among the many criticisms about Work Capability Assessment were those from the mental health lobby. One campaign launched to take on Work Capability Assessment was by Rethink Mental Illness. The charity had been arguing for some time that the test was unfair to people with mental health conditions for a number of serious and specific reasons. Speaking after three judges at a tribunal found the assessment to be unfair (the government was appealing the ruling at the time of), the charity's chief executive, Paul Jenkins, wrote:[23]

> The WCA is riddled with problems but this judicial review focused on one specific issue – that of gathering supporting evidence. Under the current system, no matter how ill or even delusional you may be, you are responsible for proactively gathering your own medical evidence and sending it to the Department for Work and Pensions (DWP). If you fail to do this, it simply won't be looked at. This means your ability to work will be judged from a one-off 15 minute assessment by a stranger who may well have no mental health training whatsoever and has no idea what your GP, psychiatrist or Community Psychiatric Nurse has to say about your illness. It means all the paperwork documenting your long history of severe and enduring mental illness can be simply ignored.

The Work Capability Assessment was causing so much distress, in fact, that DPAC launched a separate campaign, '10,000 Cuts and Counting', with a goal of discrediting of policy and seeing it abolished. As the organisation put it:

> ... there is no point in just replacing ATOS with another corporate monster and the WCA must be scrapped in its entirety. Why should any private firm rake in millions and millions of pounds of taxpayers' money to provide a totally flawed service which could be provided by civil servants for a fraction of the cost as has been the case until recently? The WCA was put in place to cut the number of claimants by 1 million either through miracle cures or death it seems.

By April 2013 it was clear that appeals against the assessment had reached astounding levels. Government figures showed that between April 2012 and April 2013, 465,000 individuals launched appeals – up from 279,000 in 2009/10 under the previous Labour administration.[24] In July 2013 it emerged that the annual cost of appeals on ESA decisions had shot up from £21 million in 2009/10 to £66 million in 2012/13, with new judges and tribunal staff also having to be recruited to deal with the backlog. This led, unsurprisingly, to questions about how any of this could possibly be justified as saving money due to austerity.[25] In addition, the process of challenging the test results was extremely stressful in its own right due to the uncertainty of outcome and also because appeals tended to take long periods of time to be resolved, leaving many people more ill than they were to begin with. And just in case there wasn't enough strain to go round in 2013 it emerged that some GPs were charging up to £130 for evidence to help people with appeals.[26]

The extent of the problem was also evident in reactions from other quarters. While ministers and the Department for Work and Pensions routinely defended the system, local councils, many of which were battling with how to deal with savage cuts to their own budgets and which were facing their own criticism for cuts, were speaking out against the assessments. Islington Council in London called them 'shocking'[27] while Bradford Council announced it would investigate them for being 'discriminatory'.[28] Meanwhile staff were abandoning the Atos ship – and they weren't going quietly either. In May 2013, Greg Wood, a former Navy doctor, revealed that he was leaving Atos because, among other criticisms, the tests were based on "medical nonsense". His whistleblowing lifted the lid on a host of deficiencies and made national headlines.[29] (Wood now blogs at worktestwhistleblower.blogspot.co.uk)

Such was the unfurling catastrophe with Work Capability Assessment that Atos lost its monopoly to deliver the assessment in July 2013 after a government audit found their work to be of an unacceptable standard in over 40 per cent of reports sampled.[30] Other companies were anticipated to be delivering the assessments by the middle of 2014.[31] (The Labour Party committed to firing Atos if it won the general election in 2015, something welcomed by campaigners but criticised for not going far enough in pledging to abandon the assessment altogether.)

After the government finally admitted Atos's performance was substandard, this is what Richard Hawkes of Scope had to say:

> "It's about time the government told Atos to smarten up its act. But, it's also strikingly clear to disabled people that whole £112 million per year system is broken. The cost of appeals has skyrocketed, assessors have resigned in disgust, and the test has received criticism from the Public Accounts Committee[32] and National Audit Office.[33] We have also witnessed shocking undercover footage of how ATOS assessors are trained and heard horror stories of disabled people inappropriately found fit to work."

One of the most disturbing aspects to all of this was that behind the vocal public criticisms were, as the interviewees quoted earlier illustrate, some of the most deeply unsettling stories imaginable. A deluge of reports poured forth of seriously sick and disabled people who had been unfairly treated but, most shocking of all, who had been declared fit for work only to die within days or weeks of the assessment, having endured extraordinary stress in their final days. Below are just a few examples of reports of where people were declared fit for work when they were patently incapable and where they died quickly after being told to begin searching for employment. There was:

- The young Scottish mother of three who died of a brain tumour she had already been diagnosed with a few weeks after Atos told her she should be looking for work.[34]
- Larry Newman who, after years in employment, developed a serious lung condition that saw his weight plummet from 10 to 7 stone who died while appealing an Atos decision declaring him fit for work.[35]
- Cecilia Anim, who, despite needing constant one-to-one care and having to attend classes in order to carry out basic tasks such as making a cup of tea, was told she could work in the near future.[36]
- Linda Wootton who lay dying in hospital after a double lung and heart transplant, when the letter came to inform her that benefits were being removed. She died nine days after being declared fit to work.[37]
- In a heated House of Commons debate, Labour MP, Michael Meacher, brought up the case of a young man with epilepsy who died due to a massive seizure shortly after he was classified fit for work. Mr Meacher told the Commons: "A month after he died, the DWP rang his parents to say that it had made a mistake and his benefit was being restored."[38]

Incredibly, despite the criticisms, regardless of the trail of despair it left and even in light of the government's own negative evaluations, ministers continued to claim the process was improving. Work and Pensions Secretary, Iain Duncan Smith, was castigated from multiple directions and yet showed no signs of his fervour diminishing. Duncan Smith announced in July 2013 that he was 'proud' of his record in slashing benefits. "I don't apologise for attempting to do what previous governments have shied away from, bringing in major changes to make the welfare state fair to both the people who use it and the taxpayers who pay for it", he said. "We have been ambitious and will continue to push ahead with these reforms, but we will do so in a safe and responsible way."[39]

(At the time of writing the Department for Work and Pensions had just announced yet another new initiative whereby people on sickness benefits would be required to have regular meetings with health professionals [again through private companies – not their own GP] to help them 'address their barriers to work' or face further sanctions.[40])

As if only to gnaw further at people's dignity, a series of mini-scandals emerged from the Department for Work and Pensions in relation to back-to-work initiatives. In September 2013 leaked documents showed that Iain Duncan Smith had been looking at ways to give jobcentre staff more powers to make people with disabilities take additional tests to prove they were 'trying as hard as possible' to find work,[41] and even discussed how to force sick and disabled people with time-limited but serious conditions to take up offers of work or be stripped of benefits. The controversy erupted within weeks of another leak that led to the cancellation of a planned 'celebration' by the Department of its 'success' at implementing so many 'fair' sanctions. And as if all of this wasn't disturbing enough, it was revealed that staff and organisations involved in the Work Programme had been planning a 'Conditionality Week' to celebrate 'how far we have come since new tougher sanctions rules were introduced.'[42]

Charities and trades unionists were apoplectic. Mark Serwotka of the PCS union called these sanctions celebrations "grossly offensive" while Paul Farmer, chief executive of the mental health charity, Mind – one of the charities that had early on objected to Workfare – condemned them, saying the government's "repeated response" to people trying to access help was to "crank up the pressure and potential punishments". He added: "This pressure often exacerbates people's mental health problems and pushes them further from work rather than closer to it."

Independent Living Fund

But there was more. Radical changes to benefits for severely disabled people and those with very serious long-term health conditions such as dementia, Multiple Sclerosis and arthritis and cuts to the social care services on which many people had come to rely[43] meant yet even more pain was being meted out. The closure of the Independent Living Fund[44] was one of the most shocking. It was a 'ring-fenced' discretionary fund established to help severely disabled people live independently in the community who might otherwise be left in institutional residential settings.

The Fund's closure to new applicants (there were on average around 20,000 beneficiaries annually) was announced at the beginning of the austerity drive back in June 2010; two-and-a-half years later, in December 2012, after being declared 'financially unsustainable', the government confirmed its intention to close the Fund as of 31 March 2015, after which local authorities in England and the devolved administrations in Scotland, Wales and Northern Ireland were to be responsible for determining what kind of support could be made available from local coffers for Fund users.

In what was turning out to be a typically weak political ruse, central government insisted the closure wasn't technically 'a cut' because responsibility was being transferred to local government.[45] However, campaigners countered that with the transfer meaning funds would no longer be ring-fenced, and as local councils buckled under the weight of their own budget cuts, the chances of adequate cash being found locally would at best be a 'lottery' or – in the worst case scenario – would mean no support at all. The closure of the Fund highlighted just how significant the escalating pressure on social care budgets was becoming for local authorities. Councils were tightening their own care 'eligibility criteria' to fund only people who had 'substantial or critical' care needs.[46]

Even where commitments to provide care were in place, it didn't guarantee sufficient provision – as numerous first-hand accounts had been documenting.[47] All the while a debate was raging about the level at which eligibility should be set,[48] but there was little comfort for those affected. FOI figures collected by False Economy (the campaigning group challenging cuts[49]) in 2012 revealed that around 7,000 elderly and disabled people in the UK had already lost some or all of their state-funded support due to changes in eligibility criteria.[50] Some councils were even taken to court[51] – for attempts to restrict care and for increasing charges.[52] According to the learning disability charity, Mencap, by the end of 2013 the revision of eligibility criteria was having a "devastating" effect on disabled, sick and older people. Speaking in November 2013, a spokeswoman for the charity stressed:

> "When it comes to social care it's been a bit of a lottery
> so far. Local government is having budgets slashed and if
> [a benefit] isn't ring-fenced there are no guarantees. The
> changes to eligibility criteria are extremely significant. Our
> worries are that for many people with mild or moderate

learning difficulties the support will no longer be there. This is about the fundamental things – being able to live with independence and dignity."

According to Mencap, viewing any cut or reform in isolation led to a diminished understanding of the true consequences for those affected by multiple policies. A worrying feature of the cuts to social care and benefits was that eliminating what might, on the face of it, seem like a non-essential care package could precipitate a complex chain reaction. A charity spokeswoman told me:

"One woman we know of [with a moderate learning disability] is a [good] example of what's been happening. She is in her late 20s and was able to visit a day centre two days a week that made a huge difference to her ability to live independently. It helped boost her confidence and she had contact with others. It doesn't seem like much but when the funding criteria was tightened [by her local council] and she couldn't attend any more she ended up getting lonely and depressed. She had to move back in with her parents and her mother had to give up her job to care for her. There are so many effects. And the awful thing is that unless someone is personally affected they don't really understand what these cuts mean. For disabled people it is an enormous problem and we are having to fight harder than ever as more [cuts] are to come."

The upshot for Independent Living Fund recipients of the combined loss of the 'protected' benefit and shrinking social care budgets was an intensifying dread that in future they would be left isolated, alone and neglected without, for example, being able to pay for 'at home' carers – placing even greater pressure on families. Others were worried it would mean no longer being able to live independently at all. Writer and journalist Penny Pepper told the *New Statesman* as part of its 'Secret Cuts' series:[53]

> "The direct fear we have is that they will impose going in an institution on us – which [could also mean] imposing moving out of the borough."

And, as public sector blogger Kate Belgrave wrote in *The Guardian* in early 2013:

> Anyone who says councils will be able to finance these complex care packages in this appalling funding environment, with these monumental care funding gaps, is either dreaming, or lying.[54]

As this book was being completed at the end of 2013 there was one significant and positive development for those condemning the government's closure of the Fund – a legal challenge by five Fund recipients that had originally been lost at the High Court in April 2013 when the court declared the closure lawful was overturned by the Court of Appeal.[55] The claimants had argued that the government failed to properly consult about the changes and was therefore in breach of the 2010 Equality Act, which requires that governments follow a process that ensures the effects of a policy decision on a specific group are lawful. As the BBC's legal correspondent wrote on the day: 'The Court of Appeal unanimously quashed the decision to close the fund and devolve the money to local councils, on the basis that the minister had not specifically considered duties under the Equality Act, such as the need to promote equality of opportunity for disabled people and, in particular, the need to encourage their participation in public life.'

Not only was the previous decision quashed, however, the judges also emphasised that rights under the 2010 Act were not optional just because austerity policies were in place. The law firms Deighton Pierce Glynn and Scott-Moncrieff & Associates, which represented the claimants, welcomed the ruling, calling it "powerful". A statement said the claimants had 'feared that the loss of their ILF support would threaten their right to live with dignity, and that they could be forced into residential care or lose their ability to work and participate in everyday activities on an equal footing with other people.'

Within days of the ruling, the Department for Work and Pensions announced it would not be seeking leave to appeal the Court's decision and that the Fund would continue for now while ministers considered their options.[56] In a statement following the government's decision not to challenge the ruling, the three people who had taken the case to court, Anne Pridmore, Gabriel Pepper and Stuart Bracking, issued a statement. It read:

> Rather than being the 'privileged group' referred to in the High Court judgement, the Appeal Court has acknowledged the potentially very grave impact the closure of the Fund would have on its users, putting seriously in peril the ability of a large number of people to live independent lives in their own homes, and pursue activities such as employment and education.... For a generation, the Independent Living Fund has provided funding to support disabled people with complex conditions who need personal assistance to live in the community....

They warned:

> Until a decision is taken to save the Independent Living Fund and open it to new applicants with adequate funding to meet people's individually assessed needs, the fear many disabled people have expressed about their future will not disappear.[57]

Disability Living Allowance

Even a minor victory such as that with the Independent Living Fund was obscured in a sea of additional austerity-related cuts inflicted on people with disabilities. Tracy Dearing in Hull was one of a number of interviewees who drew attention to one of the most vexing reforms of all: the government's planned move from DLA – a benefit that some three million disabled and sick people claimed to support additional needs associated with disability – to the new Personal Independence Payments (PIPs). There were several aspects of the change that were generating unease and uncertainty and which were putting "terrible stress" on people, Dearing pointed out.

> "It's not clear what the assessment criteria is going to be [for
> PIP]. The initial indication is that it's going to be quite fixed
> and rigorous … and there's a real worry that lots of people
> will fall through the net and they won't be able to get the
> extra help that they need for the extra costs that they have."

Dearing was reflecting the views of campaigners all over the country who argued that the government's aim was to slice a hefty chunk from the total number of people claiming DLA (the benefit was estimated by government to cost £13 billion annually, with payments – subject to the severity of the disability – awarded to approximately 3.3 million people), making people's lives a misery in the process. So what was it exactly that was causing such consternation? DLA – a non-means-tested benefit for adults with disabilities of working age and for children with disabilities to assist with additional needs such as mobility (despite being a millionaire, the Prime Minister had received DLA for his disabled son Ivan before his death) – had for a long time been one of the most misunderstood and hotly debated disability benefits. When politicians talked about people being 'dependent' on welfare, they were often referring to this since it was widely believed among the public to be one of the most abused benefits,[58] even though fraud (running at 0.5 per cent) was negligible.[59]

Stories of people on DLA playing sport or doing physically demanding work were often paraded in the tabloid press as evidence of rampant benefits fraud.[60] Against this backdrop it was probably inevitable that it would be a target for cuts, and indeed in December 2010 one of the Chancellor's first moves in his Spending Review was to announce an intention to shave a fifth – £2 billion – from the DLA budget. The government's own estimates predicted 600,000 people would be removed from DLA by 2018 – or in other words, according to the charity Scope, individuals could lose between £20.55 and £131.50 per week in vital financial support (depending on their circumstances).[61] Opponents of the way the reform was being carried out argued that tighter conditions of entitlement and qualifying assessments (to be carried out by private companies) would inevitably (and paradoxically) prevent many who were keen to work from doing so. In addition, for sick and disabled people who were especially vulnerable, poor, or perhaps not as well educated or informed as others, the stress induced by many of the changes could be truly devastating.

This is how Dearing summed it up:

> "There's real worry because if you lose out on your DLA – it's like a passport to other things; to work, that's one important thing. For myself, I'm a single parent. Although I have got a really good job – and I work really hard ... because the job situation in Hull is so bad I commute a long distance to do that job. And my Access to Work Package is absolutely fundamental for me to do that. I get help with my mobility within work and mobility around getting to the station and back. Plus I get a lot of help with equipment. Now what

I've seen is a re-categorisation of what my impairment actually means.

"When I first [got] Access to Work it was fantastic. That wasn't really hard to get but I've just been reassessed recently when I got my new job and it was just so much harder. The difference from two years ago was huge. I worry that if I lose my DLA – and if the current criteria stays in place I won't qualify for it – it would mean for me that I wouldn't qualify instantly for Access to Work. If I don't get that package that means my employer would have to take that cost on. Maybe with RNIB that would be reasonable. However, with small organisations, how on earth could they?"

(Access to Work is a flexible grant designed to provide support for those with a disability, health or mental health condition to start working, stay in work or start a business. The amount depends on circumstances and the grant is only available in England, Scotland and Wales.[62])

In Northern Ireland the change to PIP was spoken of by a lot of interviewees. One disability campaigner summed the situation up thus:

"The change from DLA to PIP will have a negative impact on 117,000 households. That's what we reckon just from that one change. There is an immediate fear of what impact it will have say on me or my family but in the longer term … government may adopt policies where there are [easy] cuts they can make and services to the disabled community is one of the low hanging fruit. And they might look for families [for more] carers rather than dedicated professionals."

Not only were people worried about no longer qualifying for the DLA replacement at all, many of those who would – particularly those most in need of specialist mobility equipment –

faced stricter tests to qualify. And to make matters worse, once the government had begun its process of reassessing people to reduce the number of DLA claimants and transfer claimants to PIP it was beset by delays and problems with implementation that were leaving many people without essential support.[63] There were concerns about the companies given contracts to assess claims, complaints (as with Work Capability Assessment) that the system was unfairly weighted against people with fluctuating health conditions, and criticism that appeals against decisions were taking too long. By the end of October 2013[64] the government announced that PIP was to be phased in "more gradually", starting with Wales, East Anglia and the Midlands. This was on top of an earlier adjustment to the original timetable, which had proposed rollout from April 2013 with full transfer from DLA completed by April 2016.

This is how Polly Toynbee in *The Guardian* described the situation after the government's announcement:[65]

> Another mishap yesterday rammed into the back of Iain Duncan Smith's pile-up of car crashes, as his roll-out of new disability benefits was delayed, yet again. His Work Programme and his universal credit are in intensive care, now joined by his tougher personal independence payments (PIP) for disability. "The end-to-end claiming process is taking longer than expected," said the Department for Work and Pensions.

She continued:

> Delays for PIP are already shocking. Kate Green, Labour's shadow disability minister, says terminally ill constituents who claimed in May still receive nothing. Disability claims demand filling in a 55-page online form: how many give up? No one knows how or where 3.1 million people can be

tested with adequate disabled access: many need home visits, which take time. Do Atos and Capita staff have the skills to test 3.1 million people? The delay is no surprise.

By October 2013 not only were people exasperated by the chaos of the policy's implementation and the announcement of yet more delays to rollout, their pleas that the rigid assessment criteria be moderated had resolutely fallen on deaf ears. A hard-fought-for consultation with the government, to which well over 1,000 disabled and sick people made submissions and that it was hoped would guarantee a reasonable version of the 'enhanced mobility component' of PIP, ended in profound disappointment. The government had originally set criteria for qualifying for the enhanced element of the benefit at a much lower threshold than activists were arguing for. Ministers had wanted to set it at 20 metres versus 50 metres, meaning that only people judged as unable 'to move around' for 20 metres qualified for the enhanced rate mobility component – for example, provision of a 'motability' vehicle or money to run a private car. The government ended up being challenged by judicial review (which prompted the consultation).[66] Despite the consultation, in October 2013, the government confirmed that the threshold would stay at 20 metres.

Three-and-a-half years into austerity it was undeniable that disabled and sick people were at the epicentre of a maelstrom of cuts that were disproportionately and deliberately targeted and incompetently administered. In the name of austerity, disabled people's human rights were being eroded and their place as equal citizens was threatened. As one campaigner told me:

> "I cannot believe that we're are having to go back to talking about basic human rights again. We had come so far and now because of cuts we are having to resort to the language

of human rights to try to get dignity and independence on the agenda."

SEVEN

A life lived in fear is a life half lived

Austerity pushes people to the edge

"This government will not cut [the] deficit in a way that hurts those we most need to help, that divides the country, or that undermines the spirit and ethos of our public services." (David Cameron, in a speech in June 2010)

"If austerity were tested like a medication in a clinical trial, it would have been stopped long ago, given its deadly side effects.... One need not be an economic ideologue – we certainly aren't – to recognise that the price of austerity can be calculated in human lives." (David Stuckler and physician Sanjay Basu, authors, *The body economic: Why austerity kills*, 2013)

The mental strain unleashed by cuts

Helpline caller number 1: 'David' is getting more anxious and more agitated the more calls he makes to the suicide helpline. He has mental health problems. He tells the volunteer manning the phone that he is finding it difficult to cope. He is terrified. His benefits 'situation' is causing him enormous distress. It is early March 2013 when he first calls after being

———

told that from April he would have to pay the 'Bedroom Tax'. There is no way he can find the money from his incapacity benefits. He doesn't eat for days at a time. The benefits office doesn't seem to take any notice of what he is telling them. He can't sleep. It is the end of March. The call log ends.

Helpline caller number 2: 'Geoff', a father who lives with his partner, their young son and her parents, talks of how the family has lost their home because they fell into debt after benefits changes and delays to payments. They now have mounting, unmanageable debts and no home of their own, he explains. He has made several suicide attempts.

Helpline caller number 3: 'Alison' rings asking if the helpline knows how she can get a food parcel or if they can tell her where to get money to purchase some food. Her benefits have been stopped. She has no money left to buy food. She is afraid of what lies ahead.

I was given access to a summary of logged calls to a suicide helpline during 2013. The callers and their locations were anonymised to protect their identities. Scrolling through the summarised transcripts of plea after plea for help, the desperate circumstances of the people reaching out were laid bare.

By their nature, calls to suicide helplines are always from people in crisis. However, the organisation running this helpline told me that the calls they were receiving during austerity were different to those that had come before. Growing numbers of calls were from people who were under escalating financial strain, with many desperate callers saying they were at breaking point as a result of specific austerity measures such as the 'Bedroom Tax'. A large proportion was distraught at the prospect of losing their homes if they could no longer afford the rent. In fact, the people calling were doing so for many of the same reasons people were turning to food banks – only by the time a person was picking up the phone to a helpline as a last resort, their circumstances had brought them to a dangerous precipice.

If there was one word to capture the mood during the months that I travelled the country, it was 'fear'. I talked to people afraid of cuts that had yet to be fully felt, of losing their home, of disability benefits being snatched away, of being unable to take care of their children or sick or elderly relatives, of essential local services being eliminated – and of their mental health deteriorating. As the months passed, it was as if these fears had taken root deep beneath people's feet. The more the shockwaves of austerity were absorbed, the more initial fears about what might happen mutated into a daily dread about how to survive.

This is how J.J. Tatten of the Goodwin Trust in Hull explained what he was seeing all around him as austerity took hold:

> "When Aneurin Bevan and his people were setting about the task of ensuring that we could all live in safe community their phrase was 'in place of fear'. What we have returning now is fear – fear of the unknown, fear of destitution [and] fear of poverty. We are seeing increasingly anecdotal and hard evidence that this is the case."

Also in Hull, this is what Tracy Dearing had to say:

> "Are people losing hope? I think it's worse than that. I think [many] people's mental health is deteriorating very quickly and it could be because there's a lack of hope....They see the economic climate worsening. They see the benefits safety net untangling. It's more hopelessness impacting on their mental health. I think in Hull mental health services are going to be under huge amounts of strain."

—

Throughout 2012 and 2013 there was little doubt about the degree of the mental strain unleashed by austerity across the UK. In its November 2013 report, *Maxed out*, even the right-wing Centre for Social Justice concluded that, as well as poorer people bearing the brunt of financial strain of increased personal debt, the corollary was an 'immense' impact on their mental health and wellbeing.[1] The lead author of the report said:

> The costs to those affected in stress and mental disorders, relationship breakdown and hardship is immense.

In the summer of 2013, the UK's largest mental health charity, Mind, reported an unprecedented 50 per cent rise in calls to its national helpline for the 12 months up to March 2013[2] (this was on top of a rise of 100 per cent in the previous year for money-related calls[3]). The distinguishing feature of the calls was, first, that more of the callers said they were contemplating suicide compared with pre-recession figures and, second, that 'severe financial worries' were increasingly being cited. The charity said:

- Calls to the helpline rose from 46,000 in 2011/12 to 68,000 in 2012/13.
- The number of calls relating to suicidal feelings jumped by 30 per cent in a year.

Mind's chief executive, Paul Farmer, summarised the trend thus:

> "Today many people face the stark reality of severe financial pressures – be it through employment worries, benefit cuts, increased cost of living, or a lethal combination of all three."

The mental and emotional strain of austerity was everywhere. From as early as 2011, charities including Sane and the Depression Alliance were reporting concerns about links between financial woes and rising stress and depression.[4] According to the Samaritans, the largest suicide prevention organisation in the UK, by early 2013 one in six of its helpline calls was about escalating financial pressures.[5] In June that year the charity warned that economic problems were highly likely to have an impact on the number of suicides, since people living in poverty were already at higher risk of suicidal behaviour even without the additional tension wrought by an economic downturn as severe as that of 2008[6] or the unprecedented cuts of austerity policies after 2010.

Accurate trend figures for suicides can take a number of years to come through as the complexity of collating statistics and inquest rulings makes it difficult to gauge early impact. It is also important to note that the reasons behind suicidal behaviour are complex and rarely down to a single 'trigger'. That said, the Samaritans reported that there were already indications of a 'significant increase' in UK suicides between 2010 and 2011 (running at its highest level since 2004, up from 11.1 to 11.8 per 100,000[7]). Such was the severity of what people in Austerity UK – and especially the poorest – were enduring that this is what the Samaritans concluded:

> Distinctive to the current recession are the simultaneous cuts to public spending and social welfare systems: to social security benefits, benefits for sick and disabled people, and any introduction of universal credit. Thus, in the context of extremely hard financial times and increasing economic stress, especially for those at the bottom of social ladder, there is simultaneously a rolling back, rather than investment in, welfare safety nets; as well as political and public discourse which is at best unsympathetic and at worst potentially vilifying of the poor and socially excluded.

In April 2012, in a move that reflected the role of jobseeking and benefits changes on people's state of mind, senior jobcentre managers took the unorthodox approach of warning staff to be alert to the risk of claimants attempting suicide.[8]

There was also evidence emerging of a rise in the number of anti-depressants being prescribed. Figures for NHS England for 2011 showed a leap of 23 per cent in the number of anti-depressants prescribed since 2010 at a cost of £1 million extra a year to the NHS.[9] (In November 2013 figures released by the OECD showed a surge in anti-depressant usage across richer nations in the previous decade. It concluded that rises of 20 per cent or more in countries such as Spain that had introduced a harsh austerity programme could be down to the ramifications of the financial crisis.[10]) And GPs were reporting more people coming to them for help with money and job insecurity worries – suggesting rising levels of individual desperation – while evidence was also mounting that older people were becoming progressively more isolated as support services were cut and they were turning to GPs for someone to talk to.[11]

In their book, *The body economic: Why austerity kills*,[12] published in 2013 and perhaps the most comprehensive analysis to date of the health risks associated with austerity, economist David Stuckler and physician Sanjay Basu probed the health impacts of austerity globally. The book estimated that around 10,000 additional suicides in Europe and the US were attributable to government cuts introduced in the wake of the Great Recession. The authors mined decades' worth of global data to assess the links between economic shocks and health. Writing in *The New York Times*, they explained why it was crucial to understand that it wasn't merely the economic reverberations of recession that was devastating for health, but how governments reacted. They wrote:

> If suicides were an unavoidable consequence of economic downturns, this would just be another story about the human toll of the Great Recession. But it isn't so. Countries that slashed health and social protection budgets, like Greece,

Italy and Spain, have seen starkly worse health outcomes than nations like Germany, Iceland and Sweden, which maintained their social safety nets and opted for stimulus over austerity. As scholars of public health and political economy, we have watched aghast as politicians endlessly debate debts and deficits with little regard for the human costs of their decisions.

They concluded:

If austerity were tested like a medication in a clinical trial, it would have been stopped long ago, given its deadly side effects.... One need not be an economic ideologue – we certainly aren't – to recognize that the price of austerity can be calculated in human lives.

Throughout the time I was interviewing people, news reports of mental distress, suicides or attempted suicides connected to austerity and cuts came thick and fast. Even taking into account the necessary caution about exaggerating causal links, it seemed that something extreme was happening as individuals affected and their families called on the government to acknowledge the pressures pushing people to a mental edge. In one horrific case, a man 'doused' himself with a flammable liquid and tied himself to railings at a jobcentre in Birmingham after being declared 'fit for work' and experiencing benefits delays.[13] Luckily, the police arrived soon enough after he set himself alight to prevent really serious injury.

The *London Evening Standard* reported on the inquest of a woman who died two days after attempting to take her own life. The inquest heard from her doctor that a letter saying her incapacity benefits were to be withdrawn had precipitated her suicide attempt. The attempt failed, but she died two days later (the court ruled it was from natural causes). An unopened letter was found at the woman's house after her death indicating that she might not lose her benefits after all.[14] In other incidents, the *Liverpool Echo* reported on the story of a 31-year-old mother who attempted suicide following Housing Benefit cuts and 'Bedroom Tax' charges;[15] and the *Mirror* reported on an inquest into the death of an older man, a pensioner in his 70s, who was believed to have taken his own life due to fears about the 'Bedroom Tax'. Even though he was exempt because of his age, witnesses testified at the inquest that he had been frightened by the news reports of people possibly losing their homes.[16] Another story in the *Mirror* told of a 53-year-old disabled former nurse who took her own life days before a second appeal against her benefits being stopped.[17] These are mere snapshots.

In the background to all of this was growing concern around the state of mental health service provision. For decades seen as the 'Cinderella Service' within the NHS and deprived of vital funding year after year,[18] mental healthcare (as with the rest of the NHS) had seen funding rise under the Labour administration after 1997.[19] With mental health accounting for half of all illness for the under-65s, it was certainly not a marginal concern, yet 13 per cent of NHS budgets typically went towards mental healthcare when it accounted for 23 per cent of the overall health burden.[20] Even after the Coalition government came to power there were some encouraging overtures, including discussions around 'parity' of care and ensuring mental health was given equal status with physical health (especially from Liberal Democrat Health Minister Norman Lamb[21]). Nevertheless, warning flares were being fired pretty soon after austerity came into force about how rising demand and 'spending efficiencies' within the health service were manifesting.[22] Meanwhile, evidence accrued of cuts to one of the flagship therapy programmes introduced under New Labour, IAPT (Improving Access to Psychological Therapies), which had been improving access to psychological therapies.[23]

One major issue of concern was around acute care – when people require a hospital stay if in crisis or when sectioned. Drawing on information garnered from a FOI request, an investigation by *Community Care* magazine and the BBC in late 2013 found that, by October 2013, NHS England actually had nearly 2,000 fewer acute mental health beds than in April 2011, and that most wards were running at 100 per cent occupancy.[24] According to the investigation, patients in great distress were often being transported hundreds of miles in search of a bed. Problems with acute care combined with increased workloads for GPs and long waiting lists for other provision, such as psychological therapies, meant that the situation was reaching crisis point.

Dr Martin Baggaley, medical director of the South London and Maudsley NHS Trust, who spoke to the BBC at the time, said pressure on mental health services was going up. He said:

> "There seems to be a genuine increase in demand. That's partly explained by a reduction in beds, by resources coming out of the health system, the squeeze on social services budgets, and by the general economic situation."

Marjorie Wallace, chief executive of the charity SANE, told the broadcaster: "It is all too easy to find the cuts demanded by NHS efficiency savings in mental health. If a patient has heart failure or is in a coma, a bed has to be found. But for a person in mental distress, this is not seen to be as necessary. Being turned away when seeking help only reinforces patients' feelings of rejection and hopelessness and can in our experience drive them to suicide."

People's distress during austerity was predicated on multiple and often overlapping forces, with financial worries typically at the epicentre. Not everyone affected was reaching out to mental health services, of course, but that there were daily anxieties sapping people's ability to cope was undeniable. It became clearer the more I moved around the country that some of the reasons people were crying out for support was directly related to a number of key austerity measures that were stoking a particular variety of fear – one rooted in a profound insecurity about what the future might bring. As many people repeatedly reminded me, as bad as things had been since 2010, with another wave of austerity cuts in the offing for 2014 and beyond, there was a widespread impression that 'the worst was yet to come'. Indeed, similar unease about the future was identified by numerous studies over the first three years of austerity.[25]

Local government and communities

One of the fears gaining momentum as I travelled was to do with cuts to services at a regional, local and community level. From the outset of austerity there was an explicit intention on the part of the government to slash local authority budgets.[26] Indeed, as the cuts unfolded, barely a month passed without a bucket load of estimates or analysis about how much was being chopped from local authority budgets and what the fallout was likely to be.[27] Central and local government were often at loggerheads about the scale and distribution of cuts, with councils in some poorer regions arguing they had been disproportionately affected.[28] Other groups, ranging from trades unions[29] to women's organisations[30] to homeless shelters[31] were battling to highlight the human cost as services were cut back or vanished as funding dried up – especially in areas where demand was highest due to high levels of deprivation even before austerity.

As with other cuts, the Coalition's core retort to criticism around local government budget slashing was that it was unavoidable, rounded off with a brazen reassurance that, where possible, ministers had ensured emergency funds were available to those who needed additional support[32] (even though there was ample evidence to the contrary[33]). (It should be noted that the devolved administrations in the UK meant in the first three years of austerity that the impact was uneven when it came to cuts to local services in the different nations. The Welsh Assembly, for example, had a policy of protecting their local authorities from the impact of central government cuts for as long as possible.[34] Both the Welsh and Scottish devolved governments also tried to soften the blow of funding cuts by, for example, funding the Council Tax Benefit themselves for the first year after it was cut in April 2013.)

So, just how big and how significant were these cuts? And who were they having most impact on? Right from the first Comprehensive Spending in October 2010 and announcements in the Local Government Settlement in December the same year, it was apparent that the extent of 'savings' local authorities were going to be expected to make was, as the Local Government Association (LGA) referred to it, "the worst in living memory".[35]

Calling the review a 'massacre', Unite Joint General Secretary, Derek Simpson, said: "It's totally perverse to claim that cutting half a million jobs and razing our public services to the ground is good for this country. No matter how often it repeats that its actions are fair, this government is making a political choice to attack the public sector and, by doing this now damaging the whole of the economy long into the future."

The realisation spawned fears that some councils would not be able to meet their long-term funding requirements (even if they had substantial reserves to begin with) without drastically decreasing frontline services, many of which would affect their most vulnerable citizens.[36] Worries were raised as austerity was being introduced as to exactly where the axe would fall, with many campaigners highlighting that adult social care (something already seeing increased demand due to, among other things, structural demographic shifts such as an ageing population) would inevitably suffer.[37] Professional bodies and trades unions were also warning of drastic impacts on services. In its 2012 survey of social workers, the British Association of Social Workers (BASW) found that over two thirds (77 per cent) of the profession believed their caseloads were 'unbearable' while the same percentage reported that cuts were meaning vacant positions were being left unfilled. Nine out of ten said lives were being put at risk as a result of cuts.[38]

In September 2013, *The Telegraph* newspaper reported on an escalating concern for many people – that care for the elderly was being 'rationed' so that increasingly only those with more severe needs were being catered for.[39] One graphic illustration of how cuts were having an impact on older people three years in to the austerity drive came from The College of Social Work and the charity Age UK.[40] In June 2013, a survey of social workers found that 90 per cent who responded feared life would become even harder for older people who used social care services as more cuts hit the front line, while seven out of ten said the cuts were increasing isolation. Flagging up how there was a ripple effect of cuts emanating from adult social care, 80 per cent of social workers said there was growing evidence of families feeling the strain of additional caring responsibilities.

We saw earlier in Chapter Six how shifting eligibility criteria for care was having a significant impact, but by early 2013 a group of leading charities, Scope, Mencap, the National Autistic Society, Sense and Leonard Cheshire Disability, were pointing to a much wider crisis. In a landmark report, *The other care crisis*, they stressed that there was an urgent need for government to reassess how disabled people's needs would be met over the longer term.[41] The report concluded that 40 per cent of people with disabilities were not having their basic social care needs met – such as help with washing, dressing or leaving the house – and that the £1.2 billion funding gap in social care support for people with disabilities under the age of 65 was a glaring indication of a system 'on the brink of collapse'. The situation was so dire, the charities said, that hundreds of thousands of people with disabilities and their carers were left worried sick about how they would manage.

Clare Pelham, chief executive of Leonard Cheshire Disability, said of the situation:

> "This new research reveals for the first time how many people are living in the care 'gap' and it is a disgrace. No government and no right-thinking person should allow this to continue in their street, their town, their country."

In November 2013, spending watchdog the Audit Commission (itself due to shut down in 2015 as part of the government's 'quango cull'[42]) published the third in a series of annual Tough Times reviews of how English councils had been responding to the new financial constraints they were under. It offered a robust overview of what had occurred to date.[42] The report, which surveyed local authority auditors in England, found that from 2010/11 to 2013/14 central government funding to local government had been reduced by £6 billion in real terms – a whopping 19.6 per cent cut. While containing some positive news – mainly that most councils had shown what the auditor called a 'high degree of financial resilience' and were managing to meet strict budget requirements despite the dual strains of funding cuts and declining income from local sources such as council tax – it also stressed where the main pressure points were:

- Three in 10 councils (29 per cent) experienced some kind of 'financial distress' in 2012/13.
- Those councils most dependent on government income to fund spending had seen a proportionally greater reduction in funding.

- From 2010/11 to 2013/14 Council Tax revenues fell by a third of a billion pounds (1.7 per cent in real terms), putting additional pressure on cash-strapped authorities.
- Staff cuts had been the single biggest source of savings for councils with social services responsibilities.
- Adult social services took the greater hit as other avenues for cuts were increasingly exhausted, potentially storing up additional service delivery problems (as the disability charities and others had been pointing out). In 2010/11 adult social services accounted for 14 per cent of total spending reductions but for 2013/14 this had shot up to 52 per cent. This shift increased concerns that in future councils would have much less leeway to shield social care from future cuts.
- Further reductions in central government funding planned for 2014/15 and 2015/16 and ongoing uncertainties around other revenue, such as business rates (while the economy rebounded slowly from an extended period of low growth) would make it difficult to calculate future financial burdens.

Also in November 2013 JRF published a paper, *Coping with the cuts? Local government and poorer communities*,[44] assessing the 'scale and pattern' of spending cuts in local government in England and Scotland since 2010 – in particular, on disadvantaged people and places. It shed further light on the effects for the most vulnerable. While Scottish government policy offered a degree of protection north of the border (at least initially), the paper concluded that: 'local government is one of the foremost casualties of austerity in the UK' and was set to remain so. It was a sobering indication of what was occurring on the front line, reflecting what many had feared was happening to varying degrees all over the UK as more cuts were implemented: that as councils exhausted their ability to make 'back office efficiency savings', such as staffing, many core services were being scaled back or cut altogether and that, in future, those that didn't come with a legal obligation were in danger of disappearing. Provision such as youth services,[45] children's centres, arts and culture activities,[46] street cleaning[47] and community wardens[48] – which had already seen cuts since 2010 – were facing further threat in 2015 and beyond.

Summing up what had transpired since 2010 and assessing the situation going forward it reported:

- By 2015 local government spending in England (excluding the police, schools, Housing Benefit) was set to fall by nearly 30 per cent in real terms from 2008.
- Cuts in spending in both Scotland and England were 'systematically greater in more deprived local authorities than in more affluent ones', with the North of England and the Midlands in England generally seeing more cuts.
- Rising costs and increased demand for services were exacerbating the pressure on local authority budgets caused by cuts. Cultural services such as libraries, sports, transport and housing services, saw larger cuts.
- Cuts affected different services 'differentially', meaning that while some had a level of protection, others did not.
- Local authorities had taken 'significant steps' to protect the most vulnerable groups, but cuts were still affecting those most in need and those on lower incomes.

It concluded:

> Poorer groups have enjoyed a degree of protection from the worst effects of budget contraction thus far. But poor people and places still stand to lose the most from austerity now and as it rolls out in the coming years. It needs to be constantly borne in mind that public services play a much more important role in the lives of people on low incomes compared to those living in more affluent circumstances.

In the summer of 2013 the LGA issued its own stark appraisal of what was happening and what lay ahead.[49] The fear that the full force of budget pressures had yet to be fully appreciated was plain to see. Updating its annual Funding Outlook in July after cuts for 2015/16 were announced by the government a month earlier, the body warned of a 'black hole' for local government finances that would reach £14.4 billion by 2020, harming some of the UK's most vulnerable citizens. It concluded:

> …The money available to deliver all other local services, including leisure and cultural facilities, school support services, fixing the roads, building new homes and promoting economic growth will shrink by 46% by 2020, down from £26.6 billion in 2010/11 to £14.3 billion by the end of the decade.

The organisation also warned of a huge knock-on effect on other public services already reeling from a welter of budget reductions that would mean 'increased costs for our hospitals, prisons, police service and welfare system', as people increasingly could not access the support they needed – from drugs and alcohol services to mother and baby groups.

LGA chair, Sir Merrick Cockell, said at the time:

> "We are in danger of losing entirely some services, with significant reductions right across the board. This is a false economy which threatens to shunt additional costs onto the reactive parts of the public sector, particularly our hospitals, prisons and welfare system."

So what were people saying on the ground? There appeared to be two prisms through which people understood local authority cuts: there were the anxieties surrounding cuts they were witnessing or experiencing directly (including job losses in many cases), and then there were the fears surrounding those cuts that had yet to come or be fully felt. People with disabilities were almost immediately cognisant of the impact of cuts because their quality of life was affected. Less well-off older people, generally heavy users of community facilities such as libraries[50] or public toilets,[51] were also conscious of where provision was being shaved. Many women – usually those at the lower end of the income scale – were also aware of cuts as they unfolded because they tended to rely more on state-run services.[52] If a playground was no longer there, or if recreation activities for children with disabilities or funding for a playgroup was suddenly withdrawn, then mothers felt the effects right away.

One of the most prominent cuts to local frontline services affecting mothers and carers in particular was the decimation of Sure Start – among the most valued community-based service in the UK since its introduction by the previous Labour government in 1998.[53] An early intervention programme aimed at enhancing the wellbeing of younger children and their families with a focus on education, childcare, health and family support, Sure Start was immensely popular and yet, despite government pledges that it was committed to keeping the programme up and running, by the end of 2013 it had been drastically scaled back. It seemed like a very long time indeed from the day before the 2010 general election when the soon-to-be Prime Minister, David Cameron, when asked by a voter what would become of Sure Start, replied:

> "Yes, we back Sure Start. It's a disgrace that Gordon Brown has been trying to frighten people about this. He's the Prime Minister of this country but he's been scaring people about something that really matters."

The Labour Party estimated that by the end of 2013 there were almost 600 fewer Sure Start centres (out of just over 3,000) than when the Coalition came to power.[54] While, at the end of 2013, the government was claiming that just 45 centres had closed (which, as George Eaton pointed out in the *New Statesman*,[55] would still be a lot of centres), their own figures suggested the number was much higher[56] – and even the Prime Minister's own constituents were protesting about closures.[57]

In the autumn of 2013, Labour Leader, Ed Miliband, attacked the government's record on childcare policy, saying that a promise had been patently and unashamedly broken:

> "Millions of parents are facing a childcare crunch. The cost of a nursery place is now the highest in history, at more than £100 a week to cover part-time hour…. Rising prices have been matched only by falling numbers of places. And hundreds of Sure Start centres have been lost, contributing to a total of 35,000 fewer childcare places under David Cameron."

It was particularly galling that many campaigners and columnists[58] had predicted the loss of Sure Start centres as soon as the government's changes to local government financing were announced. In 2010, as part of its 'localism' agenda, central government removed the 'ring-fencing' from 80 grants to local government, including the one for Sure Start. (The budget for the centres was rolled into a new Early Intervention Grant.) While instructing local authorities to 'prioritise' Sure Start,[59] under the auspices of giving local authorities greater 'flexibility' it, in effect, removed an obligation to allocate funds to pay for the programme. Needless to say, cash-strapped councils foraging for savings wherever they could began targeting it for cuts.[60]

Vigorous local and national campaigns to save local schemes gathered momentum during 2012 and 2013.[61] The Family and Daycare Trust launched its own campaign, highlighting how families that had come to rely on the centres were left without valuable support that (ironically) they now needed even more as other austerity-related cuts hit home. The charity warned that in some areas there was no alternative nursery provision available, leaving parents without childcare options.[62]

The loss of services was having a significant human cost. Many of the people I spoke to felt the cuts on a deeply personal level because of the degree to which their quality of life was affected. The fact that they tended to be introduced incrementally may have decreased their visibility on the national radar, but this didn't stop them from filling people with fear for their own wellbeing and that of their neighbourhoods.[63] I certainly found this to be the case in Hull. In the spring of 2013, the older ladies (and one older gentleman) gathered at the Tuesday Club on the Thornton estate in Hull had just finished their exercises with a volunteer fitness instructor and were about to begin their weekly bingo session. Before that, however, they were eager to talk about how life in the area was changing as local government cuts began to take hold.

This group of people in their 70s and 80s met weekly at a premises in a parade of shops provided by the Goodwin Development Trust.[64]. They were concerned about losing a number of local services, but chief among them was the possible loss of local 'community wardens', a community outreach service funded by the local council and managed by Goodwin. By checking in on these older people and escorting them to gatherings like the Tuesday Club, the wardens operated as a kind of guarantee against isolation and helped them to feel part of the wider community. "At the moment we've got the wardens but how long for? That's the main worry", a woman in her late 70s volunteered. Another interjected: "Previously for anyone who was elderly or disabled there were one or two wardens that were assigned to ring us and see if we were okay. That was a friendly word but it's all being cut back."

According to Stuart Spandler, the chair of the board of trustees at Goodwin and a resident of the Thornton estate his whole life, the Tuesday Club's anxieties were symptomatic of broader problems due to cuts to local authority budgets. "We've been fighting like mad to keep the community wardens," Spandler told me. "We've got an extension of the wardens [for now] but the future is uncertain. One of the biggest problems on the estate is going to be isolation."

It was the same all over. In place after place local residents talked about vital local services disappearing. Some of these, such as day centres or social activities, may have been deemed 'non-essential', but for the most vulnerable people these were often regarded as lifelines. Other provision such as libraries, sports centres, youth clubs and parks were basic amenities widely regarded as part and parcel of what local government was there to do.[65] In Bristol parents and grandparents at a local after-school club were concerned about the loss of youth services and outdoor areas for their children. Putting it bluntly, one mother said: "What's actually going to be left when these children grow up? There's going to be absolutely nothing and then they are going to wonder why [youngsters] get into trouble."

In Rhondda, Bethan Dally, a young community volunteer and carer who has Down's syndrome, explained that she was becoming increasingly anxious the more she heard about cuts that were on the way. As a carer for her elderly, disabled parents, Dally was especially worried that help looking after them would be harder to find and about isolation if public transport was cut. "I have to watch my father doesn't fall. I'd love to have a bit more [help]. I [have to] think about my health and other people's as well. I worry about what will happen."

In Luton, mother-of-four Jackie Jenkins summed up the fears of many people at a local level, especially women:

"The cuts are going to rip the ass out of communities that are already poverty-stricken. It's not just personal benefits cuts. It's the cuts in and around the community. Mums and tots groups will have to stop [because there's funding cuts] so that [single] day a week that a mum might get [access to something] which helps her with her children is gone. And that might sound like nothing to someone who doesn't understand what it's like cooped up on a 14th floor with three children where your only release is maybe two days a week at a nursery. That has a massive impact. Cutting things in and around the society is all going to have a knock-on effect."

She continued:

"I've seen the amount of money [the council] are going to have to lose. There's not even enough money to cover the essentials. So the non-essentials, which you could say are the mums and tots groups, or sports centres – those sorts of things that aren't necessities – if they're going as well it scares the life out of me."

Women and the cuts

Women, especially those already on the breadline, reported a whole range of serious and multiplying fears. As the managers of household finances in most families and main caregivers, they had a lot to contend with. The rising cost of childcare, public sector pay freezes and massive jobs cuts, benefits and tax credit changes and obstinate levels of low pay all conspired to make women's lives tougher. This is how a report from Oxfam at the end of 2013 summed up the overall impact of austerity cuts on women – and their children.[66]

Of the £8.1bn in net personal tax increases and benefits cuts an estimated £5.8bn (72%) will impact on women. Since the 2008 financial crisis female unemployment has risen from 678,000 to 1.08 million in 2013. This is expected to rise further to 1.5 million by 2018 as the remainder of public sector cuts take effect.

It continued:

Women typically use public services more than men for a variety of reasons and will therefore be more significantly impacted by their closure, both in their own right and as principal carers. The combination of these impacts from austerity measures will have long-term consequences for both gender equality, and most likely, child poverty, in the UK.

After the Coalition came to power a slew of reports emerged demonstrating the ongoing impact of government policies on women and drew attention to the long-term consequences.[67] These included one from the House of Commons Library[68] that concluded women were enduring the lion's share of cuts (more than three quarters). The Women's Budget Group, an alliance of academics, non-governmental organisation (NGO) professionals and trade unionists, tracked the gender implications of austerity from the start, and in a series of reports documented the cumulative effects as the cuts kept coming. In its response to the government's announcement of its next round of cuts in June 2013, the organisation pleaded for tax increases instead of further public spending cuts which, it argued, could only do more harm to women.[69] It concluded:

"The WBG calls on the coalition government to stop and reverse these cuts, which put the poorest and most vulnerable women, and their children, at risk of deep poverty, physical harm or worse."

In 2011 the leading women's equality campaigners, the Fawcett Society, argued in a report published in conjunction with 20 other charities, *A life raft for women's equality*, that such was the severity of austerity measures from the get-go that women's human rights as well as their financial security was under threat.[70] A few months later, in 2012, it published a detailed evaluation on 'The impact of austerity on women',[71] which revealed the alarming degree to which women were affected and concluded that the cuts were so unprecedented they would 'turn back the clock' on gender equality. Collating a battery of academic and other evidence, the charity criticised the government for failing to generate policies that would benefit women, and declared that they faced 'a triple jeopardy' under austerity. It said:

- Women are being hit hardest by cuts to public sector jobs, wages and pensions.
- Women are being hit hardest as the services and benefits they use more are cut.
- Women will be left 'filling the gaps' as state services are withdrawn.

Significantly, the report echoed many other studies that were warning of the fallout from the loss of basic services such as playgroups and holiday childcare assistance and of the widespread pressures on local children's charities related to cuts.[72] Services that vulnerable and poorer women, in particular, saw as vital – ranging from rape crisis centres and refuges, to groups advising women from black and minority ethnic backgrounds and those catering for recent immigrants or trafficked women – were disappearing. This is how it described the situation:

A wide range of voluntary sector organisations provide for the specific needs of women. Such services often fill gaps in statutory provision, particularly in meeting the needs of marginalised women; for example, violence against women services, specialised support services for low-income and BME women and those that provide outreach to isolated and deprived women.

Many voluntary sector organisations currently face grave uncertainties about the future of their funding due to a toxic combination of central and local government funding cuts, the removal of ring-fencing, reductions in independent grant giving combined with increased competitiveness for these funds, and a reduction in the levels of personal donations. Women's organisations face greater barriers to obtaining funds/sustaining themselves than voluntary sector organisations as a whole.

In the face of ongoing criticism, the government produced a 'gender analysis' of tax and welfare measures in the 2013 budget,[73] but women's groups rejected it for being "partial", "insufficient" and "inconsistent". Campaigners, including Fawcett, argued for a 'comprehensive, global gender impact analysis'[74] that would accurately record how women were affected and therefore provide a useful tool for policy-makers. The Fawcett report had highlighted the plight of women struggling to cope with ongoing financial difficulties. It garnered national attention because of its powerful and sweeping critique of austerity and its focus on the most vulnerable women. A host of campaign groups, including women's organisations such as Refuge and Women's Aid, as well as grassroots groups like Southall Black Sisters and The North East Women's Network, had been stressing all along that the impact of austerity on 'vulnerable groups within vulnerable groups' was too often being ignored and that it led to some terrifying consequences – especially when it came to violence and abuse.[75]

Figures released in 2012 showed a 17 per cent increase in reported incidents of domestic abuse in England and Wales in just two years – up by more than 2,000 a week – prompting campaigners to warn that financial problems could be exacerbating abuse, while funding cuts to services such as refuges could lead to more women remaining in abusive relationships because they had nowhere else to go.[76] In November 2012, Women's Aid reported that in a single year almost 30,000 women had been turned away by the first refuge they approached.[77] Research by the University of Lancaster published the same year[78] provided a stark illustration of the fallout from cutting services dealing directly with violence against women (VAW). It found:

- 31 per cent of the funding to VAW services from local authorities was cut between 2010/11 and 2011/12.
- 230 women, almost 9 per cent of those seeking refuge, were turned away by Women's Aid on a typical day in 2011 due to lack of space. This led to support workers being forced to suggest places for women to sleep outside, such as the 'Occupy' camps, A&E departments or night buses.
- Smaller organisations were being hit harder: the average cut for organisations with local authority funding of less than £20,000 was 70 per cent, compared with 29 per cent for those receiving over £100,000.

Meanwhile a report from the Women's Resource Centre in March 2013 probing the situation in London found that demand for services was soaring just as availability was shrinking. It painted a picture of acutely overstretched services with long waiting lists, and stress among staff and volunteers rising as more women in distress approached them for help.[79]

Legal aid

If all of this wasn't frightening enough, it represented but a fraction of the difficulties being generated by austerity for at-risk women. Not only were there fewer women's services to seek help from, there was yet another tier of budget slashing that was, in the most extreme cases, leading women to fear for their lives. Cuts to legal aid introduced in May 2013 had to be one of the most under-reported of the government's austerity measures, yet its consequences were potentially among the most adverse. Around the country, women, women's groups and lawyers I spoke to were enraged by reforms that were reducing access to justice for the most vulnerable.[80] In the run-up to a government review of both criminal and civil legal aid for England and Wales there was outcry from many in the legal profession and threats of strikes by barristers.[81]

Women's groups were outraged by cuts that would make it harder for those in danger to find legal representation.[82] A coalition of over 100 legal and voluntary groups, the Justice Alliance,[83] joined forces in June 2013 to present a collective challenge to the changes. Members, including human rights organisations, unions, mental health and disability charities, children's charities, immigration and asylum groups, and numerous women's organisations, protested at the many ways in which a whole range of vulnerable people – including the very poorest and marginalised – would be denied access to justice in civil and criminal proceedings.

At the time of writing, the Ministry of Justice was undertaking a review of criminal legal aid, *Transforming legal aid*, with the goal of slashing £220 million from the annual £1 billion criminal legal aid budget by 2018. This was the focus of many of the most public protests (and there were no signs of any kind of government U-turn by the end of 2013). However, for women, the cause of widespread alarm was the Legal Aid, Sentencing and

Punishment of Offenders Act (LASPO),[84] which came into force in England and Wales in April 2013 with the aim of culling a quarter (£320 million) of the civil legal aid budget by 2014/15. LASPO meant that, for the first time in its 60-year history, civil legal aid was removed (with some specific exceptions) from the majority of cases involving divorce, welfare benefits, clinical negligence and child contact. The Bill itself had a tortuous passage through Parliament (mainly due to vocal critics in the House of Lords[85] claiming it would remove access to justice for whole swaths of vulnerable people, including domestic abuse victims, and that it would put women at risk).

Multiple amendments were tabled in the House of Lords only to be overturned later in the Commons, although there were concessions around domestic violence along the way.[86] (For example, the Ministry of Justice – after vociferous representations from women's groups and others – finally agreed to broaden its original definition of domestic violence beyond solely physical to take in other forms such as psychological and emotional abuse.) That an argument even had to be made that abuse could be more than physical was astonishing. Among the obstacles that reduced access to justice for victims of domestic violence (male or female) was a 'residency test', meaning that before qualifying for legal aid assistance, an applicant had to present evidence of how long they had lived in the UK – something not all women would have to hand, especially if fleeing a violent partner. A new requirement that victims produce specific 'evidence' that they had been domestically abused – such as a criminal conviction of the abusive partner – before qualifying for legal aid was another reform that campaigners believed was putting women at risk. And a new limit of 24 months for victims to come forward with evidence was also introduced. Given that many victims take years to come forward about abuse, women's advocates argued that this was a particularly unnecessary and cruel stipulation.

As a result, campaigners and many legal aid lawyers reported that victims (almost always female) were increasingly not getting the help they needed and that many weren't coming forward for help at all because they didn't have the necessary 'proof' (or it fell outside the new time limit). The result? Victims were being put in greater danger of prolonged or future abuse. Cris McCurley, a legal aid lawyer and partner at the firm Ben Hoare Bell, explained the situation this way to me:

> "Before April 1st 2013 victims of domestic violence were never expected to have to represent themselves. Now a victim has to either prove they are a victim, with very exacting and hard to acquire evidence (all of which have complex requirements to meet), pay privately, or represent themselves. For many, this is out of the question."

In some instances, McCurley and other advocates pointed out, women were being charged by GPs for letters of evidence – money that poorer victims in need of access to legal aid were highly unlikely to possess. One manager at a women's refuge in Bishop Auckland told me how the combination of cuts to services and reduction in access to justice was putting domestic violence victims' physical and mental health in peril.

> "It's bad enough that things have got so bad that women are having to turn to food banks but with fewer refuges to turn to when they are in danger? That's extremely serious. And now that they can't get legal aid the way they used to – I really worry that it's going to lead to greater violence [against women and children]."

'Jennifer Smith' had to turn to a refuge in Bishop Auckland with her teenage daughter to escape a violent partner. This is what she had to say about the strain on places of safety and the changes to legal aid.

> "I'd worked every day of my life and suddenly I had nothing. No home. I was terrified. If it wasn't for the refuge I don't know where me and my daughter would be right now. How could a government take something as fundamental as this away and put women at risk? How could they cut legal aid? It's scandalous."

Housing and homelessness

Other than threats to life or limb it would be hard to imagine something more frightening for people than the possibility of losing the roof over their heads – yet under austerity the Coalition government in the UK managed to conjure up policies that did just that, catapulting such fears to a whole new level. Throughout 2012 and 2013, as the pace of austerity measures accelerated, the brutal fusion of soaring rents along with multiple policies including the 'Bedroom Tax', changes to Housing Benefit and Council Tax Benefit – and the debt they fostered – was having a huge impact on housing security. To a degree, homeowners were protected by historically low interest rates between 2010 and 2013, which enabled many to hang on to their properties who otherwise might not have, but the financial pressures on millions of households during austerity was such that increasingly people were struggling to pay rent, falling into arrears or even facing eviction.

Thousands, including young families, were forced to live in sub-standard accommodation as rents surged and the supply of public housing remained static, with some parts of the country – especially London – increasingly unaffordable for people on low incomes or benefits.[87] In one of the most notable reactions following the decision by some London councils to consider moving Housing Benefit recipients out of the capital altogether, the Conservative Mayor of London, Boris Johnson, who was running for re-election, ignited controversy when he accused councils of instigating a 'Kosovo-style social cleansing' of the capital's poor. (Johnson, not averse to controversy, sparked a storm of criticism in late 2013 when giving a speech at the annual Margaret Thatcher lecture he invoked fictional banker Gordon Gekko, announcing 'greed is good' and claiming that people who were successful were so because they had higher IQs.[88]) He later backtracked on the reference to Kosovo but the point about housing affordability nevertheless resonated.[89]

Housing was a hot button issue in the UK for years prior to austerity and for a range of Gordian-like reasons including a shortage of properties in the social and private sectors, property price bubbles and soaring rents. (In the autumn of 2013 JRF reported that Britain would have one million properties less than it needed unless a radical housebuilding programme was instituted.[90]) It also emerged at the end of 2013 that private landlords were issuing eviction notices to Housing Benefit recipients in growing numbers, citing benefit caps as a key reason.[91] Writing in *The Guardian*, Patrick Collinson called spiralling private rents 'Britain's social scandal that is being ignored'.

He wrote:

> Rage [from tenants] is being met with almost total silence from the political and economic establishment. How many MPs have rented their family home all their lives from a private landlord? I'd wager almost none.

According to the National Housing Federation, by the end of 2013 the housing crisis in England was so terrible that the country was left with 'two broken housing markets' – house prices were spiralling upwards and at risk of overheating in some areas, while others were still reeling from the recession.[92] It also pointed out that rents were surging in 'growth areas' (and projected to grow by a staggering 37 per cent by 2020), which was not only squeezing household incomes further but also increasing the very Housing Benefit Bill the government was attempting to slash, with an extra 310 people every day applying for Housing Benefit in 2013.

David Orr, chief executive of the Federation, concluded: "Billions of pounds of taxpayers' money is wasted, lining the pockets of private landlords, when it could be better spent building more homes people can afford."

Meanwhile, the housing charity, Shelter, was reporting record calls to its helpline[93] – up by 40 per cent in a year in England – with callers needing help with issues including arrears. Campbell Robb, chief executive of the charity, warned:

> "This research highlights the frightening lack of options available to people who are fighting to keep a roof over their head. Sadly, with little remaining of the housing safety net meant to support them in tough times, many can quickly find themselves at risk of losing their home."

It was clear three-and-a-half years into austerity that not only had homelessness risen, but corresponding budget cuts – mainly by local government – were leaving those who found themselves destitute with fewer places to turn to for help. According to the umbrella body for homelessness charities, Homeless Link, the number of homeless households leapt by 33 per cent between 2010 and 2013, while services were disappearing. It reported that 133 homelessness services had closed by autumn 2013 while there were over 4,000 fewer beds available in shelters. There was also a decline in staff numbers.[94] The charity also cautioned that the risks of young people becoming homeless had increased as a result of welfare changes such as capping their housing allowance.[95]

In November 2013, Shelter warned that 80,000 children across the UK could face living in 'shocking conditions' as the number of families in emergency accommodation – often no more than a single room – reached a 10-year-high.[96] A month later an analysis of homelessness published by Crisis and JRF reported that homelessness had risen for three years running, and called the housing situation a 'pressure cooker'. It found year-on-year increases in 'rough sleeping', 'hidden homeless' such as overcrowding as well as those in temporary accommodation.[97]

The government defended its record, insisting it was giving £1 billion a year to councils to tackle homelessness, but according to the LGA, the problem was worsened in part by a dire shortage of affordable housing in which to place families. To make matters worse, there were numerous social security-related changes that were having a grossly negative impact on people who were already homeless.[98] For example, homeless people were disproportionately affected by benefit sanctions, leaving them in financial chaos. According to one study, a third of homeless people (many with learning disabilities, a mental health diagnosis or substance abuse problems) who were unemployed had been sanctioned compared to approximately 3 per cent of ESA and Jobseeker's Allowance claimants. For younger people the figure was even worse, with the research finding that 60 per cent of under-25s who were homeless and claiming Jobseeker's Allowance had been sanctioned.[99]

The fear of losing a home or never finding one that was affordable and habitable was by the end of 2013 becoming an embarrassing indictment of the government and of its austerity agenda. All too often it was people made vulnerable by policies unrelated to housing, such as women losing legal aid or young people without a job, who were in the firing line. The human cost of losing a home, of children being uprooted or forced to live in bed and breakfasts or cold, damp properties, is almost inconceivable to someone who hasn't faced that threat. As Ally Fogg so eloquently put it in *The Guardian*:

> Homelessness is many problems woven together into a human calamity and a social catastrophe: lack of housing; lack of jobs; lack of money; lack of social support; lack of mental health care; but above all, lack of compassion where it matters.

Or, as a homeless teenager in East Sussex told me about the consequences of someone falling foul of multiple austerity policies at once:

> "I think you don't understand the severity of the situation unless you're in the situation. I can't get a job because I don't have any experience so I can't get the money to be able to live somewhere and because of that I don't eat very well. You can say to someone as much as you like 'this is what is happening' but you have to be there to fully understand it."

Conclusion

"I don't think the effects are seen until maybe the next generation. The legacy we leave these kids, it's not going to be a good one." (Jackie Jenkins, mother, Luton, spring 2013)

"Just because people are not screaming, it does not mean that people are not desperate. It does not mean there isn't a crisis." (Bal Athwal, worker at Bradford Resource Centre, interviewed by Oxfam)[1]

Picking up the pieces

This book was inspired by a year-long journey I made around Austerity UK and the people I met while on it. It is an exploration of the policies and people that brought austerity about, and of how the devastating consequences of a regressive strategy altered a country. Some of the profound and destabilising outcomes of the most radical transformation of the welfare state in the UK since its inception have been examined. The chapters have looked at how, against the backdrop of a 'Great Recession', historic declines in real incomes, entrenched deprivation, soaring personal debt and gaping wealth inequalities, the UK's government took a course of action aimed at dismantling the social security safety net in which millions of its citizens were invested.

The chapters have documented how whole swaths of the population – the poorest, people with disabilities, women, carers, older people, poorer people from black and minority ethnic backgrounds, children and young people – have been made more financially insecure and increasingly vulnerable as a result. They have illustrated how, for many, their very dignity has been stripped away as essential state-supported services and benefits have been slashed and how some were even driven to suicide.

The final part of this book looks at two related and pivotal aspects of the austerity landscape: the role of people who have been picking up the pieces, and the rise of those who have refused to be cowed and have been fighting back. With so much misery triggered by austerity, the individuals and groups all over the UK assisting those most in need – either through grassroots support or by protesting – were proving to be a precious resource. They offered a modicum of hope in an otherwise bleak political panorama. More than this, however, since the beginning they have been a tangible example of collective efforts to confront the austerian agenda as well as providing a barometer for what alternatives might lie ahead. They have been evidence that the script could yet be rewritten.

As we saw in earlier chapters, there have been legions of unseen, overstretched informal carers, often sacrificing their own health and wellbeing (to say nothing of earnings and careers) to look after family members, being forced to take on yet greater responsibilities as services have shrunk – all the while themselves falling victim to cuts. Alongside these undervalued societal linchpins have been the thousands of small voluntary and community organisations that, as I learned on my travels, have been performing herculean tasks despite cuts to their own income often due to the loss of local government contracts. In many ways these groups have done the Coalition an unintended favour by obscuring the full force of cuts on the ground in the initial phase as they endeavoured to keep providing vital services as austerity was blowing the lives of people in their communities to smithereens.

On a freezing cold day in the winter of 2012 I was driving around an English inner city with the chief executive of a small voluntary organisation who was explaining how the area she worked in – one of longstanding deprivation with well above average levels of child poverty – had seen some improvements prior to 2010 thanks in part to cash injections courtesy of government neighbourhood renewal programmes. There were physical indicators of development such as well-maintained public spaces and less visible (but no less vital) proof of how government grants had helped cultivate projects including youth services run by her organisation with the help of local volunteers. She was immensely proud of what had been achieved.

When the conversation moved on to what was happening under austerity, she choked up. Her eyes began to moisten. She bit her bottom lip. She asked not to be put on camera for her interview. I asked why. She replied candidly: "Because I will cry." This was a person with a long and accomplished career in the voluntary sector, who had worked with people in poverty for many years. Tough times were nothing new to her. But the fact that the community organisation she was running had to terminate some of its most effective services and lay off staff due to cuts in government grants was clearly getting to her.

"It's different this time", she said of the government's austerity masterplan. "It's deliberate. We are doing the best we can, making what we have stretch as far as possible, but I'm not sure how much longer we can keep doing that."

I met with a lot of voluntary organisation heads, their staff and their volunteers. The more I interviewed the more I found myself in awe of what these people were doing – invisible to most of us and with scarce resources even before austerity – they were making people's lives better. And they were making communities stronger. In fact, for anyone who has never gone near what would be classified as a 'deprived community' it might come as a surprise to learn how much these workers talked about the solidarity and resilience within the neighbourhoods in which they operated. The smile that crossed a volunteer's face when speaking of resident-led initiatives spoke volumes of a shared sense of community spirit that was a small but significant antidote to the hardships many people were experiencing. The slightest accomplishment was celebrated.

In Northumberland there was the small charity that set up its own chocolate factory in the back of its premises, and established it as a social enterprise employing local people who were long-term unemployed in a high unemployment area. In Croxteth there was the community education initiative, Communiversity, which helped adults improve their skills; and in Rhondda there was the online bookselling scheme that sold rare books on the internet while training workers. All over there were people grafting to make youth services, women's groups, work experience projects for people with learning disabilities, after-school clubs and much more as good as they could be.

People using these services would tell me spontaneously of how much the local organisations meant to them. The value they brought to those most in need was undeniable. As young mum Alea Khanam in the East End of London explained about her local community organisation: "If [they] go where should I go? I need this centre, truly. Because me, myself, my family, need the advice centre."

A group of people at Birmingham Settlement who had access to a range of services including wellbeing sessions and financial advice were effusive about what the organisation provided. They were also distraught at the thought that cuts might derail it.

"It has so much to offer. When the service is shut you are kind of lost", 'Susan' explained. "It's more like your core family", 'Fred' added. "If it's not there it's like part of your life, part of your family has gone missing. If funding is taken away it kind of has a backlash on everything. From mental wellbeing to getting people outside and into the community."

Every voluntary organisation and community group I visited reported a huge increase in the number of local residents turning to them for help, be it with debt or emotional problems, and every one of them added that they saw no sign of this changing any time soon. And no matter how enterprising these organisations were, or how many income-generating initiatives they came up with, or how well they had stretched their budgets or leveraged the good will of volunteers, there was deep uncertainty about what lay ahead.

Talk of 'crisis' as more cuts came down the line was on everyone's lips. These were the type of organisations that David Cameron once claimed would be the engine of his 'Big Society' venture, yet they were battling – just like the people they catered to – for survival.

As Alex Kittow, general manager at the Southmead Development Trust in Bristol, put it:

> "Demand for all our services is increasingly rapidly but the resources are decreasing rapidly. The sources of income or of grants or of support or advice are just diminishing or disappearing."

Karen Buttigan at St Peter's Partnership in Manchester's Ashton district had this to say:

> "Up until now, through a mix of income-generated surplus and grant funding, St Peter's Partnerships has been able to provide services free at the point of delivery to those most in need. However, a 100 per cent cut in our local authority grant funding has put our work and the organisation at risk, leaving deprived communities vulnerable."

In the spring of 2013, Martin Holcombe, chief executive of Birmingham Settlement, said that his organisation had been doing the best it could to juggle diminishing funds despite surges in requests for help – but he was worried that as reserves depleted in 2014 and 2015, it would be tougher then ever. A small hardship fund administered by the charity was "eaten up right away", he said, after they were "swamped" with applications. He added: "We've seen a massive rise in terms of people coming to us, not just in terms of this area but from across the city as a whole."

According to Steve Wyler, chief executive of the charity Locality, which has hundreds of small community organisations all over the country in its network, many voluntary groups were able to "rise to the challenge" by innovating and generating new funding streams such as social enterprises. However, he concluded that the pressures were escalating – including from large corporations winning government contracts away from local groups. He said:

> "It seems in many places that the tide of the state is withdrawing, leaving an exposed foreshore littered with debris and the casualties of the cuts. We have seen an increase in demand on [community organisations'] services – a rise of 7 per cent compared to 2012. There is mounting concern and anger over the consequences of public sector cutbacks. Community organisations are working hard to respond. At the same time many … are themselves struggling financially. [They] have also suffered from the introduction of government's prime contracting models which shift resources from local agencies to large corporates such as Serco, G4S and Capita."

As of the end of 2013, Wyler added, a survey of members revealed the true nature of the difficulties faced:

"Thirty per cent of Locality members have had to make staff
redundancies, and 37 per cent say that they are facing possible
closure or there are significant risks to their future viability."

As austerity unfolded, similar tales of rising demand and
vanishing or drastically scaled-back services emerged from
national, regional and local voluntary organisations. In the
North East – the English region most hit by cuts – the impact
of austerity on voluntary organisations was shattering. In April
2013 research by Voluntary Organisations' Network North
East (or Vonne, as it is known), *Surviving not thriving*, catalogued
the effects.[2] It reported that 59 per cent of voluntary groups
in the region had seen a decrease in fund over the previous 12
months, while a third (33 per cent) had lost staff. Two thirds
(62 per cent) had seen a rise in demand for services, while 39
per cent expected to, or were considering, closing their service.
The report concluded:

> The patterns over the last three years illustrate an increasing
> reliance on reserves, loss of substantial funding, and a number
> of organisations shrinking. It is clear that third sector
> organisations have faced the brunt of cuts, despite the pleas
> from all sides not to cut the sector disproportionately.

In December 2013 Judy Robinson, chief executive of Involve
Yorkshire & Humber, reported that her organisation's research
showed groups in that region were doing their best against
incredible odds.[3] She said:

> "Voluntary organisations and charities report increased
> demand for services at a time when resources have been
> reduced. While the future for many looks uncertain."

And it wasn't just the budget constraints and pressing needs of desperate clients that community organisations were grappling with. Because of their place right on the front line of austerity, embedded in communities, staff and volunteers were beginning to witness a broader problem – the physical deterioration of some districts as regeneration funds dried up and businesses failed to stay afloat in an economy that hadn't improved at all in the poorest parts of the country. Issues such as boarded-up shop fronts when businesses went bust, or homes that stood empty due to eviction, were rendering once buzzing streets in some areas scarred and desolate. And, as a number of reports pointed out, numerous high streets were being colonised by betting shops, pawnbrokers and payday loan firms moving into vacant shops and preying on vulnerable residents.[4] Steve Wyler of Locality argued that it would be disingenuous to ignore these manifestations of austerity, adding that, taken alongside the loss of valuable community-based projects such as youth clubs, it was "storing up major problems for the future" and made the work of grassroots groups much harder. He said:

> "When people are living on the margins it takes little to tip them over the edge, and the fastest growing industry in deprived neighbourhoods has been the credit sector, legal and illegal, including the payday lenders, pawnbrokers and loan sharks, closely matched by a rise in neighbourhood betting shops."

Community activists and residents I spoke to frequently brought up the worries about the longer-term repercussions this increased 'visibility' of deprivation and the corresponding depletion of social cohesion it might bring. Colin Lynch, a community organiser in inner-city Hull, was a typical example. He contended that should the physical spaces around people fall into long-term decline, the effects would be enduring.

"Retail on Hessle Road is suffering quite badly at the moment from a lot of businesses that are failing, a lot of shop units that are empty, shutters down", he said of one of the areas he works in. "It makes for what looks like a very bad area and it's not. [People] are seeing their area, their community, slowly going down and down. It's that anxiety over the change that's causing a lot of problems."

In Liverpool in the spring of 2013 Phil Knibb, executive director of Alt Valley Community Trust, was, like many others in the voluntary sector, interested in what the future held because, also like many others, he was convinced that the government was grossly underestimating or ignoring the true extent of the impact of austerity – especially on the country's most deprived communities. If things didn't change, if austerity wasn't halted, if the economy failed to bounce back sufficiently – and benefit everyone – Knibb concluded that even with the best efforts of individuals and voluntary groups, the future would be much harder than anyone anticipated. Reflecting on the situation he said unequivocally: "It's only the tip of the iceberg as we see it now."

The fightback

One of the curious things about observing people, communities and organisations as they responded to the rapid and destructive whirlwind of austerity was the co-existence of seemingly antithetical reactions. On the one hand, there was the abject despair at what was unfolding, the sense of being railroaded by an unstoppable juggernaut, and a deep disillusionment with politics and 'out-of-touch' politicians. I can't count the number of times people asked me the question: 'But what can we do about it?'

That said, however, there was a discernible reluctance to descend into defeatism and a refusal to be made to feel lesser than other people because of being poor or marginalised, or to be told there was no choice but to acquiesce. Nowhere was this latter reaction more embodied than by the disparate and determined guerrilla-like opponents who had sprung up in villages, towns, cities and social media to take on the government.

There was a short period in 2010 running into 2011 after austerity was officially proclaimed as *the* way forward that could only be described as a kind of 'limbo'. It was a surreal time when there appeared to be a surfeit of government rhetoric around the inevitability of cuts, of necessary 'belt-tightening' and everyone being 'in this together', yet for a while at least, austerity as a lived reality didn't seem to register because the big cuts had yet to come. At the same time, opposition to austerity was at best patchy. In part this was explained by the fact that most of the cuts would come after 2011, but it was also to a large degree because the government was dictating the terms of engagement.

This is how Owen Jones summed up the situation:

> "What wrong-footed a potential anti-austerity movement [at the start] was the way [government] very cleverly redirected people's anger away from those responsible to people's neighbours. To turn people against unemployed people, immigrants, public sector workers. That has proved a very clever firewall I think for the elite in this country."

The recession had, of course, taken a toll right away – on jobs in particular[5] – but it was only when it truly began to sink in just how gigantic the Coalition's programme of cuts and roll back of the state would be that something shifted in people's consciousness, and the genesis of an 'anti-austerity' movement began to take shape. Earlier chapters have looked at the advent of, in particular, disability campaigners including DPAC, We are Spartacus and the Wow Petition, as well as numerous bloggers who have capitalised on social media to challenge austerity.

They also referred to some of the public demonstrations that took place exposing the disproportionate effect austerity was having on people living with long-term illnesses and disability, and highlighted some of the more inventive anti-poverty campaigners such as Jack Monroe, who helped catapult the issue of food poverty into the mainstream.

Broader movements that emerged in the wake of the banking crisis were also mentioned, including 'Occupy', with its spectacularly apposite slogan 'We are the 99%', and 'UK Uncut', with its clever sporadic tactics such as staging impromptu occupations of high street bank premises serving to raise awareness of escalating wealth disparities. So too was how churches and some mainstream charities were doing much of the anti-austerity heavy lifting: churches through clergy speaking out on the immorality of poverty-inducing policies or through work within communities and charities by campaigning, lobbying, fronting legal challenges and evidence gathering on the spiralling crisis.

For anyone consuming only mainstream media it was entirely possible to not have been aware of the sheer variety of protests and fledgling campaigns that were taking root. Mass demonstrations such as the early ones by students and those supported by the trade union movement[6] may have attracted considerable media coverage, as did some of the 'Uncut'[7] and disability protest actions, but in the main the austerity battle was also being fought on a small scale or hyper-local level. There were so many fronts on which austerity was being fought, it was hard to keep track. There were residents banding together to save local A&E departments from closure,[8] and lawyers and groups representing victims of domestic violence, minority ethnic groups and prisoners fighting against legal aid cuts. There were lone bloggers taking on a host of issues, as well as coordinated efforts such as Boycott Workfare,[9] denouncing the unfairness of unpaid work allied to the government's back-to-work scheme Workfare.

There were grassroots initiatives such as Movement for Change,[10] which, among its many campaigns, was 'Shark Stoppers', calling for an end to extortionate rates of interest on credit and loans. All were playing a part. There were also groups emerging that shed light on the issues directly affecting people from black and minority ethnic backgrounds including Black Activists Rising Against Cuts. And there were evolving local groups too, such as Communities Against the Cuts,[11] campaigns for a 'Living Wage' which had new life breathed into them[12] and brand new approaches such as Who Benefits?[13] that set about counteracting the negative messages propagated around benefits by collecting and publicising the positive experiences of people whose lives had been improved by the welfare state. Many burgeoning groups spawned local chapters, often run on a 'franchise' basis, where local or regional issues could be targeted while enjoying the back-up of a wider network and feeding into national campaigns. These groups grew organically and flourished as support climbed.

One initiative that came to prominence in 2012 and 2013 as the cuts really began to bite was False Economy.[14] A trade union-backed project, it was set up to provide an online platform for alternatives to austerity to be hosted and discussed, but also to create an environment where anti-austerity campaigners could post directly, and where campaigns could be disseminated and shared. 'A public-facing, grassroots facility for people to publish, post events and ideas' is how Kate Belgrave, a journalist working on the project, described it. According to Belgrave, False Economy offered an alternative to the sort of mainstream narratives that promote the 'skiver versus striver' picture, and acted as a countervailing force to what she referred to as 'the largely woeful' response of the official opposition in Parliament.

Summing up the situation on the fight against austerity by the end of 2013, this is what Belgrave told me:

> The pressures people are now under is absolutely incredible. There have been some successes and some good campaigns such as challenges to the Independent Living Fund. Social media has been good at putting a lot of the issues on the map. So many people are organizing. The story is far from over yet.

However, arguing that the anti-austerity efforts needed a strong ally in mainstream politics, she added: 'There will still be a political vacuum until Ed Miliband wakes up from his coma.'

In June 2013, another front on the anti-austerity fight emerged with the launch of a new national group, the People's Assembly.[15] According to Owen Jones, a founding member, while still in its infancy the organisation was attempting to bring a number of fragmented groups together including progressive MPs, trade unionists and other activists to "weld together a national movement or coalition" and present a united front against cuts. Jones pointed out that by 2013 public opinion was shifting in favour of policies such as renationalising the railways and against individual austerity policies such as the 'Bedroom Tax'. If there had been complacency in the past, he argued, there were signs of that altering in the run-up to the 2015 general election.

> "There isn't a public consensus for the things [the government] is doing. People don't want the NHS to be privatised, they don't want taxes on the rich to be cut. The question is: how do you mobilise it? It's people organising from below – that's the only way things can change. It's a hope issue. The anger is there but anger is not enough."

As I travelled I encountered a type of anger and resistance that had no direct connection to any of the anti-austerity groups or protestors. These weren't the people going on marches or waving placards or joining campaigns. These were the people working on the front line or silently existing at the sharp end who, when someone finally put a microphone in front of them and sought their opinion, grasped the opportunity because they were too busy day-to-day coping, caring and providing to speak out otherwise. But they were no less ardent in their opposition. They could see what was happening to them, their neighbours and their communities and were crying out for a voice. Many people had constructive ideas to put forward for how things could be improved, and many were adamant that if things did not change for the better soon – especially for young people – serious episodes of social unrest like the English riots of 2011, where hundreds of primarily people from disadvantaged areas took to the streets during days of violence and looting,[16] could happen again. As one person in Birmingham told me: "All it will take is one, long hot summer."

In Glasgow David Martin expressed the views of a number of interviewees:

> "In their eyes they did not create [the crisis]. We have the bankers' pay rises of millions and the super rich cut in tax rates. This seems to the people on the street [as] the government looking after their own. People are angry at this and I think if things keep going the way they have and people's anger rises then there may very well be people out on the streets."

What the myriad opposition to austerity represented was something much bigger than the sum of their parts. The groups and individuals speaking out held a moral mirror up to the politicians who were the architects of austerity, and to those in society who remained silent or complicit as injustice grew. Most importantly they were a reminder with each interview, each campus upset, each arrest, each petition and each wheelchair chained to another that the belts being tightened were not those of the rich but of the poorest, most marginalised and most vulnerable in society. We were *not* all in this together. We never were. And if austerity was to be allowed to become a permanent fixture of the British state, as David Cameron wished, then what was at stake was that we never would be.

If there was one overriding message from the journey I made around Austerity UK it was this: people were only prepared to take so much. The women I interviewed in Croxteth were resolutely of this view, and it is to them that this book gives the final word:

Sharon: "There's the prime example of the ants and the polar bear. The ant comes over and says 'Excuse me, can you move?' And the polar bear just [ignores him]. So he goes away and comes back with 3,000 of his friends and he says 'Excuse me!' and the polar bear gets up and moves. And I think that's what it is with people. People feel they are on their own and they're not going to get listened to. They need to get together to make people listen to them."

Debbie: "If Mr Cameron thinks he's getting away with this he's got another thing coming. It may take people to hit rock bottom but we'll fight him. We'll end up fighting him – definitely. We can't constantly let him to that to us. We are good people. We're nice people. We want our children to have the best. We bring our children up with good values. None of us is lazy. If he thinks he's getting away with it he's not. End of."

Notes

Introduction

[1] Martin Wolf, 'Osborne has now been proved wrong on austerity', *Financial Times*, 26 September 2013 (www.ft.com/cms/s/0/c2fc7352-25de-11e3-aee8-00144feab7de.html?siteedition=uk#axzz2olteZTCg).

[2] Mark Blyth, 'Eternal austerity makes complete sense – if you're rich', *The Guardian*, 15 November 2013 (www.theguardian.com/commentisfree/2013/nov/15/eternal-austerity-makes-sense-if-rich-david-cameron).

[3] Tracy Shildrick et al, *Poverty and insecurity: Life in low-pay, no-pay Britain*, Bristol: Policy Press, 2012.

[4] Carys Afoko and Daniel Vokins, *Framing the economy: the austerity story*, London: New Economics Foundation, 11 September (www.neweconomics.org/publications/entry/framing-the-economy-the-austerity-story).

[5] Phillip Inman, 'UK avoided double-dip recession in 2011, revised official data shows', *The Guardian*, 27 June 2013 (www.theguardian.com/business/2013/jun/27/uk-avoid-double-dip-recession-ons-data).

[6] Allister Heath, 'Sorry to be a party-pooper, but this is the wrong kind of growth', *City AM*, 1 November 2013 (www.cityam.com/article/1383270044/sorry-be-party-pooper-wrong-kind-growth); Aditya Chakrabortty, 'London's economic boom leaves the rest of England behind', *The Guardian*, 23 October 2013 (www.theguardian.com/business/2013/oct/23/london-south-east-economic-boom).

[7] The Centre for Welfare Reform, *A fair society?*, Sheffield (www.centreforwelfarereform.org/library/type/pdfs/a-fair-society1.html).

[8] Shane Croucher, 'UK just half way through age of austerity as spending cuts set to deepen', *International Business Times*, 6 December 2013 (www.ibtimes.co.uk/uk-austerity-cuts-george-osborne-autumn-statement-528143).

[9] "The end of local government as we know it," was how Birmingham City Council Leader, Sir Albert Bore, described the impending cuts to adult social care and children's services. See Alex Blyth, 'Adult social care and children's services

– what next?', *Local Government Chronicle*, 25 April 2013 (www.lgcplus.com/news/adult-social-care-and-childrens-services-what-next/5057870.article).

[10] The Centre for Welfare Reform, op cit.

[11] This is Money, 'Two-thirds of a million: the number of public sector workers who have lost their jobs since the Coalition came to power', 21 November 2012 (www.thisismoney.co.uk/money/news/article-2236301/660-000-public-sector-workers-lost-jobs-Coalition-came-power.html).

[12] 'For the first time in history welfare benefits and tax credits will not rise in line with inflation and will instead for the next three years rise by 1%. Had there been no change benefits would have risen by 2.2%.' Quoted in Patrick Wintour, 'The day Britain changes: welfare reforms and coalition cuts take effect', *The Guardian*, 1 April 2013 (www.theguardian.com/politics/2013/mar/31/liberal-conservative-coalition-conservatives).

[13] Nick Owens, 'Working poor worse off than ever despite Coalition tax cuts designed to boost their income', *Mirror*, 23 June 2013, citing research by the Joseph Rowntree Foundation (www.mirror.co.uk/money/personal-finance/working-poor-worse-ever-despite-1983094).

[14] New Policy Institute, *Monitoring poverty and social exclusion 2013*, York: Joseph Rowntree Foundation (http://npi.org.uk/files/9613/8634/5794/MPSE_Findings_2013_FINAL.pdf).

[15] Rupert Neate, 'Pay workers more, CBI chief tells thriving firms', *The Guardian*, 30 December 2013 (www.theguardian.com/money/2013/dec/30/pay-workers-more-cbi-firms).

[16] Larry Elliott and Phillip Inman, 'Living standards to be lower in 2015 than in 2010, IFS warns', *The Guardian*, 6 December 2013 (www.theguardian.com/business/2013/dec/06/ifs-living-standards-lower-osborne-autumn-statement).

[17] Rupert Neate, for *The Guardian*, 30 December 2013, op cit.

[18] Rupert Jones, 'Household finances at breaking point, says Shelter', *The Guardian*, 3 January 2014 (www.theguardian.com/money/2014/jan/03/household-finances-breaking-point-shelter).

[19] The Staggers, 'Unemployment falls sharply but the living standards crisis continues', *New Statesman*, 18 December 2013 (www.newstatesman.com/politics/2013/12/unemployment-falls-sharply-living-standards-crisis-continues); Chris Johnes, 'Autumn Statement: The poorest pay twice', Oxfam Policy & Practice blog, 6 December 2013 (http://policy-practice.oxfam.org.uk/blog/2013/12/autumn-statement-2013-the-poorest-pay-twice).

[20] Joana Martinho, 'The impact of austerity – and the alternatives', Oxfam blogs, 11 September 2013 (www.oxfam.org.uk/blogs/2013/09/the-impact-of-austerity); Scriptonite Daily, 'Wealth inequality in UK now equal to Nigeria,

UN report', 5 August 2013 (www.scriptonitedaily.com/2013/08/05/wealth-inequality-in-uk-now-equal-to-nigeria-un-report).

[21] Heather Stewart, 'Shocking figures reveal the growth in UK's wealth gap', *The Observer*, 10 February 2013 (www.theguardian.com/society/2013/feb/10/uk-super-rich-richer-as-majority-squeezed).

[22] Mark Blyth, *Austerity: The history of a dangerous idea*, Oxford: Oxford University Press, 2013

[23] Joana Martinho, for Oxfam, 11 September 2013, op cit; Naomi Klein, *The shock doctrine: The rise of disaster capitalism*, New York: Picador, 2007.

[24] 'The austerity drive in Britain isn't really about debt and deficits at all; it's about using deficit panic as an excuse to dismantle social programs.' Quoted in Paul Krugman, 'The austerity agenda', *The New York Times*, 31 May 2012 (www.nytimes.com/2012/06/01/opinion/krugman-the-austerity-agenda.html?_r=2&hp&).

[25] Mark Blyth, *Austerity: The history of a dangerous idea*, op cit.

[26] George Eaton challenges claims by David Cameron that the cuts are not about 'ideological zeal'; see George Eaton, 'Cameron is wrong: the spending cuts are ideological', *New Statesman*, 31 December 2010 (www.newstatesman.com/blogs/the-staggers/2010/12/spending-cuts-tax-ideological).

[27] Author and academic Mark Blyth outlines his rebuttal to austerity on video; see www.youtube.com/watch?v=JQuHSQXxsjM

[28] www.youtube.com/watch?v=JQuHSQXxsjM

[29] Kate Alexander and Jonathan Hopkin, 'Breaking away from "the austerity state"', Policy Network, 12 September 2013 (www.policy-network.net/pno_detail.aspx?ID=4456&title=Breaking-away-from-'the-austerity-state).

[30] Aditya Chakrabortty, 'Mainstream economics is in denial: the world has changed', *The Guardian*, 28 October 2013 (www.theguardian.com/commentisfree/2013/oct/28/mainstream-economics-denial-world-changed?CMP=twt_gu).

[31] Mary O'Hara, 'Magdalena Sepúlveda: "Austerity is devastating for the world's poorest"', *The Guardian*, 26 February 2013 (www.theguardian.com/society/2013/feb/26/magdalena-sepulveda-austerity-devastating-worlds-poorest).

[32] UNICEF, 'UNICEF calls on austerity Britain not to harm children', Press release (www.unicef.org.uk/Media-centre/Press-releases/UNICEF-calls-on-austerity-Britain-not-to-harm-children).

[33] Paul Krugman, 'How the case for austerity has crumbled', *The New York Review of Books*, 6 June 2013 (www.nybooks.com/articles/archives/2013/jun/06/how-case-austerity-has-crumbled).

[34] Andrew Grice, 'George Osborne braced for IMF challenge over austerity plans', *The Independent*, 8 May 2013 (www.independent.co.uk/news/uk/politics/george-osborne-braced-for-imf-challenge-over-austerity-plans-8606818.html).

[35] Paul Krugman, *End this depression now*, New York: W.W. Norton & Company, Inc, 2012.

[36] Joseph Stiglitz, 'Stagnation by design', Project Syndicate, 6 February 2014, (https://www.project-syndicate.org/commentary/joseph-e--stiglitz-argues-that-bad-policies-in-rich-countries--not-economic-inevitability--have-caused-most-people-s-standard-of-living-to-decline).

[37] Office for National Statistics, Economic Review, November 2013 (www.ons.gov.uk/ons/rel/elmr/economic-review/november-2013/art-novemberer.html?format=print).

[38] John Cassidy, 'By George, Britain's austerity experiment didn't work', *The New Yorker*, 7 December 2013 (www.newyorker.com/online/blogs/johncassidy/2013/12/by-george-britains-austerity-experiment-didnt-work.html).

[39] Ibid.

[40] Martin Wolf, for the *Financial Times*, 26 September 2013, op cit.

[41] Ian Traynor, 'Austerity pushing Europe into social and economic decline, says Red Cross', *The Guardian*, 10 October 2013 (www.theguardian.com/world/2013/oct/10/austerity-europe-debt-red-cross).

[42] Martin Wolf, 'We still need to learn the real lessons of the crisis', *Financial Times*, 19 December 2013 (www.ft.com/cms/s/0/25f004e6-673a-11e3-a5f9-00144feabdc0.html?siteedition=uk#axzz2olteZTCg).

[43] Graham Hiscott, 'Critics claim that government's Help to Buy scheme will actually WORSEN Britain's housing crisis', *Mirror*, 9 October 2013 (www.mirror.co.uk/news/uk-news/critics-warn-new-help-buy-2351714).

[44] Daniel Boffey, 'Mortgage rise will plunge a million homeowners into "perilous debt"', *The Guardian*, 28 December 2013 (www.theguardian.com/money/2013/dec/28/mortgage-rise-homeowners-perilous-debt).

[45] David Blanchflower, 'David Cameron has shown his hand – austerity is really all about shrinking the size of the state', *The Independent*, 17 November 2013 (www.independent.co.uk/voices/comment/david-cameron-has-shown-his-hand--austerity-is-really-all-about-shrinking-the-size-of-the-state-8945387.html); Dylan Matthews, 'British austerity was even worse than you thought', *The Washington Post*, 9 September 2013 (www.washingtonpost.com/blogs/wonkblog/wp/2013/09/09/british-austerity-was-even-worse-than-you-thought/?wprss=rss_ezra-klein&clsrd).

[46] 'The austerity drive in Britain isn't really about debt and deficits at all; it's about using deficit panic as an excuse to dismantle social programs.' Quoted in Paul Krugman, *The New York Times*, 31 May, op cit.

[47] George Eaton, 'Cameron's declaration that the cuts are permanent reveals the Tories' true agenda', *New Statesman*, 12 November 2013 (www.newstatesman. com/politics/2013/11/camerons-declaration-cuts-are-permanent-reveals-tories-true-agenda).

[48] Denis Campbell, '7,000 key NHS clinical staff made redundant amid enforced cuts', *The Guardian*, 31 December 2013 (www.theguardian.com/society/2013/dec/31/nhs-staff-laid-off-amid-savings-drive).

[49] Tom Clark and Rowena Mason, 'Fury with MPs is the main reason for not voting – poll', *The Guardian*, 26 December 2013 (www.theguardian.com/politics/2013/dec/26/fury-mps-not-voting-poll).

[50] *Prospect*, 'Poverty in the UK: Can it be eradicated?', 2013 (www.prospectmagazine.co.uk/magazine/free-download-poverty-in-the-uk/#.UtAXMfad5_k).

[51] The Sutton Trust, 'The private schools produce a tenth of the country's elite', Press release, 20 November 2012 (www.suttontrust.com/news/news/ten-private-schools-produce-a-tenth-of-the-countrys-elite).

[52] Daniel Dorling, *Injustice: Why social inequality persists*, Bristol: Policy Press, 2009.

Chapter One

[1] www.fareshare.org.uk

[2] Archived information on the New Deal for Communities is available at http://collections.europarchive.org/tna/20090106142604/http://www.neighbourhood.gov.uk/page.asp?id=617

[3] Hélène Mulholland, 'Cameron challenged by Miliband on poverty and rise in use of food banks', *The Guardian*, 19 December 2012 (www.theguardian.com/politics/2012/dec/19/cameron-miliband-poverty-food-banks).

[4] www.independent.co.uk/news/uk/home-news/food-banks-are-sign-of-return-to-dickensian-world-warns-food-expert-8604629.html

[5] 'In 2010, 17.1 per cent of the UK population was defined as being at risk of poverty, equivalent to 10.7 million people.' From Office for National Statistics, 'Comparison of UK and EU at-risk-of-poverty rates 2005-2010', 7 June 2012 (www.ons.gov.uk/ons/rel/household-income/comparison-of-uk-and-eu-at-risk-of-poverty-rates/2005-2010/rep--uk-and-eu-at-risk-of-poverty-rates.html).

[6] Office for National Statistics, 'Comparison of UK and EU at-risk-of-poverty rates 2005-2010, Overall at-risk-of-poverty rates' (www.ons.gov.uk/ons/rel/household-income/comparison-of-uk-and-eu-at-risk-of-poverty-rates/2005-2010/rep--uk-and-eu-at-risk-of-poverty-rates.html#tab-Overall-at-risk-of-poverty-rates).

[7] Tom MacInnes, Peter Kenway and Anushree Parekh, *Monitoring poverty and social exclusion 2009*, York: Joseph Rowntree Foundation, 3 December 2009 (www.jrf.org.uk/publications/monitoring-poverty-2009).

[8] 'PSE: UK [Poverty Social Exclusion] research identifies people falling below what the public agrees is a minimum standard of living and measures poverty and exclusion using a wide range of rigorous methods. This first report reveals a detailed picture of the extent of deprivation, low living standards and financial insecurity in the UK today.... Independent surveys of poverty using this methodology were first conducted in 1983 and again in 1990, 1999, 2002/03 and 2012. The report examines trends over this thirty year period and that the proportions of the population falling below the standards set by society at the time across a range of items and activities are higher today than in 1983, 1990 and 1999.' Quoted in David Gordon, Joanna Mack, Stewart Lansley, Gill Main, Shailen Nandy, Demi Patsios, Marco Pomati et al, *The impoverishment of the UK*, PSE UK first results: Living standards, 28 March 2013 (www.poverty.ac.uk/pse-research/pse-uk-reports).

[9] Robert Joyce, *Child poverty during the recession and beyond*, London: Institute for Fiscal Studies (www.ifs.org.uk/economic_review/fp271.pdf).

[10] 'Although in the last decade the number of children living in poverty has reduced, progress has not been fast enough for us to reach the goal of ending child poverty by 2020 that all the main political parties signed up to in the Child Poverty Act' (www.endchildpoverty.org.uk).

[11] Office for National Statistics, 'Gross domestic product preliminary estimate, Q3 2013' (www.ons.gov.uk/ons/rel/gva/gross-domestic-product--preliminary-estimate/q3-2013/stb-gdp-preliminary-estimate--q3-2013.html).

[12] Amelia Gentleman, 'Food banks: a life on handouts', *The Guardian*, 18 July 2012 (www.theguardian.com/society/2012/jul/18/food-banks-on-handouts?INTCMP=SRCH).

[13] Brian Reade, 'Our hidden poor: the desperate families begging for food handouts to keep alive', *Mirror*, 30 April 2012 (www.mirror.co.uk/news/uk-news/our-hidden-poor-the-desperate-families-begging-81187).

[14] In June 2013, several charities called on the government to monitor the levels of referrals from jobcentres to food banks. See Katherine Trebeck, 'When is a food bank referral not a food bank referral? When it's from the DWP', Oxfam Policy & Practice blog, 3 July 2013 (http://policy-practice.oxfam.org.uk/blog/2013/07/foodbank-referrals-from-the-dwp). However, by September 2013,

it appeared that the government response was to stop referrals in order to reduce the numbers of people using food banks (Mum v Austerity, 5 September 2013, http://mumvausterity.blogspot.co.uk/2013/09/dwp-pull-foodbank-lifeline-from-poorest.html; James Lyons, 'Food banks: Ministers accused of breaking agreement to help hungry jobseekers', *Mirror*, 5 September 2013, www.mirror.co.uk/news/uk-news/food-banks-ministers-accused-breaking-2252405#.UihVcJVWh2A.twitter).

[15] 'In 2012-13 [Trussell Trust] foodbanks fed 346,992 people nationwide. Of those helped, 126,889 were children. Rising costs of food and fuel combined with static income, high unemployment and changes to benefits are causing more and more people to come to foodbanks for help.' Trussell Trust figures show an exponential growth in foodbank clients: 2005-06: 2,814; 2006-07: 9,174; 2007-08: 13,849; 2008-09: 25,899; 2009-10: 40,898; 2010-11: 61,468; 2011-12: 128,697; 2012-13: 346,992 (see www.trusselltrust.org/foodbank-projects).

[16] Church Action on Poverty, *Walking the breadline*, co-published with Oxfam (www.church-poverty.org.uk/foodfuelfinance/walkingthebreadline).

[17] Citizens Advice, 'Citizens Advice reports "alarming" 78% rise in foodbanks enquiries', 19 August 2013 (www.citizensadvice.org.uk/press_office20130819).

[18] FareShare, 'FareShare now feeds more people', 1 May 2013 (www.fareshare.org.uk/fareshare-feeds-more-people-than-ever-before).

[19] Patrick Butler, 'Number of people turning to food banks triples in a year', *The Guardian*, 24 April 2013 (www.theguardian.com/society/2013/apr/24/number-people-food-banks-triples).

[20] 'Parents skipping meals so children don't go hungry as families struggle with longest cost of living squeeze in 60 years:

· One in ten families are skipping meals or relying on charity and hand-outs

· Mothers are putting their health at risk by eating only every other day.' Quoted in Sean Poulter, 'Parents skipping meals so children don't go hungry', *Daily Mail*, 22 November 2012 (www.dailymail.co.uk/news/article-2236633/Parents-skipping-meals-children-dont-hungry-families-struggle-longest-cost-living-squeeze-60-years.html#ixzz2fhmuldLk).

[21] See, for example, JRF's mapping of long-term trends in poverty at http://data.jrf.org.uk/data/long-term-view-poverty/; see also Neil Wrigley, '"Food deserts" in British cities: Policy context and research priorities', *Urban Studies*, October 2002 (http://usj.sagepub.com/content/39/11/2029.short).

[22] Charlie Cooper, 'Look back in hunger: Britain's silent, scandalous epidemic', *The Independent*, 6 April 2012 (www.independent.co.uk/life-style/health-and-families/health-news/look-back-in-hunger-britains-silent-scandalous-epidemic-7622363.html).

[23] Kellogg's News Release, 5 March 2013 (http://pressoffice.kelloggs.co.uk/index.php?s=20295&item=122399).

[24] James Lyons, 'Soaring number of starving Britons who rely on food banks is national "emergency", experts warn', *Mirror*, 4 December 2013 (www.mirror.co.uk/news/uk-news/food-banks-soaring-number-starving-2880044).

[25] See www.turn2us.org.uk/information__resources/benefits/working_or_looking_for_work/jobseekers_allowance/jsa_sanctions_-_turn2us.aspx#howmuch.

[26] www.gov.uk/government/news/independent-reviewer-of-benefit-sanctions-announced

[27] Matthew Taylor, 'Osborne's signing on delay plan met by anger and bemusement at job centre', *The Guardian*, 26 June 2013 (www.theguardian.com/politics/2013/jun/26/osborne-jobseekers-allowance-seven-day-wait).

[28] TheyWorkForYou.com, 'Food: Food banks: Question', 2 July 2013 (www.theyworkforyou.com/lords/?id=2013-07-02a.1071.0&s=speaker%3A13554#g1071.1).

[29] Niall Cooper, 'Archbishop of Canterbury takes up the cudgels', 9 July 2013 (http://niallcooper.wordpress.com/2013/07/09/archbishop-of-canterbury-takes-up-the-cudgels).

[30] Patrick Butler, 'Huge rise in use of food banks since welfare changes, says aid body', *The Guardian*, 11 July 2013 (www.theguardian.com/society/2013/jul/11/food-bank-rise-welfare-changes).

[31] Matt Chorley, 'Poor forced to use food banks', Mail Online, 10 September 2013 (www.dailymail.co.uk/news/article-2416737/Poor-forced-use-food-banks-Theyve-got-blame-says-Michael-Gove.html).

[32] Martin Shipton, 'Vale of Glamorgan MP Alun Cairns in food bank row after claims drug addicts use them', Wales Online, 19 September 2013 (www.walesonline.co.uk/news/wales-news/vale-glamorgan-tory-mp-alun-6060730).

[33] Luciana Berger, 'We must not normalise food banks. Their proliferation is a mark of shame on this country', *The Independent*, 18 December 2013 (www.independent.co.uk/voices/comment/we-must-not-normalise-food-banks-their-proliferation-is-a-mark-of-shame-on-this-country-9013489.html).

[34] Quoted in Charlie Cooper, 'Food banks are "sign of return to Dickensian world", warns food expert', *The Independent*, 5 May 2013 (www.independent.co.uk/news/uk/home-news/food-banks-are-sign-of-return-to-dickensian-world-warns-food-expert-8604629.html).

[35] Figures from the Church Urban Fund's Poverty in England research (www.cuf.org.uk/povertyinengland).

[36] Patrick Butler, 'Homeless and penniless – the food bank users with nowhere else to turn', *The Guardian*, 11 July 2013 (www.theguardian.com/society/2013/jul/11/food-bank-homeless-penniless).

[37] *The Huffington Post UK*, 'Half a million Brits turning to food banks as poverty crisis deepens', 30 May 2013 (www.huffingtonpost.co.uk/2013/05/29/food-poverty-benefit-delays_n_3352178.html).

[38] Dennis Ellam, 'Food bank Britain: Scandal of 1/4 million surviving on food handouts', *Sunday Mirror*, 9 December 2012 (www.mirror.co.uk/news/uk-news/food-bank-britain-scandal-of-14-1481587#ixzz2g6SJy3Fh).

[39] Sandra Webster, 'Food Banks cash in on poverty', NewsNetScotland.com, 19 June 2013 (http://newsnetscotland.com/index.php/scottish-opinion/7616-food-banks-cash-in-on-poverty).

[40] BBC News, 'Darling unveils borrowing gamble', 24 November 2008 (http://news.bbc.co.uk/1/hi/7745340.stm).

[41] Danny Alexander: 'This coalition will continue until the end of this Parliament as we promised for the very simple reason that we have a very big job to do – to clean up the economic mess that Labour left behind and entrench the recovery we are starting to see', quoted in Sky News, 17 September 2013 (http://news.sky.com/story/1142749/cables-early-coalition-split-talk-dismissed).

[42] Tim Ross, 'Ed Balls plans to keep Coalition spending cuts', *The Telegraph*, 3 June 2013 (www.telegraph.co.uk/news/politics/labour/10096793/Ed-Balls-plans-to-keep-Coalition-spending-cuts.html).

[43] BBC News, 'Ed Miliband: Labour would freeze energy prices', 24 September 2013 (www.bbc.co.uk/news/uk-politics-24213366).

[44] Natalie Evans, 'Food banks debate: Recap updates as Tory ministers WALK OUT of MPs' discussion on hunger', *Mirror*, 18 December 2013 (www.mirror.co.uk/news/uk-news/food-banks-debate-recap-updates-2939576).

[45] BBC News, 'Economic growth in the UK during the second quarter of the year has been revised up to 0.7% by the Office for National Statistics (ONS)', 23 August 2013 (www.bbc.co.uk/news/business-23807182).

[46] Patrick Collinson, 'George Osborne is missing the link between economic and personal prosperity', *The Guardian*, 5 December 2013 (www.theguardian.com/money/2013/dec/05/george-osborne-economic-recovery-personal-debt).

[47] Karel Williams, 'National recovery? Don't believe the hype', *The Guardian*, 8 September 2013 (www.theguardian.com/commentisfree/2013/sep/08/national-recovery-dont-believe-hype); Phillip Inman, 'George Osborne's speech on the econony: seven ways he rewrote history', *The Guardian*, 9 September 2013 (www.theguardian.com/business/economics-blog/2013/sep/09/george-osborne-economy-speech-seven-ways-he-rewrote-history); Simon Kirby, 'Households are increasing their borrowing in order to maintain their standard

of living', Pieria, 19 August 2013 (www.pieria.co.uk/articles/households_are_increasing_their_borrowing_in_order_to_maintain_their_standard_of_living); Michael Burke, 'Did austerity lead to recovery? No, GDP was increased by government spending', 9 September 2013 (http://socialisteconomicbulletin. blogspot.co.uk/2013/09/did-austerity-lead-to-recovery-no-it.html?spref=tw); Ben Chu, 'New figures cast doubt on George Osborne's claims that Coalition austerity programme has been vindicated', *The Independent*, 10 September 2013 (www.independent.co.uk/news/uk/politics/new-figures-cast-doubt-on-george-osbornes-claims-that-coalition-austerity-programme-has-been-vindicated-8807518.html).

[48] Patrick Wintour, 'George Osborne claims economic argument is won: "Britain is turning a corner"', *The Guardian*, 9 September 2013 (www.theguardian.com/politics/2013/sep/09/george-osborne-economy).

[49] Robert Watts, '"To revive the economy, cut spending", Spending cuts are more effective than raising taxes at restoring shattered public finances, a new report claims', *The Telegraph*, 4 April 2013 (www.telegraph.co.uk/news/politics/9972723/To-revive-the-economy-cut-spending.html).

[50] Adam Smith Institute, 'Cut business taxes and public spending to stave off UK bankruptcy', Press release, 4 August 2009 (www.adamsmith.org/news/press-releases/cut-business-taxes-and-public-spending-to-stave-off-uk-bankruptcy).

[51] 'The country's most powerful mandarin has been accused of breaching civil service political neutrality by publicly advocating austerity measures more "extreme" than George Osborne has enacted', quoted in Mehdi Hasan, 'Cabinet Secretary Jeremy Heywood accused of advocating "extreme" austerity', *The Huffington Post UK*, 3 July 2013 (www.huffingtonpost.co.uk/2013/07/03/jeremy-heywood_n_3538983.html); see also Gerri Peev, 'Economic recovery "will take 20 years", warns Britain's top civil servant', Mail Online, 3 July 2013 (www.dailymail.co.uk/news/article-2354231/Economic-recovery-20-years-warns-Britains-civil-servant.html).

[52] The Trussell Trust, 'Tripling in foodbank usage sparks Trussell Trust to call for an inquiry', Press release, 16 October 2013 (www.trusselltrust.org/foodbank-numbers-triple).

[53] Charlotte McDonald-Gibson, 'Exclusive: Red Cross launches emergency food aid plan for UK's hungry', *The Independent*, 11 October 2013 (www.independent.co.uk/news/uk/home-news/exclusive-red-cross-launches-emergency-food-aid-plan-for-uks-hungry-8872496.html).

[54] Citizens Advice Bureau, 'Citizens Advice Bureau set to give out more than 100,000 vouchers for emergency food this year', Press release, 16 December 2013 (www.citizensadvice.org.uk/index/pressoffice/press_index/press_20131216.htm).

[55] http://agirlcalledjack.com

[56] David Millward, 'Jamie Oliver sparks poverty row after he attacks families for eating junk food and buying expensive TV sets', *The Telegraph*, 27 August 2013 (www.telegraph.co.uk/news/celebritynews/10266648/Jamie-Oliver-sparks-poverty-row-after-he-attacks-families-for-eating-junk-food-and-buying-expensive-TV-sets.html).

[57] In an article on Left Futures website, Jilly Luke writes of Jack Monroe being 'an acceptable benefits claimant because she reminds the middle classes of themselves ... her version of poverty is the cosy frugality of a Beatrix Potter book' (www.leftfutures.org/2013/08/lentils-and-lager-why-we-forgive-tax-evaders-but-not-benefit-claimants).

[58] EightEights, 'Perhaps you've heard of a girl called Jack, a much feted face of "poverty porn", the acceptable face of "impoverished" people. What you won't have heard is how intensely problematic the tropes she plays into are', 26 August 2013 (http://eightdiverging.blogspot.co.uk/2013/08/much-ado-about-girl-called-jack.html).

[59] Xanthe Clay, 'My 49p lunch with a girl called Jack', *The Telegraph*, 4 March 2013 (www.telegraph.co.uk/foodanddrink/9900773/My-49p-lunch-with-a-girl-called-Jack.html).

[60] Richard Littlejohn, 'Ah Pesto! These poverty poster girls of Welfare Britain want the gravy too ... without having to pay for it', Mail Online, 31 October 2013 (www.dailymail.co.uk/debate/article-2482111/RICHARD-LITTLEJOHN-Ah-Pesto-Meet-poverty-poster-girls.html).

[61] Jack Monroe, 'Dear Richard Littlejohn –here are all the things you got wrong about me', *The Guardian*, 1 November 2013 (www.theguardian.com/commentisfree/2013/nov/01/richard-littlejohn-wrong-about-jack-monroe-daily-mail).

[62] Steve White, 'Austerity Britain: Starving families "stealing meat and cheese" as cuts continue to bite', *Mirror*, 24 September 2013 (www.mirror.co.uk/money/personal-finance/austerity-britain-starving-families-stealing-2296520).

[63] Natalie Evans, for the *Mirror*, 18 December 2013, op cit.

[64] 'Welfare reform and cuts threaten to worsen poverty' (www.jrf.org.uk/austerity-Manchester).

Chapter Two

[1] Hugo Gye, 'D-Day for the welfare state: Government launches biggest benefits shake-up in history (but new age of austerity means families will "be £5,000 worse off")', *Daily Mail*, 1 April 2013 (www.dailymail.co.uk/news/article-2302260/Welfare-cuts-D-Day-Government-attempts-save-billions-today-new-age-austerity-means-families-5-000-worse-off.html#ixzz2gSxfEDii).

[2] BBC News, 'Radical shake-up of benefits to cut spending', 22 June 2010 (www.bbc.co.uk/news/10380692).

[3] Dom Aversano, '£53/wk? Prove it IDS', Change.org petition (www.change.org/en-GB/petitions/iain-duncan-smith-iain-duncan-smith-to-live-on-53-a-week).

[4] Christopher Hope, 'Exclusive: Cabinet is worth £70million', *The Telegraph*, 27 May 2013 (www.telegraph.co.uk/news/politics/9290520/Exclusive-Cabinet-is-worth-70million.html).

[5] BBC News, 'Battle over plan to cap benefits ahead of Commons vote', 2 January 2013 (www.bbc.co.uk/news/uk-politics-20886192).

[6] David Gordon, Joanna Mack, Stewart Lansley, Gill Main, Shailen Nandy, Demi Patsios, Marco Pomati et al, *The impoverishment of the UK*, PSE UK, Economic and Social Research Council (www.poverty.ac.uk/sites/default/files/attachments/The_Impoverishment_of_the_UK_PSE_UK_first_results_summary_report_March_28.pdf).

[7] Sean Farrell, 'Squeezed households cut energy use by a quarter as prices soar', *The Guardian*, 16 August 2013 (www.theguardian.com/money/2013/aug/16/households-cut-energy-use-prices-soar?CMP=twt_fd).

[8] Tracy Shildrick, Robert MacDonald, Colin Scott Webster and Kayleigh Garthwaite, *Poverty and insecurity: Life in low-pay, no-pay Britain*, Studies in Poverty, Inequality & Social Exclusion Series, Bristol: Policy Press, 2012.

[9] Hannah Aldridge and Adam Tinson, *How many families are affected by more than one benefit cut this April?*, London: New Policy Institute (http://npi.org.uk/publications/social-security-and-welfare-reform/how-many-families-are-affected-more-one-benefit-cut-april/#sthash.yLdVAd4o.dpuf).

[10] Connect Community Trust (www.wellhouseha.org.uk/index.php?id=97).

[11] See *Herald Scotland*, 'How Iain Duncan Smith came to Easterhouse and left with a new vision for the Tory party', 23 March 2002 (www.heraldscotland.com/sport/spl/aberdeen/how-iain-duncan-smith-came-to-easterhouse-and-left-with-a-new-vision-for-the-tory-party-1.155218).

[12] http://birminghamsettlement.org.uk

[13] www.artsfactory.co.uk

[14] Office for National Statistics figures from 1997 to 2011 show Northern Ireland with the lowest income per head of the UK countries in all years.

[15] James Browne, Andrew Hood and Robert Joyce, *Child and working-age poverty in Northern Ireland from 2010 to 2020*, London: Institute for Fiscal Studies (www.ifs.org.uk/comms/r78.pdf).

---

[16] Sunny Hundal, 'Cameron the worst PM for living standards in history', Liberal Conspiracy, 6 August 2013 (http://liberalconspiracy.org/2013/08/06/cameron-is-the-worst-british-pm-for-living-standards-in-recorded-history).

[17] Danny Dorling, 'New Labour and inequality: Thatcherism continued?', *Local Economy*, vol 25, nos 5-6, August-September 2010, pp 406-23.

[18] Oxfam, 'Work no longer pays for Britons caught in "perfect storm" of falling incomes and rising costs', Press release, 14 June 2012 (www.oxfam.org.uk/media-centre/press-releases/2012/06/work-no-longer-pays-for-britons-caught-in-perfect-storm-of-falling-incomes-and-rising-costs).

[19] 'A global super-rich elite had at least $21 trillion (£13tn) hidden in secret tax havens by the end of 2010', according to BBC News, 'The price of offshore revisited', 22 July 2012 (www.bbc.co.uk/news/business-18944097); Sean O'Hare, 'Tax haven abuse costs the UK government £16 billion per year', *The Telegraph*, 13 July 2011 (www.telegraph.co.uk/finance/personalfinance/expat-money/8635370/Tax-haven-abuse-costs-the-UK-government-16-billion-per-year.html).

[20] Matthew Whittaker and Alex Hurrell, *Low pay Britain 2013*, London: Resolution Foundation (www.resolutionfoundation.org/media/media/downloads/Low_Pay_Britain_2013.pdf).

[21] Moussa Haddad, *The perfect storm: Economic stagnation, the rising cost of living, public spending cuts, and the impact on UK poverty*, Oxfam GB (http://policy-practice.oxfam.org.uk/publications/the-perfect-storm-economic-stagnation-the-rising-cost-of-living-public-spending-228591).

[22] David Gordon et al, op cit.

[23] James Browne, Andrew Hood and Robert Joyce, *Child and working-age poverty in Northern Ireland from 2010 to 2020*, IFS Report R78, London: Institute of Fiscal Studies (www.ifs.org.uk/comms/r78.pdf); Randeep Ramesh, 'One in four UK children will be living in poverty by 2020, says thinktank', *The Guardian*, 7 May 2013 (www.theguardian.com/society/2013/may/07/uk-children-poverty-2020-thinktank).

[24] The Children's Society, *Through young eyes*, 2013 (www.childrenssociety.org.uk/sites/default/files/tcs/poverty_commission_2pp_summary_final.pdf).

[25] Children's Commissioner, *A child rights impact assessment of budget decisions*, London: The Office of the Children's Commissioner, 2011 (www.childrenscommissioner.gov.uk/content/publications/content_676).

[26] Gingerbread, *Paying the price: Single parents in the age of austerity*, London: Gingerbread, 2013 (www.gingerbread.org.uk/content/1813/Paying-the-price).

[27] 'Minimum wage rises as rogue firms targeted.... The Resolution Foundation think-tank said the minimum wage will be falling in real terms for the fifth year in a row despite the increase, because it is not keeping pace with rising prices',

Sky News, 1 October 2013 (http://news.sky.com/story/1148596/minimum-wage-rises-as-rogue-firms-targeted).

[28] Randeep Ramesh, 'Minimum wage "being poorly policed"', *The Guardian*, 3 December 2013 (www.theguardian.com/society/2013/dec/03/minimum-wage-poorly-policed).

[29] http://blackactivistsrisingagainstcuts.blogspot.co.uk

[30] Moussa Haddad, op cit.

[31] Sky News, 'Cameron refuses to rule out tax cut for the rich', 29 January 2014, http://news.sky.com/story/1203071/cameron-refuses-to-rule-out-tax-cut-for-rich

[32] Nigel Morris, 'Up to 450,000 face court over council tax arrears', *The Independent*, 11 October 2013 (www.independent.co.uk/news/uk/politics/up-to-450000-face-court-over-council-tax-arrears-8872515.html).

[33] Lorna Hankin, 'Council tax rise for low-income families', BBC News, 31 January 2013 (www.bbc.co.uk/news/uk-politics-21272688).

[34] See www.telegraph.co.uk/news/politics/spending- review/10144312/Spending-Review-Council-tax-frozen-for-two-years-until-2016.html

[35] False Economy blog, 'Our latest Guardian research: bankruptcy and repossession threat as council tax benefit cuts hit' (http://falseeconomy.org.uk/blog/our-latest-guardian-research-bankruptcy-and-repossession-threat-as-council).

[36] Welfare Reform Act 2012, c 5 (www.legislation.gov.uk/ukpga/2012/5/pdfs/ukpga_20120005_en.pdf).

[37] Susan Himmelwelt, 'The welfare reform bill will erode women's financial independence', *The Guardian*, 23 January 2012 (www.theguardian.com/commentisfree/2012/jan/23/welfare-reform-bill-women-independence).

[38] Gavin Kelly, 'Stealth cuts are making universal credit toxic to the working poor', *The Guardian*, 12 December 2013 (www.theguardian.com/commentisfree/2013/dec/12/stealth-cuts-universal-credit-working-poor).

[39] Mike Brewer, James Browne and Wenchao Jin, *Universal credit: A preliminary analysis*, London: Institute for Fiscal Studies (www.ifs.org.uk/bns/bn116.pdf).

[40] Alex Stevenson, 'Single parents "biggest losers" from IDS' welfare reforms', Politics.co.uk, 30 October 2013 (www.politics.co.uk/news/2013/10/30/single-parents-biggest-losers-from-ids-welfare-reforms).

[41] Department for Work and Pensions, 'Simplifying the welfare system and making sure work pays' (www.gov.uk/government/policies/simplifying-the-welfare-system-and-making-sure-work-pays/supporting-pages/introducing-universal-credit).

NOTES

[42] James Kirkup, 'Cameron raises fears of more delays for IDS benefit reforms', *The Telegraph*, 10 September 2013 (www.telegraph.co.uk/news/politics/david-cameron/10300800/Cameron-raises-fears-of-more-delays-for-IDS-benefit-reforms.html); Anne Perkins, 'Universal credit and a very public mess', *The Guardian*, 12 November 2013 (www.theguardian.com/society/2013/nov/12/universal-credit-public-mess-iain-duncan-smith?commentpage=1); Johnny Void, 'DWP reveals the real agenda behind universal credit and welfare reform', 18 September 2013 (http://johnnyvoid.wordpress.com/2013/09/18/the-real-dwp-reveals-the-real-agenda-behind-universal-credit).

[43] Kathleen Hall, 'DWP hits back at criticism over universal credit IT systems', ComputerWeekly.com, 17 September 2012 (www.computerweekly.com/news/2240163346/DWP-hits-back-at-criticism-over-Universal-Credit-IT-systems).

[44] Bryan Glick, 'DWP writes off millions of pounds on universal credit IT, damning NAO report reveals', ComputerWeekly.com, 5 September 2013 (www.computerweekly.com/news/2240204715/DWP-writes-off-millions-of-pounds-on-Universal-Credit-IT-damning-NAO-report-reveals); George Eaton, 'Duncan Smith can't avoid the blame for the universal credit disaster', *New Statesman*, 5 September 2013 (www.newstatesman.com/politics/2013/09/duncan-smith-cant-avoid-blame-universal-credit-disaster).

[45] National Audit Office, *Universal credit: Early progress* (www.nao.org.uk/report/universal-credit-early-progress).

[46] Shiv Malik, 'Universal credit: £120m could be written off to rescue welfare reform', *The Guardian*, 31 October 2013 (www.theguardian.com/politics/2013/oct/31/universal).

[47] Nigel Morris, 'Universal credit scheme faces withering criticism from MPs', *The Independent*, 7 November 2013 (www.independent.co.uk/news/uk/politics/universal-credit-scheme-faces-withering-criticism-from-mps-8925364.html).

[48] Ross Hawkins, 'Universal credit may not hit 2017 deadline, says Duncan Smith', BBC News, 5 December 2013 (www.bbc.co.uk/news/uk-politics-25230158).

[49] Alison Roche, 'Universal credit and "real time information": Uncertainty for low paid workers?', ToUChStone, 9 August 2013 (http://touchstoneblog.org.uk/2013/08/universal-credit-and-real-time-information-uncertainty-for-low-paid-workers); Claire Munro, 'Delays to universal credit cause concern', Scottish Federation of Housing Associations, 5 December 2013 (www.sfha.co.uk/sfha/news/delays-to-universal-credit-cause-concern-sfha).

In addition, by December 2013, it emerged that another impact of the uncertainty was the increased unwillingness of landlords to take on benefits claimants as tenants – the number of landlords prepared to let properties to people on benefits had halved in the preceding three years from 46 to 22 per cent (see http://news.sky.com/story/1179638/landlords-avoid-tenants-on-universal-credit).

[50] Amy Tarr and Dan Finn, *Implementing Universal Credit: Will the reforms improve the service for users?*, York: Joseph Rowntree Foundation (www.jrf.org.uk/sites/files/jrf/universal-credit-benefits-summary.pdf).

[51] Amelia Gentleman, 'Universal Credit: the essential guide', *The Guardian*, 29 April 2013 (www.theguardian.com/society/2013/apr/26/universal-credit-the-essential-guide).

[52] National Housing Federation, *Social tenants' finances and vulnerability to direct payments* (www.housing.org.uk/publications/browse/social-tenants-finances-and-vulnerability-to-direct-payments).

[53] National Housing Federation, 'Impact of welfare reform', Blog (www.housing.org.uk/media/blog/impact-of-welfare-reform).

[54] National Housing Federation, *Impact of welfare reform on housing association tenants – baseline report* (www.housing.org.uk/publications/browse/impact-of-welfare-reform-on-housing-association-tenants-baseline-report).

[55] Social Market Foundation, *Sink or swim? The impact of universal credit*, London (www.smf.co.uk/research/welfare-reform/sink-or-swim-impact-universal-credit/sink-or-swim-the-impact-of-the-universal-credit).

[56] 'The UK faces the "longest, deepest, sustained period of cuts to public services spending at least since World War II", said an economic think tank. It is the first time that six years of consecutive spending cuts will have been endured, the respected Institute for Fiscal Studies (IFS) said', quoted in BBC News, 22 June 2010 (www.bbc.co.uk/news/10393585).

[57] Randeep Ramesh, 'NHS faces unexpected £500m cuts, say hospitals', *The Guardian*, 3 October 2013 (www.theguardian.com/society/2013/oct/03/nhs-cuts-frontline-services-hospitals).

[58] HM Government, *The Coalition: Our programme for government*, London: Cabinet Office, 2010 (www.gov.uk/government/uploads/system/uploads/attachment_data/file/78977/coalition_programme_for_government.pdf).

[59] BBC News, 'Benefits cap of £500 a week rolls out across Britain', 15 July 2013 (www.bbc.co.uk/news/business-23311578).

[60] Martin Bentham, 'Londoners support government's £26,000 benefits cap', *London Evening Standard*, 29 May 2013 (www.standard.co.uk/news/london/londoners-support-governments-26000-benefits-cap-8635771.html).

[61] Rowena Mason, 'Benefits cap does work, Iain Duncan Smith insists', *The Telegraph*, 15 July 2013 (www.telegraph.co.uk/news/politics/10179385/Benefits-cap-does-work-Iain-Duncan-Smith-insists.html); Patrick Butler, 'Benefit cap is failing to achieve its aims, study concludes', *The Guardian*, 23 October 2013 (www.theguardian.com/society/2013/oct/23/benefit-cap-

failing-achieve-aims); Claire Kober, 'The benefit cap just shunts welfare costs on to councils', *The Guardian*, 23 October 2013 (www.theguardian.com/society/2013/oct/23/benefits-cap-welfare-costs-to-councils); Giles Sheldrick, '16,500 find jobs after clamp on benefits', *Express*, 5 October 2013 (www.express.co.uk/news/uk/434431/16-500-find-jobs-after-clamp-on-benefits).

[62] Trade Unions Congress, 'Support for benefit cuts dependent on ignorance, TUC-commissioned poll finds', 2 January 2013 (www.tuc.org.uk/social/tuc-21796-f0.cfm).

[63] For information on tax credits, refer to BBC News, 'Q&A: Tax credits', 5 April 2007 (http://news.bbc.co.uk/1/hi/business/3198211.stm).

[64] Aleks Collingwood and Marguerite Owen, *Monitoring poverty and social exclusion*, York: Joseph Rowntree Foundation (www.jrf.org.uk/work/workarea/monitoring-poverty-and-social-exclusion).

[65] Child Poverty Action Group, *The cost of a child in 2013* (www.cpag.org.uk/content/cost-child-2013).

[66] The Family & Parenting Institute was responding to the Family Matters report from Ipsos MORI in April 2013 (www.familyandparenting.org/news/Press-releases/2013+Press+Releases/Family+Matters+New+Research).

[67] Plans to scrap EMA were announced in October 2010, with the Commons vote on 19 January 2011 resulting in the decision to end the scheme (see www.gov.uk/government/news/plans-to-end-the-education-maintenance-allowance-ema-programme).

[68] 'EMA: Student numbers fall blamed on allowance cut.... Almost half of England's further education colleges have seen a decline in student numbers – with the drop blamed on the scrapping of the Education Maintenance Allowance (EMA)', BBC News, 13 October 2011 (www.bbc.co.uk/news/education-15273410).

[69] Christopher Chantrill, 'The total education spend was around £90bn in 2011' (www.ukpublicspending.co.uk/spending_chart_2002_2022UKb_13c1li111mcn_20t).

[70] *Express*, 'Thousands in "bedroom tax" protest', 24 August 2013 (www.express.co.uk/news/uk/424319/Thousands-in-bedroom-tax-protest).

[71] Anna Edwards, '"Axe the bedroom tax!": Thousands of protesters join demonstrations against levy on spare rooms in council houses', Mail Online, 30 March 2013 (www.dailymail.co.uk/news/article-2301575/Axe-bedroom-tax--Thousands-protesters-join-demonstrations-cut-benefits.html). See also the Anti-Bedroom Tax & Benefit Justice Federation (http://antibedroomtax.org.uk).

[72] BBC News, 'Merseyside hit hard by housing benefit cuts, says study', 5 July 2013 (www.bbc.co.uk/news/uk-england-merseyside-23183352).

[73] www.itv.com/news/update/2013-02-01/two-thirds-of-those-hit-by-bedroom-tax-are-disabled; *Epilepsy Today*, 'Bedroom tax exemptions not enough', 13 March 2013 (www.epilepsy.org.uk/news/news/bedroom-tax-exemptions-not-enough); Chris Mallett, 'Disabled people among 2,300 in Derby hit by "bedroom tax"', *Derby Telegraph*, 20 November 2013 (www.derbytelegraph.co.uk/Disabled-people-2-300-Derby-hit-bedroom-tax/story-20103824-detail/story.html).

[74] Frances Ryan, 'Bedroom tax: pushing those "getting by" over the edge', *New Statesman*, 13 March 2013 (www.newstatesman.com/voices/2013/03/bedroom-tax-pushing-those-getting-by-over-edge).

[75] Roswynne Jones, 'From child of courage to bedroom tax victim', *Mirror*, 10 July 2013 (www.mirror.co.uk/news/uk-news/child-courage-bedroom-tax-victim-2041253).

[76] Citizens Advice, 'Cuts to Housing Benefit if your social housing is too large' (www.adviceguide.org.uk/england/benefits_e/benefits_welfare_benefits_reform_e/housing_benefit_cuts_for_social_housing_tenants_from_april_2013/cuts_to_housing_benefit_if_your_social_housing_is_too_large.htm).

[77] National Housing Federation, 'Bedroom tax' (www.housing.org.uk/policy/welfare-reform/bedroom-tax).

[78] Channel 4 News, '"Bed tax" forces people out of homes', 23 January 2013 (www.channel4.com/news/bed-tax-forces-people-out-of-homes); Emily Dugan, 'Exclusive: 50,000 people are now facing eviction after bedroom tax', *The Independent*, 19 September 2013 (www.independent.co.uk/news/uk/politics/exclusive-50000-people-are-now-facing-eviction-after-bedroom-tax-8825074.html); James Bloodsworth, '1 in 3 council tenants face eviction over bedroom tax', Left Foot Forward, 19 September 2013 (www.leftfootforward.org/2013/09/tenants-face-eviction-bedroom-tax).

[79] Roswynne Jones, '25 reasons your MP must kill David Cameron's bedroom tax', *Mirror*, 12 November 2013 (www.mirror.co.uk/news/uk-news/bedroom-tax-vote-25-reasons-2781904); 'Decline starting to show as cuts hit and debts mount' (www.jrf.org.uk/austerity-liverpool).

[80] Department for Work and Pensions, 'Housing Benefit reform: Removal of the spare bedroom subsidy: fact sheet', 27 February 2013 (www.gov.uk/government/news/housing-benefit-reform-removal-of-the-spare-room-subsidy-fact-sheet).

[81] Because of a dire shortfall of smaller properties in Wales, it was deemed to be harder hit than any other part of the country by the 'Bedroom Tax'; see Dawn Foster, 'Bedroom tax traps Welsh tenants into arrears and misery', *The Guardian*, 20 November 2013 (www.theguardian.com/society/2013/nov/20/bedroom-tax-hardest-hit-wales-uk).

[82] Patrick Collinson, 'Renting – Britain's social scandal that is being ignored', *The Guardian*, 4 January 2014 (www.theguardian.com/money/blog/2014/jan/04/renting-scandal-ignored-politicians?CMP=twt_gu).

[83] Amelia Gentleman, 'Bedroom tax: stress and struggle as benefits clawback hits home', *The Guardian*, 27 November 2013 (www.theguardian.com/society/2013/nov/27/bedroom-tax-benefits-claimants-smaller-homes).

[84] Disabled People Against Cuts (http://dpac.uk.net/tag/bedroom-tax); Tyrone Marshall, 'Human cost of bedroom tax "incalculable" says disabled Nelson man', *Lancashire Telegraph*, 1 August 2013 (www.lancashiretelegraph.co.uk/news/10586868.Human_cost_of_bedroom_tax__incalculable__says_disabled_Nelson_man).

[85] Scottish Federation of Housing Associations, *'Bedroom tax': Early impacts*, June 2013 (www.housingnews.co.uk/images/75158_FINAL%20Bedroom%20Tax%20Early%20Impacts%20June%202013.pdf); Dawn Foster, for *The Guardian*, 20 November 2013, op cit; National Housing Federation, 'Monitoring the impact of welfare reform' (www.housing.org.uk/policy/welfare-reform/monitoring-the-impact-of-welfare-reform).

[86] Daniel Boffey, 'Affordable homes facing demolition because of bedroom tax', *The Guardian*, 10 November 2013 (www.theguardian.com/society/2013/nov/10/bedrooom-tax-affordable-homes-face-demolition).

[87] Patrick Butler's Blog, 'Social housing boss: I'm a big supporter of welfare reform … but the bedroom tax is simply unfair', *The Guardian* (www.theguardian.com/society/patrick-butler-cuts-blog/2013/nov/13/housing-communities).

[88] National Housing Federation, 'New data shows how many North East families are really being hit by the bedroom tax', Press release, 19 November 2013 (www.housing.org.uk/media/press-releases/new-data-shows-how-many-north-east-families-are-really-being-hit-by-the-bed); National Housing Federation, 'New report reveals impact of bedroom tax – 100 days on', Press release, 5 July 2013 (www.housing.org.uk/media/press-releases/new-report-reveals-impact-of-bedroom-tax-100-days-on); Amelia Gentleman, for *The Guardian*, 27 November 2013, op cit; Alan Wilson, '"Bedroom tax" costs Dundee City Council more than £250,000', *The Courier*, 2 July 2013 (www.thecourier.co.uk/news/local/dundee-bedroom-tax-costs-dundee-city-council-more-than-250-000-1.108896).

[89] Shelter Cymru, 'Bedroom tax snapshot', November 2013 (www.sheltercymru.org.uk/bedroom-tax-snapshot-nov-2013).

[90] Steve White, 'Bedroom tax tragedy: Mum faces sending autistic son into care due to charge on room used by respite carer', *Mirror*, 2 May 2013 (www.mirror.co.uk/news/uk-news/bedroom-tax-tragedy-mum-faces-1866215).

[91] 38 Degrees, 'Stop the bedroom tax' (http://you.38degrees.org.uk/petitions/stop-the-bedroom-tax-3).

[92] Rowena Mason, 'Liberal Democrat activists condemn bedroom tax', *The Guardian*, 16 September 2013 (www.theguardian.com/society/2013/sep/16/lib-dem-activists-condemn-bedroom-tax); Vox Political (http://mikesivier.wordpress.com/2013/09/29/rising-tide-of-protest-marks-start-of-tory-conference).

[93] www.netmums.com/coffeehouse/general-coffeehouse-chat-514/news-current-affairs-topical-discussion-12/877671-bedroom-tax-tory-lives-8-bed-country-mansion-all.html

[94] Keir Mudie, 'Loads of room to talk! Bedroom tax Tory Lord Freud lives in eight-bedroom country mansion', *Mirror*, 19 January 2013 (www.mirror.co.uk/news/uk-news/bedroom-tax-tory-lord-freud-1545677).

[95] 'From bedroom to courtroom: challenging the "bedroom tax"', CPAG (www.cpag.org.uk/content/bedroom-courtroom-challenging-'bedroom-tax'); *Herald Scotland*, '"Bedroom tax" doesn't discriminate against disabled people, High Court rules', 30 July 2013 (www.heraldscotland.com/news/home-news/high-court-dismisses-bedroom-tax-discrimination-challenge.1375179905); Sam Adams, 'Bedroom tax: disabled win right to appeal against "unjust" benefits law', *Mirror*, 26 September 2013 (www.mirror.co.uk/news/uk-news/bedroom-tax-disabled-win-right-2305584); Sky News, '"Bedroom tax" victory for disabled woman', 3 October 2013 (http://news.sky.com/story/1149885/bedroom-tax-victory-for-disabled-woman).

[96] Amelia Gentleman, '"Shocking" bedroom tax should be axed, says UN investigator', *The Guardian*, 11 September 2013 (www.theguardian.com/society/2013/sep/11/bedroom-tax-should-be-axed-says-un-investigator).

[97] www.bbc.co.uk/programmes/b039q5dl/live

[98] www.itv.com/news/update/2013-09-26/un-insists-rapporteur-broke-no-rules-over-bedroom-tax

[99] Channel 4 News, 'Bedroom tax row: Grant Shapps v "woman from Brazil"', 11 September 2013 (www.channel4.com/news/bedroom-tax-un-grant-shapps-brazil-row).

[100] Michael Seamark, 'Raquel Rolnik: a dabbler in witchcraft who offered an animal sacrifice to Marx', Mail Online, 12 September 2013 (www.dailymail.co.uk/news/article-2418204/Raquel-Rolnik-A-dabbler-witchcraft-offered-animal-sacrifice-Marx.html).

[101] Theo Usherwood, 'Nick Clegg orders independent study into bedroom tax', *The Independent*, 15 October 2013 (www.independent.co.uk/news/uk/politics/nick-clegg-orders-independent-study-into-bedroom-tax-8881861.html); Diary of a Benefit Scrounger, 'Scrap the bedroom tax – vote in Parliament', 6 November 2013 (http://diaryofabenefitscrounger.blogspot.co.uk/2013/11/scrap-bedroom-tax-vote-in-parliament.html).

[102] www.itv.com/news/2013-09-20/labour-government-would-scrap-controversial-bedroom-tax

[103] See 'Bedroom tax hypocrisy', 14 November 2014 (http://bellacaledonia.org.uk/2013/11/14/bedroom-tax-hypocrisy).

[104] www.publications.parliament.uk/pa/cm201314/cmhansrd/cm131112/debtext/131112-0002.htm

[105] Vox Political (http://mikesivier.wordpress.com/2013/11/13/bedroom-tax-tories-what-they-said-and-why-they-were-wrong).

[106] Rowena Mason, 'Labour criticises Iain Duncan Smith for missing bedroom tax debate', *The Guardian*, 12 November 2013 (www.theguardian.com/society/2013/nov/12/labour-criticises-iain-duncan-smith-missing-bedroom-tax).

[107] Patrick Grafton-Green, 'VIDEO: Bob Stewart "sleeps" in parliament during bedroom tax debate', *Oxford Mail*, 13 November 2013 (www.oxfordmail.co.uk/news/10805292.VIDEO__Bob_Stewart__sleeps__in_parliament_during_bedroom_tax_debate/?ref=rc).

[108] Samantha Lewis, 'St Albans MP clarifies stance on "bedroom tax" after comments cause fury', *The Herts Advertiser*, 15 November 2013 (www.hertsad.co.uk/news/st_albans_mp_clarifies_stance_on_bedroom_tax_after_comments_cause_fury_1_3007631).

[109] Jessica Best, 'Live: Bedroom tax protest and debate as Labour calls vote on controversial policy', *Mirror*, 12 November 2013 (www.mirror.co.uk/news/uk-news/live-bedroom-tax-protest-debate-2783462).

Chapter Three

[1] BBC News, 'Vince Cable backs Church plans to "compete" with Wonga', 25 July 2013 (www.bbc.co.uk/news/business-23433955).

[2] Jacob Rees-Mogg, 'Why I support Justin Welby's battle with Wonga', *The Telegraph*, 30 July 2013 (www.telegraph.co.uk/news/politics/10211028/Why-I-support-Justin-Welbys-battle-with-Wonga.html); Brian Milligan, 'Payday lenders bite back: "Don't call us loan sharks"', BBC News, 23 September 2013 (www.bbc.co.uk/news/business-24032952); 'Four in every five people taking out payday loans say they are forced to do so to buy food', from Simon Read, 'Most payday loans are used for buying food', *The Independent*, 30 September 2013 (www.independent.co.uk/news/uk/home-news/most-payday-loans-are-used-for-buying-food-8849785.html).

[3] Cole Moreton, 'Justin Welby's Wonga revelation', *The Telegraph*, 28 July 2013 (www.telegraph.co.uk/news/religion/10206098/Justin-Welbys-Wonga-revelation.html).

---

[4] Steve Doughty, 'Ten-year wait for Welby's Wonga: Archbishop admits Church's rival loan company will not be ready for a decade', Mail Online, 14 August 2013 (www.dailymail.co.uk/news/article-2392433/Wait-Justin-Welbys-Wonga-Archbishop-admits-churchs-rival-loan-company-ready-decade.html).

[5] BBC News, 25 July 2013, op cit.

[6] Jason Beattie, 'Payday loans summit slammed as sham as Government rules out capping interest rates', *Mirror*, 1 July 2013 (www.mirror.co.uk/money/city-news/payday-loans-summit-slammed-sham-2014078).

[7] Martin Lewis, 'Dear Archbishop ... why I disagree with you over Wonga', *The Telegraph*, 30 July 2013 (www.telegraph.co.uk/finance/personalfinance/borrowing/10209475/Martin-Lewis-Dear-Archbishop...why-I-disagree-with-you-over-Wonga.html).

[8] Adam Uren, '"All loan providers should spell out the costs in pounds and pence": Payday lenders' plea to avoid "unfair" criticism', ThisisMoney.co.uk, 18 September 2013 (www.thisismoney.co.uk/money/cardsloans/article-2424482/Payday-lenders-plea-avoid-unfair-criticism-APR-rates.html).

[9] Graham Hiscott, 'Payday loans: 15 lenders leave market ahead of deadline to prove practices are up to scratch', *Mirror*, 30 July 2013 (www.mirror.co.uk/money/city-news/payday-loans-15-lenders-leave-2105913).

[10] Citizens Advice, 'Citizens Advice exposes payday lenders' failings as OFT closes in on unscrupulous lenders', Press release, 28 May 2013 (www.citizensadvice.org.uk/index/pressoffice/press_index/press_20130528.htm).

[11] In October 2013 the practice of rolling over was challenged head on, despite industry defiance, with tougher controls proposed. See Hilary Osborne, 'Payday lenders: FCA proposes tougher controls on adverts and rollovers', *The Guardian*, 3 October 2013 (www.theguardian.com/business/2013/oct/03/payday-lenders-fca-tougher-controls-adverts-rollovers).

[12] Citizens Advice, 'Payday loans' (www.citizensadvice.org.uk/index/campaigns/current_campaigns/paydayloans.htm).

[13] *Halifax Courier*, 'Councils tackle "predatory" payday lenders', 4 September 2013 (www.halifaxcourier.co.uk/news/business/business-news/councils-tackle-predatory-payday-lenders-1-6011266).

[14] Will Dahlgreen, 'Time's up for payday lenders', YouGov, 1 August 2013 (http://yougov.co.uk/news/2013/08/01/times-up-payday-lenders).

[15] Patrick Collinson and Hilary Osborne, 'Wonga joins ranks of top UK lenders', *The Guardian*, 3 September 2013 (www.theguardian.com/business/2013/sep/03/wonga-joins-ranks-top-uk-lenders).

[16] Citizens Advice, Press release, 28 May 2013, op cit.

[17] Patrick Collinson and Hilary Osborne, for *The Guardian*, 3 September 2013, op cit.

[18] The OFT published *Review of high-cost credit* in June 2010 (www.oft.gov.uk/shared_oft/reports/consumer_credit/High-cost-credit-review/OFT1232.pdf).

[19] Graham Hiscott, for the *Mirror*, 30 July 2013, op cit.

[20] 'Take action against legal loan sharks', The People's Assembly, 7 September 2013 (http://thepeoplesassembly.org.uk/event/take-action-against-legal-loan-sharks).

[21] Patrick Butler, 'Carers facing debt and eviction because of bedroom tax – study', *The Guardian*, 10 July 2013 (www.theguardian.com/society/2013/jul/10/carers-debt-eviction-bedroom-tax?CMP=twt_gu).

[22] Citizens Advice, 'Consumers need assurance energy bills will be tackled', Press release, 30 November 2013 (www.citizensadvice.org.uk/index/pressoffice/press_index/press_20131129.htm).

[23] Barnardo's, *Priced out: The plight of low income families and young people living in fuel poverty*, February 2012 (www.barnardos.org.uk/pricedoutreport.pdf).

[24] Jamie Doward, 'Energy bills rise by 37% in three years', *The Guardian*, 16 November 2013 (www.theguardian.com/money/2013/nov/16/energy-prices-rise).

[25] Jennifer Rankin and Patrick Butler, 'Winter deaths rose by almost a third in 2012-13', *The Guardian*, 26 November 2013 (www.theguardian.com/uk-news/2013/nov/26/winter-deaths-rose-third).

[26] Citizens Advice, 'Energy firms profits as people face heat or eat struggle', Press release, 25 November 2013 (www.citizensadvice.org.uk/index/pressoffice/press_index/press_office-newpage-20131125.htm).

[27] BBC News, 'Ed Miliband: Government's energy plan "smoke and mirrors"', 2 December 2013 (www.bbc.co.uk/news/uk-politics-25178726).

[28] Tom Bawden, '800,000 people "lifted" out of fuel poverty – by redefining it', *The Independent*, 2 December 2013 (www.independent.co.uk/news/uk/politics/800000-people-lifted-out-offuel-poverty--by-redefining-it-8976232.html).

[29] See www.nidirect.gov.uk/changes-to-the-social-fund

[30] Sam Royston and Laura Rodrigues, *Nowhere to turn? Changes to emergency support*, The Children's Society, 2013 (www.childrenssociety.org.uk/sites/default/files/tcs/nowhere-to-turn-final.pdf).

[31] See also her article on the arguments she raised in the Today Programme at Ann Pettifor, 'No, this is not the road to recovery. It's the road to Wongaland', *The Guardian*, 16 August 2013 (www.theguardian.com/commentisfree/2013/aug/16/not-road-to-recovery-but-wongaland).

[32] Sky News, 'Debt time bomb? New record sum "on tick"', 29 November 2013 (http://news.sky.com/story/1175279/debt-time-bomb-new-record-sum-on-tick).

[33] BBC News, 'North East worst for insolvencies', 12 July 2013 (www.bbc.co.uk/news/business-23286275).

[34] Heather Stewart, 'Bank of England: consumers turn to loans, credit cards and overdrafts', *The Guardian*, 30 August 2013 (www.theguardian.com/business/2013/aug/30/bank-of-england-consumers-turn-to-loans-credit-cards-overdrafts).

[35] BBC News, 'Bailiffs called in by councils for 1.8m debts, charity warns', 22 August 2013 (www.bbc.co.uk/news/uk-23770628).

[36] The Centre for Social Justice, *Maxed out: Serious personal debt in Britain*, November 2013 (www.centreforsocialjustice.org.uk/UserStorage/pdf/Pdf%20reports/CSJ_Serious_Debt_report_WEB_final.pdf).

[37] The Money Advice Service (www.moneyadviceservice.org.uk/en/campaigns/uk-money-habits-study).

[38] Terry Macalister, 'Energy firms expected to increase prices by 8%', *The Guardian*, 20 September 2013 (www.theguardian.com/money/2013/sep/20/energy-firms-increase-prices).

[39] The Money Advice Trust gained information under the Freedom of Information Act to show how councils were overusing bailiffs as a means of recovering Council Tax arrears. 'Local councils across England and Wales referred debts to bailiffs on 1.8 million occasions in the last year, new research has found.... One of the most common debts to be referred to bailiffs was council tax arrears. In the first half of last year the charity's National Debtline took over 20,000 calls for help regarding council tax – an increase of 61pc on five years ago, and 13pc from last year', quoted in Sophie Christie, 'Councils referred 1.8m debts to bailiffs last year', *The Telegraph*, 22 August 2013 (www.telegraph.co.uk/finance/personalfinance/borrowing/10254306/Councils-referred-1.8m-debts-to-bailiffs-last-year.html).

[40] Austerity Uncovered, *Newcastle to Stockton: Drowning in debt*, 22 June 2013 (http://austerityuncovered.org/newcastle-to-stockton-drowning-in-debt).

[41] BBC News, 'Manchester loan sharks jailed after preying on young mothers', 24 September 2013 (www.bbc.co.uk/news/uk-england-manchester-24205193).

Chapter Four

[1] www.gingerbread.org.uk/content.aspx?CategoryID=1901

[2] Daniel Martin, 'The poor should take risks to get off benefit, says welfare minister as he slams "dreadful system that needs to become predictable"', Mail

Online, 23 November 2013 (www.dailymail.co.uk/news/article-2237199/ The-poor-risks-benefit-says-welfare-minister-slams-dreadful-system.html).

[3] Ed Monk and ThisisMoney.co.uk, 'The jobs scramble hot-spots: 55 applicants chase every vacancy in Hull but employers struggle to find candidates in Cambridge', 27 December 2012 (www.thisismoney.co.uk/money/news/article-2253607/55-applicants-chase-vacancy-Hull-employers-struggle-candidates-Cambridge.html#ixzz2hs7OrNsq).

[4] http://doleanimators.wordpress.com/the-research/and-more-research

[5] New Economics Foundation, *Mythbusters: Strivers versus skivers*, 11 April 2013 (www.neweconomics.org/blog/entry/mythbusters-strivers-versus-skivers). See also Tracy Shildrick et al, *Are 'cultures of worklessness' passed down the generations?*, York: Joseph Rowntree Foundation, 13 December 2012, which found the 'culture of worklessness' to be a myth (www.jrf.org.uk/publications/cultures-of-worklessness).

[6] Owen Jones, *Chavs: The demonization of the working class*, 2nd edition, London and New York: Verso Books, May 2012.

[7] Jenna Sloan, 'Help us stop £1.5bn benefits scroungers', *The Sun*, 12 August 2010 (www.thesun.co.uk/sol/homepage/features/3091717/The-Sun-declares-war-on-Britains-benefits-culture.html).

[8] BBC News, 'Billions in benefits go unclaimed, DWP figures show', 23 February 2012 (www.bbc.co.uk/news/business-17139088); Department for Work and Pensions, 'Income-related benefits: estimates of take-up', 18 June 2013 (www.gov.uk/government/organisations/department-for-work-pensions/series/income-related-benefits-estimates-of-take-up--2).

[9] *Daily Mail*, 'The only way is easy street: How Essex town of Brentwood is skiving capital of Britain', Mail Online, 21 April 2012 (www.dailymail.co.uk/news/article-2132997/The-skiving-capitals-Britain-Brentwood-tops-list-55-reassessed-incapacity-benefit-claimants-fit-work.html).

[10] Patrick Butler, 'Baskers-gate: time for the media abuse of public servants to stop', *The Guardian*, 15 November 2010 (www.theguardian.com/society/patrick-butler-cuts-blog/2010/nov/15/baskers-time-for-abuse-to-stop).

[11] George Osborne, 'George Osborne's speech to the Conservative conference: full text', *New Statesman*, 8 October 2012 (www.newstatesman.com/blogs/politics/2012/10/george-osbornes-speech-conservative-conference-full-text).

[12] Neil Tweedie, 'Benefits culture: Six children and £675 a week...', *The Daily Telegraph*, 8 October 2010 (www.telegraph.co.uk/news/uknews/8052059/Benefits-culture-Six-children-and-675-a-week....html); Steve Doughty, 'Poor white children fall further behind: Benefits culture is blamed for failures at school', *Daily Mail*, 3 September 2013 (www.dailymail.co.uk/news/article-2409433/Poor-white-children-fall-Benefits-culture-blamed-failures-school.html); *Daily*

Express, 'Is Britain's benefits culture a disgrace?', 29 February 2012 (www.express.co.uk/comment/haveyoursay/305177/Is-Britain-s-benefits-culture-a-disgrace).

[13] Dan Milmo and Hélène Mulholland, 'Osborne has insulted a million young people, says TUC leader in waiting', *The Guardian*, 19 October 2012 (www.theguardian.com/politics/2012/oct/19/osborne-insult-million-young-people-tuc-lead-in-waiting).

[14] Jane Atkinson, 'I'm mother of all scroungers', *The Sun*, 10 February 2013 (www.thesun.co.uk/sol/homepage/news/4787421/Scrounging-mum-admits-she-deliberately-has-kids-to-avoid-getting-a-job.html).

[15] David Cameron, 'Crazy situation where you earn more on benefits than you do at work', *The Sun*, 7 April 2013 (www.thesun.co.uk/sol/homepage/news/politics/4876776/Crazy-situation-where-you-earn-more-on-benefits-than-you-do-at-work-ends-NOW.html).

[16] David Cameron, 'Crazy situation where you earn more on benefits than you do at work', *The Sun*, 7 April 2013 (www.thesun.co.uk/sol/homepage/news/politics/4876776/Crazy-situation-where-you-earn-more-on-benefits-than-you-do-at-work-ends-NOW.html).

[17] Simon Duffy, *A fair society? How the cuts target disabled people*, The Centre for Welfare Reform, January 2013 (www.centreforwelfarereform.org/library/type/pdfs/a-fair-society1.html).

[18] Ned Simons, 'George Osborne branded "sick" for linking Philpott case to benefit reforms', *The Huffington Post UK*, 4 April 2013 (www.huffingtonpost.co.uk/2013/04/04/george-osborne-mick-philpot_n_3014718.html).

[19] Hayley Dixon, 'Unemployed Mick Philpott on £100,000 a year salary', *The Telegraph*, 4 April 2013 (www.telegraph.co.uk/news/uknews/crime/9970619/Unemployed-Mick-Philpott-on-100000-a-year-salary.html).

[20] From 7 January 2013, Child Benefit was reduced gradually, through the self-assessment tax system, for families with one person earning more than £50,000. In addition to proposals to reduce the benefit cap further from the limit of £26,000 in benefits for a family, the Tory chair, Grant Shapps, also suggested capping Child Benefit for jobless couples at two children. See James Chapman, 'No benefit for your third child if you're on the dole: Tories unveil controversial welfare plan', Mail Online, 15 July 2013 (www.dailymail.co.uk/news/article-2364718/No-benefit-child-youre-dole-Tories-unveil-controversial-welfare-plan.html#ixzz2hz3QDEA8).

[21] Jason Groves, 'Osborne was right about Philpott, says Cameron, as storm rages on over benefits', Mail Online, 6 April 2013 (www.dailymail.co.uk/news/article-2304804/Mick-Philpott-benefits-culture-David-Cameron-backs-George-Osborne-saying-arson-case-raises-questions-welfare-lifestyle-choice.html).

[22] Peter Walker, 'Government using increasingly loaded language in welfare debate', *The Guardian*, 5 April 2013 (www.theguardian.com/society/2013/apr/05/goverment-loaded-language-welfare).

[23] Ambrose McCarron and Liam Purcell, *The blame game must stop: Challenging the stigmatisation of people experiencing poverty*, Church Action on Poverty, January 2013 (www.church-poverty.org.uk/stigma/report/blamegamereport).

[24] Among too many examples to list here: Melanie Phillips, 'It's not just absent fathers, Mr Cameron. Family breakdown is driven by single mothers on benefits', *Daily Mail*, 20 June 2011 (www.dailymail.co.uk/debate/article-2005677/Family-breakdown-driven-single-mothers-benefits-absent-fathers.html#ixzz2hz7DxgyH).

[25] Disability Rights UK, *Press portrayal of disabled people: A rise in hostility fuelled by austerity?*, August 2012 (www.disabilityrightsuk.org/sites/default/files/pdf/disabilitypresscoverage.pdf).

[26] Ben Riley-Smith, 'Disability hate crime: is "benefit scrounger" abuse to blame?', *The Guardian*, 14 August 2012 (www.theguardian.com/society/2012/aug/14/disability-hate-crime-benefit-scrounger-abuse).

[27] Inclusion London, *Bad news for disabled people: How the newspapers are reporting disability* (www.inclusionlondon.co.uk/domains/inclusionlondon.co.uk/local/meda/downloads/bad_news_for_disabled_people_pdf.pdf).

[28] www.gov.uk/government/publications/fraud-and-error-in-the-benefit-system-preliminary-201213-estimates

[29] Scope, 'Deteriorating attitudes towards disabled people', 15 May 2011 (www.scope.org.uk/news/attitudes-towards-disabled-people-survey).

[30] Channel 4 News, 'Government majority cut in "bedroom tax" debate', 12 November 2013 (www.channel4.com/news/bedroom-tax-labour-lib-dems-vote-commons).

[31] Rafael Behr, 'Shirkers v strivers', *New Statesman*, 29 November 2012 (www.newstatesman.com/politics/politics/2012/11/shirkers-v-strivers).

[32] http://order-order.com/2013/01/09/watch-liam-byrne-caught-on-camera-attacking-shirkers

[33] www.youtube.com/watch?v=tH-OzhyNIQs

[34] Richard Seymour, 'BBC austerity survey: why the public is wrong this time', *The Guardian*, 9 October 2013 (www.theguardian.com/commentisfree/2013/oct/09/bbc-austerity-survey-public-wrong-services).

[35] Zoe Williams, 'Skivers v strivers: the argument that pollutes people's minds', *The Guardian*, 9 January 2013 (www.theguardian.com/politics/2013/jan/09/skivers-v-strivers-argument-pollutes). See also the open letter to Rachel Reeves, new Shadow Secretary for Work and Pensions, in the *New Statesman*, 15 October

2013 (www.newstatesman.com/politics/2013/10/open-letter-rachel-reeves-being-tough-welfare-wont-work-labour).

[36] Zoe Williams, op cit.

[37] Ruth Patrick, 'This is how people on out-of-work benefits actually feel', *The Guardian*, 3 April 2013 (www.theguardian.com/commentisfree/2013/apr/03/how-people-on-benefits-feel).

[38] Tracy Shildrick, Robert MacDonald, Colin Webster and Kayleigh Garthwaite, *Poverty and insecurity: Life in low-pay, no-pay Britain*, Bristol: Policy Press (www.policypress.co.uk/display.asp?K=9781847429100#sthash.NLc3sBzm.dpuf).

[39] www.cpag.org.uk/people-like-us

[40] Ipsos MORI, *Perceptions are not reality*, 9 July 2013 (www.ipsos-mori.com/researchpublications/researcharchive/3188/Perceptions-are-not-reality-the-top-10-we-get-wrong.aspx).

[41] Amelia Gentleman, 'What the welfare cuts mean for us: "The feeling of dread never goes away"', *The Guardian*, 16 December 2013 (www.theguardian.com/society/2013/dec/16/welfare-cuts-government-coalition-benefits).

[42] David Cameron's welfare speech in full, 25 June 2012 (www.telegraph.co.uk/news/politics/david-cameron/9354163/David-Camerons-welfare-speech-in-full.html).

[43] Bobby Duffy, 'The perils of perception', *The Huffington Post UK*, 9 July 2013 (www.huffingtonpost.co.uk/bobby-duffy/ipsos-mori-perils-of-perception_b_3567206.html).

[44] Anna Coote and Sarah Lyall, Mythbusters, *Strivers versus skivers: the workless are worthless*, New Economics Foundation and Tax Justice Network, April 2013 (http://dnwssx4l7gl7s.cloudfront.net/nefoundation/default/page/-/images/publications/Strivers%20vs.%20skivers_final.pdf).

[45] http://diaryofabenefitscrounger.blogspot.co.uk

[46] Sue Marsh, 'Disgraceful! The myth that criminals are claiming sickness benefits', *The Guardian*, 24 July 2012 (www.theguardian.com/commentisfree/2012/jul/24/myth-criminals-sickness-benefits).

[47] Jack Monroe, 'Middle-class people are the benefit fraudsters it's ok to like', *The Guardian*, 9 October 2013 (www.theguardian.com/commentisfree/2013/oct/09/middle-class-people-child-benefit-fraudsters).

[48] Amy Feltham, 'Don't judge those on benefits', Young Minds, 12 July 2013 (www.youngminds.org.uk/news/blog/1522_dont_judge_those_on_benefits).

[49] Amelia Gentleman, 'Buy now, regret later? The secret of BrightHouse's success', *The Guardian*, 4 October 2013 (www.theguardian.com/society/2013/oct/04/brighthouse-consumer-poverty-high-street?CMP=twt_gu).

[50] Andrew Collins, 'Poor show: TV's new poverty porn', *The Guardian*, 23 August 2013 (www.theguardian.com/tv-and-radio/2013/aug/23/tv-poverty-porn?CMP=twt_gu).

[51] Abigail Scott Paul, '"Poverty porn"? Who benefits from documentaries on recession Britain?', Joseph Rowntree Foundation blog, 23 August 2013 (www.jrf.org.uk/blog/2013/08/poverty-porn-who-benefits-britain).

[52] Gary Rae, 'Language is a weapon used to make "others" of people in poverty', Joseph Rowntree Foundation blog, 4 February 2013 (www.jrf.org.uk/blog/2013/02/language-people-poverty).

[53] Ned Simons, 'Tory MP admits party conference slogan "excludes people"', *The Huffington Post UK*, 30 September 2013 (www.huffingtonpost.co.uk/2013/09/29/conservative-party-2013_n_4014021.html).

[54] Richard Seymour, 'Why "hardworking people" are at the heart of Conservative mythmaking', *The Guardian*, 3 October 2013 (www.theguardian.com/commentisfree/2013/oct/03/hardworking-people-conservative-mythmaking).

[55] www.conservativepartyconference.org.uk/Speeches/2013_Iain_Duncan_Smith.aspx

[56] BBC News, 'George Osborne extends "work for benefit" for jobless', 30 September 2013 (www.bbc.co.uk/news/uk-politics-24327470).

[57] Patrick Wintour, 'Conservatives to withdraw key benefits from unemployed under-25s', *The Guardian*, 2 October 2013 (www.theguardian.com/politics/2013/oct/02/conservatives-housing-benefit-jobseekers-allowance-unemployed-under-25s).

[58] www.conservativepartyconference.org.uk/Speeches/2013_David_Cameron.aspx

[59] Tom Newton Dunn, Kevin Schofield and Emily Ashton, 'Earn or learn', *The Sun*, 3 October 2013 (www.thesun.co.uk/sol/homepage/news/politics/5176556/David-Cameron-tells-jobless-youth-Earn-or-learn.html); Simon Walters, 'Cameron to axe housing benefit for feckless under 25s as he declares war on welfare culture', Mail Online, 23 June 2012 (www.dailymail.co.uk/news/article-2163773/David-Cameron-axe-housing-benefits-feckless-25s-declares-war-welfare-culture.html#ixzz2hxo8aWaB).

[60] Citizens Advice, 'Welfare system must not be used to punish the long-term unemployed', Press release, 30 September 2013 (www.citizensadvice.org.uk/index/pressoffice/press_index/press_office-newpage-20130930.ht).

[61] John Wight, 'The continual hounding of the unemployed reveals that Britain is governed by a gang of rich sociopaths', *The Huffington Post UK*, 1 October 2013 (www.huffingtonpost.co.uk/john-wight/uk-unemployment_b_4021525.html).

[62] Poverty and Social Exclusion, *Breadline Britain 1983* (www.poverty.ac.uk/pse-research/past-uk-research/breadline-britain-1983).

[63] Poverty and Social Exclusion, *Breadline Britain 1990* (www.poverty.ac.uk/pse-research/past-uk-research/breadline-britain-1990).

[64] See *Public attitudes to poverty and welfare 1983-2011* using British Social Attitudes Survey data (www.natcen.ac.uk/study/public-attitudes-to-poverty-and-welfare); see also Claudia Wood et al, *'The first step towards tackling poverty is understanding it better': Poverty in perspective*, London: Demos, 2012 (www.demos.co.uk/files/Poverty_-_final.pdf?1354014565).

[65] National Centre for Social Research, *One queen, three recessions, five prime ministers: 30 years of insight into a changing Britain*, 30th British Social Attitudes report, 2013 (www.bsa-30.natcen.ac.uk).

[66] Claudia Wood et al, op cit; Ipsos MORI, *Generations*, (www.ipsos-mori-generations.com/Assets/Docs/ipsos-mori-the-generation-frame.pdf?utm_source=website&utm_medium=link&utm_campaign=generationsreport).

[67] Ally Fogg, 'Benefits "scroungers"? Britain isn't convinced', *The Guardian*, 10 September 2013 (www.theguardian.com/commentisfree/2013/sep/10/benefits-scroungers-british-social-attitudes).

[68] www.whobenefits.org.uk

[69] Maev Kennedy, 'Iain Banks: squeeze a Tory, Blairite or Lib Dem and Thatcherite pus oozes out', *The Guardian*, 14 June 2013 (www.theguardian.com/books/2013/jun/14/iain-banks-tory-thatcher-blair).

Chapter Five

[1] The New Labour government introduced the New Deal welfare-to-work programmes in 1998, which were the precursor to the Coalition's Work Programme. These were targeted at different groups (for example, young people aged 18-24, lone parents, people with disabilities). In addition to the stated aim of helping people back to work by providing training, volunteering opportunities and work placements to the long-term unemployed, the New Deal introduced sanctions for the first time. The government suspended benefits for those who refused an offer of work, or refused to participate in the New Deal (see Claudia Wood et al, *The first step towards tackling poverty is understanding it better*, Demos, 2012, www.demos.co.uk/files/Poverty_-_final.pdf?1354014565).

[2] 'At the beginning of 2013, police numbers were the lowest for 11 years, with 11,500 job losses since the Coalition came to power', quoted in Alan Travis, 'Number of police officers drops to lowest level for 11 years', *The Guardian*, 31 January 2013 (www.theguardian.com/uk/2013/jan/31/number-police-officers-drops-lowest).

[3] See the Taxpayers Alliance report from 12 October 2010, *Council savings: Unnecessary jobs*, which identifies political advisers, European officers, diversity

officers and climate change officers as positions to be cut (www.taxpayersalliance.com/unnecessaryjobs.pdf).

[4] Office for National Statistics, 'Public sector employment, Q2 2013', Statistical Bulletin, 11 September 2013 (www.ons.gov.uk/ons/dcp171778_325726.pdf).

[5] MSN Money, 'GMB: 600,000 public sector jobs cut', 1 October 2013 (http://money.uk.msn.com/news/gmb-600000-public-sector-jobs-cut).

[6] Katie Allen, 'Public sector austerity measures hitting women hardest', *The Guardian*, 1 July 2013 (www.theguardian.com/business/2013/jul/01/public-sector-austerity-measures-women).

[7] http://blackactivistsrisingagainstcuts.blogspot.co.uk

[8] Ibid.

[9] Office for National Statistics, 'The latest on the UK labour market', 11 September 2013 (www.ons.gov.uk/ons/rel/lms/labour-market-statistics/september-2013/sty-employment.html).

[10] Hannah Aldridge, Peter Kenway, Tom MacInnes and Anushree Parekh, *Monitoring poverty and social exclusion 2012*, York: Joseph Rowntree Foundation, 26 November 2012 (www.jrf.org.uk/publications/monitoring-poverty-2012).

[11] BBC News, 'UK jobless total falls by 18,000 to 2.49m', 16 October 2013 (www.bbc.co.uk/news/business-24547749); Jacob Mohun, 'Latest employment figures: what's really going on with the labour market?', New Economics Foundation Blog, 15 August 2013 (www.neweconomics.org/blog/entry/latest-employment-figures-whats-really-going-on-with-the-labour-market).

[12] Institute for Fiscal Studies (www.ifs.org.uk); Will Hutton, 'Blame austerity, not old people, for the plight of Britain's young', *The Guardian*, 23 June 2013 (www.theguardian.com/commentisfree/2013/jun/23/blame-austerity-old-plight-young-hutton).

[13] Ami Sedghi, 'Youth unemployment across the OECD: how does the UK compare?', *The Guardian*, 16 May 2012 (www.theguardian.com/news/datablog/2012/may/16/youth-unemployment-europe-oecd).

[14] Chartered Institute for Personnel Development, 'Latest figures show strong jobs growth again – but the numbers of young and long-term unemployed remain worryingly high', Press release, 16 October 2013 (www.cipd.co.uk/pressoffice/press-releases/latest-figures-show-strong-jobs-growth-again-but-numbers-young-long-term-unemployed-remain-worryingly-high-161013.aspx).

[15] Ibid.

[16] Department for Work and Pensions, 'Youth Contract' (www.dwp.gov.uk/youth-contract).

[17] George Eaton, 'Clegg's Youth Contract flops as just 4,690 jobs are delivered', *New Statesman*, 22 July 2013 (www.newstatesman.com/politics/2013/07/cleggs-youth-contract-flops-just-4690-jobs-are-delivered).

[18] Rowena Mason, 'Coalition's £1bn youth deal failing to create permanent jobs, Labour claims', *The Guardian*, 13 August 2013 (www.theguardian.com/politics/2013/aug/13/coalition-youth-contract-permanent-jobs?CMP=twt_fd).

[19] Gianluca Mezzofiore and Ian Silvera, 'Greek youth unemployment hits 55%, as labour market buckles', *International Business Times*, 10 October 2013 (www.ibtimes.co.uk/articles/512866/20131010/greece-unemployment-jobs-european-union-elstat.htm); on Spain, see Stephen Burgen, 'Spain youth unemployment reaches record 56.1%', *The Guardian*, 30 August 2013 (www.theguardian.com/business/2013/aug/30/spain-youth-unemployment-record-high).

[20] www.keele.ac.uk/depts/so/youthchron/Education/9197educ.htm

[21] BBC News, 'UK wages decline among worst in Europe', 11 August 2013 (www.bbc.co.uk/news/business-23655605).

[22] Becky Barrow, 'Public sector pay falls for first time in 12 years: BUT it's STILL higher than in the private sector', Mail Online, 16 October 2013 (www.dailymail.co.uk/news/article-2463668/Public-sector-pay-falls-time-12-years-But-STILL-higher-private-sector.html).

[23] www.theguardian.com/business/economics-blog/2013/oct/16/employment-growing-wage-slaves-ons-prices-pay

[24] Randeep Ramesh, 'Council funding cuts force care firms to pay less than the minimum wage', *The Guardian*, 22 October 2013 (www.theguardian.com/society/2013/oct/22/council-funding-cuts-care-homes-minimum-wage).

[25] King's College London, 'Less than minimum wage for some care workers', 5 October 2011 (www.kcl.ac.uk/newsevents/news/newsrecords/2011/10October/Nearly-ten-per-cent-care-workers-paid-less-than-minimum-wage.aspx).

[26] See www.livingwage.org.uk

[27] KPMG, 'One in five UK workers paid less than the Living Wage', News release, 29 October 2012 (www.kpmg.com/uk/en/issuesandinsights/articlespublications/newsreleases/pages/one-in-five-uk-workers-paid-less-than-the-living-wage.aspx).

[28] Darren Devine, 'Wales needs to create 32,000 jobs to reach pre-recession employment levels', Wales Online, 14 August 2013 (www.walesonline.co.uk/news/wales-news/wales-jobs-gap-now-32000-5697185). David Clegg, 'Scotland needs more than 100,000 new jobs for employment to get back to pre-recession levels', *Daily Record*, 12 August 2013 (www.dailyrecord.co.uk/news/politics/scotland-needs-more-100000-new-2155250).

[29] An October 2013 report from the New Policy Institute, *London's poverty profile*, found that more that a quarter of Londoners were living in poverty (www.bbc. co.uk/news/uk-england-london-24517391).

[30] Resolution Foundation, 'Zero hours contracts see workers earn 40 per cent less finds new report', Press release, 25 June 2013 (www.resolutionfoundation. org/press/2013/Jun/25/zero-hours-contracts-see-workers-earn-40-cent-less).

[31] Phillip Inman, 'Zero-hour contracts: what are they?', *The Guardian*, 30 July 2013 (www.theguardian.com/money/2013/jul/30/zero-hours-contracts-explained).

[32] Michelle Stevens, 'One million workers on zero hours contracts, finds CIPD study', 5 August 2013 (www.cipd.co.uk/pm/peoplemanagement/b/weblog/ archive/2013/08/05/one-million-workers-on-zero-hours-contracts-finds-cipd-study.aspx).

[33] Simon Neville, 'ONS to change method of calculating zero-hours contracts', *The Guardian*, 22 August 2013 (www.theguardian.com/uk-news/2013/aug/22/ ons-zero-hours-contracts).

[34] Adam Withnall, 'Buckingham Palace employs summer staff on "zero-hours" contracts', *The Independent*, 31 July 2013 (www.independent.co.uk/news/ uk/home-news/buckingham-palace-employs-summer-staff-on-zerohours-contracts-8739830.html).

[35] Asa Bennett, 'Ministers have "heads in the sand" over zero-hours contracts spread, warn critics', *The Huffington Post UK*, 2 October 2013 (www. huffingtonpost.co.uk/2013/10/02/zero-hours-contracts-_n_4028635.html).

[36] 'Zero hours contracts fuels life of "permanent uncertainty" and could perpetuate unemployment', *The Huffington Post UK*, 25 June 2013 (www. huffingtonpost.co.uk/2013/06/25/zero-hours-contract_n_3494124.html).

[37] BBC News, 'Viewpoints: Are zero-hours contracts exploitative?', 9 September 2013 (www.bbc.co.uk/news/uk-24017011).

[38] Tracy Shildrick et al, 'Are "cultures of worklessness" passed down the generations?', JRF Report, December 2012 (www.jrf.org.uk/publications/ cultures-of-worklessness).

[39] 'Iain Duncan Smith outlines plan for "radical" welfare reform', *The Telegraph*, 27 May 2010 (www.telegraph.co.uk/news/politics/conservative/7770990/ Iain-Duncan-Smith-outlines-plan-for-radical-welfare-reform.html).

[40] Tracy Shildrick et al, *Poverty and insecurity: Life in low-pay, no-pay Britain*, Bristol: Policy Press, 2012. For more information on the mechanics of the Work Programme, download the summary from the Department for Work and Pensions at www.gov.uk/government/uploads/system/uploads/attachment_data/ file/49884/the-work-programme.pdf

[41] Ned Simons, 'Work Programme cost more jobs than it has created, say MPs', *The Huffington Post UK*, 22 February 2013 (www.huffingtonpost.co.uk/2013/02/21/work-programme-cost-more-_n_2733808.html).

[42] www.bbc.co.uk/news/uk-19822669

[43] David Blanchflower, 'Why Osborne's crackpot jobs policy will not work', *The Independent*, 6 October 2013 (www.independent.co.uk/voices/comment/why-osbornes-crackpot-jobs-policy-will-not-work-8862395.html).

[44] National Audit Office, *The introduction of the Work Programme*, 2012 (www.nao.org.uk/report/the-introduction-of-the-work-programme).

[45] For the full Public Accounts Committee Report go to: www.parliament.uk/business/committees/committees-a-z/commons-select/public-accounts-committee/news/work-programme/

[46] Steven Swinford, '£5bn Work Programme "worse than doing nothing"', *The Telegraph*, 27 June 2013 (www.telegraph.co.uk/news/politics/spending-review/10146659/5bn-Work-Programme-worse-than-doing-nothing.html).

[47] Channel 4 News, 'FactCheck: The Work Programme is improving – but it still fails the sick and disabled', 26 September 2013 (http://blogs.channel4.com/factcheck/factcheck-work-programme-improving-fails-sick-disabled/15918); BBC News, 'Charity urges rethink of official back to work schemes', 8 October 2013 (www.bbc.co.uk/news/business-24437424); http://ablemagazine.co.uk/disability-news/work-programme-is-failing-disabled-people-says-government-adviser); Locality, 'Work Programme is failing the hardest to help', 1 October 2013 (http://locality.org.uk/news/work-programme-failing-hardest).

[48] Andrew Grice, 'Government's £5 billion Work Programme "still failing and failing badly" as figures reveal only one in 20 sick and disabled people have been found lasting jobs', *The Independent*, 27 June 2013 (www.independent.co.uk/news/uk/politics/governments-5bn-work-programme-still-failing-and-failing-badly-as-figures-reveal-only-one-in-20-sick-and-disabled-people-have-been-found-lasting-jobs-8677405.html); Department for Work and Pensions, 'Work Programme statistical summary, September 2013' (www.gov.uk/government/publications/work-programme-statistical-summary-september-2013); Sky News, 'Back-to-work programme "extremely poor"', 22 February 2013 (http://news.sky.com/story/1055464/back-to-work-programme-extremely-poor); www.drugscope.org.uk/Resources/Drugscope/Documents/PDF/Policy/WorkProgrammePilots.pdf

[49] David Blanchflower, for *The Independent*, 6 October 2013, op cit.

[50] Sharon Wright, 'Can welfare reform work?', *Poverty*, number 139, summer 2011, CPAG.

[51] Alex Hern, 'Workfare is not voluntary', Left Foot Forward, 22 February 2012 (www.leftfootforward.org/2012/02/workfare-is-not-voluntary); Stef Benstead,

'Policy exchange: Is community workfare fair?', *The Huffington Post UK*, Blog, 28 September 2013 (www.huffingtonpost.co.uk/stef-benstead/is-workfare-fair_b_4007795.html?utm_hp_ref=uk-politics&ir=UK+Politics).

[52] BBC News, 'Back-to-work scheme breached laws, says Court of Appeal', 12 February 2013 (www.bbc.co.uk/news/business-21426928).

[53] www.boycottworkfare.org/?page_id=16Court

[54] Ibid.

[55] The Tories announced at their 2013 Party Conference that they intended to make the conditionality even tougher. A good breakdown of the various jobseeking-related sanctions and mandatory schemes can be found at: www.adviceguide.org.uk/wales/work_w/work_self-employed_or_looking_for_work_e/government_employment_schemes.htm

[56] www.jetderby.co.uk

[57] Disabled People Against Cuts, 'JSA Benefit sanctions sky rocket under coalition!' (http://dpac.uk.net/2013/06/jsa-benefit-sanctions-sky-rocket-under-coalition).

[58] http://paulspicker.files.wordpress.com/2013/11/david-webster-evidence-to-hc-work-and-pensions-committee-20-nov.pdf

[59] http://forums.moneysavingexpert.com/showthread.php?t=4638603

[60] Yvonne Roberts, 'York strives to pay living wage as cuts bite and poverty spreads', *The Guardian*, 10 February 2013 (www.theguardian.com/society/2013/feb/10/york-living-wage-spending-cuts-poverty-spreads).

[61] https://twitter.com/PovertyAlliance/statuses/316531225198211072

[62] www.clydebankpost.co.uk/news/roundup/articles/2013/03/22/450852-mums-fears-after-benefits-stopped-/#.UU8H5_Kh6oM.twitter

[63] www.publications.parliament.uk/pa/cm201213/cmhansrd/cm130319/debtext/130319-0002.htm#13031966000011

[64] For a list of 'completely ridiculous' reasons benefits have been sanctioned, go to http://falseeconomy.org.uk/blog/a-list-of-completely-ridiculous-benefit-sanctions-people-have-experienced

Chapter Six

[1] For full coverage of the Austerity on Trial event, 1 March 2013, see www.lse.ac.uk/publicEvents/events/2013/03/LitFest20130301t1800vSZT.aspx. See also Mary O'Hara, 'Magdalena Sepúlveda: "Austerity is devastating for the world's poorest"', *The Guardian*, 26 February 2013 (www.theguardian.com/society/2013/feb/26/magdalena-sepulveda-austerity-devastating-worlds-poorest).

---

[2] Julia Slay and Joe Penny, *Everyday insecurity*, New Economics Foundation (www.neweconomics.org/publications/entry/everyday-insecurity).

[3] www.nap.edu/openbook.php?record_id=11579&page=234; Ann Logsdon, 'Depression and disability' (http://learningdisabilities.about.com/od/emotionalhealth/a/Depression-And-Disability.htm).

[4] 'Financial crisis deepens for disabled people', 22 July 2013 (www.scope.org.uk/news/financial-crisis-deepens-disabled-people).

[5] Claudia Wood, 'Destination unknown: April 2013', Demos (www.demos.co.uk/blog/destinationunknownapril2013).

[6] http://dpac.uk.net

[7] BBC News, 'Disabled people hold nationwide protests against cuts', 22 October 2011 (www.bbc.co.uk/news/uk-15399724); BBC News, 'Disabled people stage protest over spending cuts', 11 May 2011 (www.bbc.co.uk/news/uk-13348326).

[8] *Mail on Sunday*, 'Wheelchair users chain themselves together and blocked central London over welfare cuts', 6 February 2012 (www.dailymail.co.uk/news/article-2093286/Wheelchair-users-chained-blocked-central-London-welfare-cuts.html).

[9] Michael Savage, 'Disability reforms could set clock back, says Dame Tanni Grey-Thompson', *The Times*, 8 April 2013 (www.thetimes.co.uk/tto/news/politics/article3733508.ece).

[10] Benefit Scrounging Scum, 'Inside the Ethics Committee', 16 July 2013 (http://benefitscroungingscum.blogspot.co.uk/2013/07/inside-ethics-committee-august-8th-9am.html).

[11] http://wearespartacus.org.uk/about

[12] http://wowpetitionforum.co.uk

[13] Alan White, 'Why is there silence on the impact of welfare cuts on disabled people?', *New Statesman*, 19 July 2013 (www.newstatesman.com/uk-politics/2013/07/deafening-silence-impact-welfare-cuts-disabled-people).

[14] Simon Duffy, 'Ten attacks on disabled people's rights', The Centre for Welfare Reform, 2013 (www.centreforwelfarereform.org/library/by-date/ten-attacks-on-disabled-peoples-rights.html).

[15] http://dpac.uk.net/tag/atos

[16] ERSA, *Work Programme performance report*, London 2013; Simon Duffy, op cit.

[17] In late 2013, some of the biggest firms contracted to run the Work Programme were penalised for poor performance – see Frances Ryan, 'Disabled and on the Work Programme: "Cold calling companies for 8 to 16 hours a week"', *New Statesman*, 3 October 2013 (www.newstatesman.com/economics/2013/10/disabled-and-work-programme-cold-calling-companies-8-16-hours-week).

[18] Randeep Ramesh, 'Work Programme is failing disabled people, says government adviser', *The Guardian*, 8 October 2013 (www.theguardian.com/society/2013/oct/08/work-programme-disabled-people-government-adviser?CMP=twt_gu).

[19] UPDATE Disability Information Scotland, 'DWP report suggests Work Programme has failed disabled people' (www.update.org.uk/news-detail.php?page=527).

[20] Disability Rights UK, *Taking control of Employment Support* (www.disabilityrightsuk.org/policy-campaigns/reports-and-research/taking-control-employment-support).

[21] There is a useful summary of ESA at www.benefitsandwork.co.uk/employment-and-support-allowance/esa-glossary/1486-what-is-esa

[22] See www.gov.uk/employment-support-allowance/what-youll-get

[23] Rethink Mental Illness, WCA Judicial Review – FAQ (www.rethink.org/get-involved/campaigns/unfair-wca/wca-judicial-review-faq).

[24] Amelia Gentleman, 'Why I blew the whistle on Atos fitness-for-work test', *The Guardian*, 31 July 2013 (www.theguardian.com/society/2013/jul/31/atos-fitness-work-test-greg-wood).

[25] Amelia Gentleman, 'Work capability assessments decision follows years of criticism', *The Guardian*, 22 July 2013 (www.theguardian.com/society/2013/jul/22/work-capability-assessments-criticism).

[26] Rethink Mental Illness, '£130 to get medical evidence for WCA?', 26 August 2013 (www.rethink.org/news-views/2013/08/130-to-get-medical-evidence-for-wca).

[27] BBC News, 'Work fitness tests "shocking" says Islington Council', 21 October 2013 (www.bbc.co.uk/news/uk-england-london-24609466).

[28] BBC News, 'Bradford Council scrutinises disability tests in city', 9 September 2013 (www.bbc.co.uk/news/uk-england-leeds-24016967).

[29] Sophie Hutchinson, 'Disability benefit assessments "unfair", says ex-worker', BBC News, 16 May 2013 (www.bbc.co.uk/news/uk-22546036); Amelia Gentleman, for *The Guardian*, 31 July 2013, op cit.

[30] Caron Lindsay, 'ATOS lose monopoly on work capability assessments after audit shows up "unacceptable" standards', Liberal Democrat Voice, 23 July 2013 (www.libdemvoice.org/atos-lose-monopoly-on-work-capability-assessments-after-audit-shows-up-unacceptable-standards-35430.html).

[31] Patrick Wintour, 'Disabled benefits claimants test: Atos reports found "unacceptably poor"', *The Guardian*, 22 July 2013 (www.theguardian.com/society/2013/jul/22/disabled-benefits-claimants-test-atos?guni=Article:in%20body%20link).

---

[32] Commons Select Committee, *Report on the Department for Work and Pensions: Contract management of medical services*, 8 February 2013 (www.parliament.uk/business/committees/committees-a-z/commons-select/public-accounts-committee/news/contract-management-of-medical-services).

[33] Nina Lakhani, 'Atos contract does not offer value for money, says National Audit Office', *The Independent*, 17 August 2012 (www.independent.co.uk/news/uk/politics/atos-contract-does-not-offer-value-for-money-says-national-audit-office-8056412.html).

[34] Sally Hind, 'Mum-of-three was told to find a job by Atos chiefs … weeks later she died of a brain tumour', *Daily Record*, 22 July 2013 (www.dailyrecord.co.uk/news/scottish-news/mum-of-three-elenore-told-find-job-2074333#.Uez_gArlmYI.twitter).

[35] Amelia Gentleman, 'Work capability assessments decision follows years of criticism', *The Guardian*, 22 July 2013 (www.theguardian.com/society/2013/jul/22/work-capability-assessments-criticism).

[36] Amelia Gentleman, 'Get ready for work: what woman who needs constant care was told', *The Guardian*, 3 October 2012 (www.theguardian.com/society/2012/oct/03/work-woman-care?guni=Article:in%20body%20link).

[37] Ben Glaze, 'Linda Wootton: Double heart and lung transplant dies nine days after she has benefits stopped', *Mirror*, 26 May 2013 (www.mirror.co.uk/news/uk-news/linda-wootton-double-heart-lung-1912498).

[38] Amelia Gentleman, 'Atos comes under attack in emotional Commons debate', *The Guardian*, 17 January 2013 (www.theguardian.com/society/2013/jan/17/atos-attack-emotional-commons-debate).

[39] Iain Duncan Smith, 'I'm proud of our welfare reforms', *The Guardian*, 28 July 2013 (www.theguardian.com/commentisfree/2013/jul/28/proud-welfare-reforms-fair-benefits).

[40] Department for Work and Pensions, 'Pilot schemes to help people on sickness benefits back to work', Press release, 4 November 2013 (www.gov.uk/government/news/pilot-schemes-to-help-people-on-sickness-benefits-back-to-work).

[41] Shiv Malik, 'Minister looking at making it harder for sick and disabled to claim benefits', *The Guardian*, 30 September 2013 (www.theguardian.com/society/2013/sep/30/iain-duncan-smith-sick-disabled-benefits).

[42] Ibid.

[43] Simon Duffy, op cit.

[44] M. Gheera and R. Long, *Independent Living Fund*, London: House of Commons Library, 2013.

[45] www.dwp.gov.uk/ilf/news

[46] Mithran Samuel, 'Ministers urged to find £2bn to fund "moderate" care threshold', *Community Care*, 17 January 2013 (www.communitycare. co.uk/2013/01/17/ministers-urged-to-find-2bn-to-fund-moderate-care-threshold).

[47] www.youtube.com/watch?v=X4HC5-5Y-X4

[48] Mithran Samuel, for *Community Care*, 17 January 2013, op cit.

[49] http://falseeconomy.org.uk/about

[50] 'Councils' lack of cash hits 7,000 elderly and disabled people', Blog (http:// falseeconomy.org.uk/blog/councils-lack-of-cash-hits-7000-elderly-and-disabled-people).

[51] Mark Buckley, 'Birmingham decision supports Lancashire legal action', Disability Equality NW, 23 May 2011 (www.disability-equality.org.uk/news/ birmingham-decision-supports-lancashire-legal-action/n40).

[52] Daniel Lombard, 'Hammersmith and Fulham home care charges challenged in court', *Community Care*, 27 August 2008 (www.communitycare. co.uk/2008/08/27/hammersmith-and-fulham-home-care-charges-challenged-in-court/#.UnPVCaVIkfM).

[53] Quoted in Alan White and Kate Belgrave, 'The secret cuts: Part two, the Independent Living Fund', *New Statesman*, 6 June 2013 (www.newstatesman. com/politics/2013/06/secret-cuts-part-two-independent-living-fund).

[54] Kate Belgrave, 'Closing the Independent Living Fund shows how low the government will go', *The Guardian*, 27 February 2013 (www.theguardian.com/ commentisfree/2013/feb/27/closing-independent-living-fund-disabled-care).

[55] BBC News, 'Disabled people win living fund case against government', 6 November 2013 (www.bbc.co.uk/news/uk-politics-24834558).`

[56] BBC News, 'Independent Living Fund to be re-examined by ministers', 8 November 2013 (www.bbc.co.uk/news/uk-politics-24870493).

[57] Disabled People Against Cuts (DPAC), 'Victory for independent living rights in English Appeal Court', 8 November 2013 (http://dpac.uk.net/2013/11/ victory-for-independent-living-rights-in-english-appeal-court/#sthash. aaVlw1Bd.dpuf).

[58] http://benefitfraud.blogspot.co.uk/2011/11/32m-people-on-disability-living.html

[59] Amelia Gentleman, 'DLA reform: coalition is exaggerating benefit fraud for its own benefit', *The Guardian*, 14 may 2012 (www.theguardian.com/society/2012/ may/14/disability-living-allowance-reform-analysis).

[60] Kerry McQueeney, 'That will never wash! Benefits cheat who claimed £33,000 by pretending he had to use a wheelchair caught cleaning windows', Mail

Online, 23 May 2012 (www.dailymail.co.uk/news/article-2148793/Thomas-Kenny-Window-cleaner-claimed-33-000-pretending-use-wheelchair.html).

[61] 'Next phase of Government plans to abolish Disability Living Allowance', 28 October 2013 (www.scope.org.uk/news/disability-living-allowance-replaced-personal-independence-payment).

[62] See www.gov.uk/access-to-work/overview

[63] 'Next phase of Government plans to abolish Disability Living Allowance', 28 October 2013 (www.scope.org.uk/news/disability-living-allowance-replaced-personal-independence-payment); BBC News, 'Disability welfare changes delayed by assessment process', 26 October 2013 (www.bbc.co.uk/news/uk-politics-24680366).

[64] Rowena Mason, 'Controversial disability benefit changes delayed', *The Guardian*, 25 October 2013 (www.theguardian.com/politics/2013/oct/25/personal-independence-payments-postponed).

[65] Polly Toynbee, 'Ideology meets idiocy in these brutal disability cuts', *The Guardian*, 29 October 2013 (www.theguardian.com/commentisfree/2013/oct/29/tory-disability-benefits-ideology-idiocy?CMP=twt_gu).

[66] Disability News Service, 'PIP delay raises questions over government's 20 metres decision', 13 September 2013 (http://disabilitynewsservice.com/2013/09/pip-delay-raises-questions-over-governments-20-metres-decision).

Chapter Seven

[1] The Centre for Social Justice, *Maxed out: Serious personal debt in Britain*, November 2013 (www.centreforsocialjustice.org.uk/UserStorage/pdf/Pdf%20reports/CSJ_Serious_Debt_report_WEB_final.pdf).

[2] www.mind.org.uk

[3] Ian Birch, 'Mind says calls to its helpline up a quarter over past year', Mental Healthy (www.mentalhealthy.co.uk/news/1703-mind-says-calls-to-its-helpline-up-quarter-over-past-year.html).

[4] Nick Triggle, 'Money woes "linked to rise in depression"', BBC News, 7 April 2011 (www.bbc.co.uk/news/health-12986314).

[5] Samaritans, 'Statement about financial stress and suicide', 12 May 2013 (www.samaritans.org/news/statement-about-financial-stress-and-suicide).

[6] Samaritans, 'Why is a free-to-caller service important?', 26 June 2013 (www.samaritans.org/news/why-free-caller-service-important).

[7] Samaritans, 'Samaritans' comment on the 2011 Office for National Statistics suicide figures', Press release, 22 January 2013 (www.samaritans.org/news/comment-2011-ons-suicide-statistics).

[8] John Domokos and Patrick Butler, 'Jobcentre bosses warn of suicide risk among benefit claimants', *The Guardian*, 20 June 2012 (www.theguardian.com/society/2012/jun/20/jobcentre-supervisors-suicide-risk-benefit-claimants).

[9] www.theguardian.com/society/2011/apr/07/dramatic-rise-antidpressant-prescriptions-money-worries; Mark Easton, 'Is England a nation on anti-depressants?', BBC News, 3 August 2013 (www.bbc.co.uk/news/uk-23553897).

[10] Sarah Boseley, Mona Chalabi and Mark Rice-Oxley, 'Antidepressant use on the rise in rich countries, OECD finds', *The Guardian*, 20 November 2013 (www.theguardian.com/society/2013/nov/20/antidepressant-use-rise-world-oecd).

[11] 'Dramatic rise in antidepressant prescriptions linked to money worries', 7 April 2011 (www.theguardian.com/society/2011/apr/07/dramatic-rise-antidpressant-prescriptions-money-worries); Mhairi Aylott, Will Norman, Catherine Russell and Vicki Sellick, *An insight into the impact of the cuts on some of the most vulnerable in Camden*, Young Foundation, 2012 (http://youngfoundation.org/wp-content/uploads/2012/10/uts_on_some_of_the_most_vulnerable_in_Camden_2.pdf).

[12] David Stuckler and Sanjay Basu, *The body economic: Why austerity kills*, London: Allen Lane, 2013.

[13] Nick McCarthy, 'Desperate jobseeker sets himself alight outside Selly Oak jobcentre', *Birmingham Mail*, 29 June 2012 (www.birminghammail.co.uk/news/local-news/desperate-jobseeker-sets-himself-alight-187732); Shiv Malik and John Domokos, 'Man sets himself on fire outside Birmingham jobcentre', *The Guardian*, 29 June 2012 (www.theguardian.com/society/2012/jun/29/man-on-fire-birmingham-job-centre).

[14] Paul Cheston, 'Suicide bid of woman who feared losing her incapacity benefit', *London Evening Standard*, 14 August 2013 (www.standard.co.uk/news/uk/suicide-bid-of-woman-who-feared-losing-her-incapacity-benefit-8761182.html).

[15] Marc Waddington, 'Liverpool mum suicide as she struggled to cope with bedroom tax', *Liverpool Echo*, 8 June 2013 (www.liverpoolecho.co.uk/news/liverpool-news/liverpool-mum-suicide-attempt-struggled-4279433).

[16] Keir Mudie, 'Bedroom Tax: Pensioner killed himself over fears he could not afford his home', *Mirror*, 3 November 2013 (www.mirror.co.uk/news/uk-news/bedroom-tax-pensioner-charles-barden-2670737).

[17] Richard Smith, 'Sick nurse killed herself after disability benefits were cut and she was ruled "fit to work"', *Mirror*, 26 November 2013 (www.mirror.co.uk/news/uk-news/sick-nurse-jacqueline-harris-killed-2851486).

[18] Economic and Social Research Council, 'Cutting NHS costs with mental health investments', Evidence Briefing (www.esrc.ac.uk/_images/ESRC_Evidence_Briefing_Mental_health_NHS_tcm8-26241.pdf).

[19] Frank Dobson announced a third way for mental health in July 1998 (www.lgcplus.com/frank-dobson-outlines-third-way-for-mental-health/1454656.article), and in September 1999 set out ambitious plans to reform mental health services with the National Service Framework and additional funding (see www.gov.uk/government/uploads/system/uploads/attachment_data/file/198051/National_Service_Framework_for_Mental_Health.pdf).

[20] Economic and Social Research Council, op cit.

[21] Norman Lamb MP, 'Another step forwards in achieving parity for mental health', Liberal Democrat Voice, 13 November 2013 (www.libdemvoice.org/norman-lamb-mp-writesanother-step-forwards-in-achieving-parity-for-mental-health-37180.html).

[22] 'Impact of mental health service cuts', Letters, 17 October 2013 (www.theguardian.com/society/2013/oct/17/impact-mental-health-services); Rethink Mental Illness, *The Mental Health Strategy, systems reforms and spending pressures: what do we know so far?* (www.mentalhealth.org.uk/content/assets/PDF/publications/mental_health_strategy_what_do_we_know_so_far.pdf?view=Standard).

[23] Economic and Social Research Council, op cit.

[24] Michael Buchanan, 'England's mental health services "in crisis"', BBC News, 16 October 2013 (www.bbc.co.uk/news/health-24537304).

[25] Matthew Whittaker, 'Austerity after 2015: why the worst is yet to come', Resolution Foundation, Blog, 20 June 2013 (www.resolutionfoundation.org/blog/2013/jun/20/austerity-after-2015-why-worst-yet-come).

[26] BBC News, 'George Osborne outlines detail of £6.2bn spending cuts', 24 May 2010 (http://news.bbc.co.uk/1/hi/8699522.stm).

[27] IFS comments that the UK faces 'the longest, deepest, sustained period of cuts to public services spending at least since World War II.' IFS Director Robert Chote commented that the cuts would: 'more than reverse the entire increase that we saw under Labour ... likely to hit poorer households significantly harder than richer households', quoted in BBC News, 'Budget: UK faces worst cuts since World War II says IFS', 23 June 2010 (www.bbc.co.uk/news/10393585); Unite, 'Con-Dems raze public services to the ground', 20 October 2010 (http://archive.unitetheunion.org/news__events/archived_news_releases/2010_archived_press_releases/con-dems_raze_public_services.aspx).

[28] Katie Allen, 'Local government cuts unfair to north-east, say councils', *The Guardian*, 27 November 2013 (www.theguardian.com/business/2013/nov/27/local-government-cuts-unfair-to-north-east).

The leader of Derby City Council has claimed the government intends to "front load" the budget cuts for local authorities.

Harvey Jennings said: 'The Comprehensive Spending Review yesterday suggested we were going to receive spending cuts of 7.1% per year over the next four years....We've just found out that's actually not quite true, that it's going to be front loaded, which means that next year – the first— we're going to have to achieve double the savings of 14.2%', quoted in BBC News, 'Spending Review: Council cuts to be "front loaded"', 21 October 2010 (www.bbc.co.uk/news/uk-england-derbyshire-11602938).

'The North-South divide has become part of the political lexicon, although in reality the divide could be more accurately described as the Greater South East and the rest. The economies of the North grew substantially in the period leading up to the recession, but they suffered disproportionately the effects of the recession and rising unemployment', quoted in Ed Cox and Katie Schmuecker, *Well north of fair: The implications of the Spending Review for the North of England*, Institute for Public Policy Research, 25 October 2010 (www.ippr.org/publication/55/1804/well-north-of-fair-the-implications-of-the-spending-review-for-the-north-of-england).

[29] Tony Woodley, Unite Joint General Secretary: 'The coalition has no brief for the devastation it is about to unleash on this country. Cuts on this scale make no sense ... the people of this country, who most need their public services to help them during tough times, did not vote for the dismantling of their schools, hospitals and communities', quoted in Unite, 'Unite warning on cuts', 19 October 2010 (http://archive.unitetheunion.org/news__events/archived_news_releases/2010_archived_press_releases/unite_warning_on_cuts.aspx).

[30] Anushka Asthana, 'Coalition budget faces legal challenge from Fawcett Society over claims women will bear brunt of cuts', *The Guardian*, 1 August 2010 (www.guardian.co.uk/society/2010/aug/01/budget-legal-challenge-women-equality).

[31] Mike Barrett, 'Burdened with impossible choices – who would you choose to help?', Porchlight, 2 February 2011 (www.porchlight.org.uk/2011/02/02/burdened-with-impossible-choices-%E2%80%93-who-would-you-choose-to-help).

[32] With the abolition of the Social Fund, which had funded crisis loans, money was potentially available through an advance from the Department for Work and Pensions, or from funding devolved to local authorities, although as the funding was not ring-fenced, there was inconsistency of provision (see www.cpag.org.uk/content/what-replacing-social-fund).

[33] Patrick Butler, 'Will council crisis funds last the winter?', *The Guardian*, 27 November 2013 (www.theguardian.com/society/2013/nov/27/council-crisis-funds-local-assistance-schemes-last-winter?CMP=twt_gu).

[34] See www.bbc.co.uk/news/uk-wales-22979438

[35] Unite, 20 October 2010, op cit. For other reactions to the Comprehensive Spending review see www.ifs.org.uk/projects/346. The impact on young

people was highlighted by the YMCA (see www.ymca.org.uk/newsmedia/ pressreleases/48-spending-review-poor-for-young-people), and the National Council for Voluntary Youth Services (http://ncvys.org.uk/UserFiles/ NCVYS%20briefing%20on%20HM%20Treasury%20Comprehensive%20 Spending%20Review%202010.pdf), while others pointed out the disproportionate impact of the spending cuts on women (www.guardian.co.uk/politics/2010/ oct/22/cuts-women-spending-review), and on the already deprived areas in the north of England (Ed Cox and Katie Schmuecker, op cit).

[36] Andy Ford, 'Another round of austerity ahead', *Local Government Chronicle*, 26 June 2013 (www.lgcplus.com/opinion/another-round-of-austerity-ahead/5060328.article).

[37] Jonathan Carr-West, 'Political bravery is needed to plug the gap in social care', *The Guardian*, 2 November 2012 (www.theguardian.com/social-care-network/2012/nov/02/jonathan-carr-west-lgiu-social-care-funding).

[38] British Association of Social Workers, *The state of social work 2012*, 17 May 2012 (http://cdn.basw.co.uk/upload/basw_23651-3.pdf).

[39] John Bingham, 'Million more elderly outside care system than before financial crash', *The Telegraph*, 7 September 2013 (www.telegraph.co.uk/health/ elderhealth/10292562/Million-more-elderly-outside-care-system-than-before-financial-crash.html).

[40] The College of Social Work, 'Social workers raise concern for older people as frontline care services are cut', 24 June 2013 (www.tcsw.org.uk/pressrelease. aspx?id=8589934816).

[41] 'Thousands struggling to eat, wash or leave their homes', 17 January 2013 (www.scope.org.uk/news/other-care-crisis); *The other care crisis: Making social care funding work for disabled adults in England*, January 2013 (www.scope.org.uk/ sites/default/files/The_Other_Care_Crisis.pdf).

[42] David Walker, 'The quango cull: an exercise in randomness with no real savings', *The Guardian*, 20 January 2012 (www.theguardian.com/public-leaders-network/2012/jan/20/quango-cull-exercise-randomness-savings).

[43] Audit Commission, *Tough Times 2013: Councils' responses to financial challenges from 2010/11 to 2013/14*, November 2013 (www.audit-commission. gov.uk/wp-content/uploads/2013/11/Tough-Times-2013-Councils-Responses-to-Financial-Challenges-w1.pdf); Mithran Samuel, 'Councils losing ability to protect adult social care from significant cuts, says finance watchdog', *Community Care*, 28 November 2013 (www.communitycare. co.uk/2013/11/28/councils-losing-ability-protect-adult-social-care-significant-cuts-says-finance-watchdog/?cmpid=SOC%7Ctwitter%7CMithran%20 Samuel%7C2013112810832905#.UppxK6U2EfP).

[44] Annette Hastings, Nick Bailey, Kirsten Besemer, Glen Bramley, Maria Gannon and David Watkins, *Coping with the cuts? Local government and poorer*

communities, JRF Programme Paper, Austerity, November 2013 (www.lgcplus. com/Journals/2013/11/26/g/p/x/JRF-Coping-with-cuts.pdf).

[45] Tom Barton, 'Eastern region youth services spend cut by £20m in two years', BBC News, 17 November 2013 (www.bbc.co.uk/news/uk-england-24980262).

[46] Alistair Smith, 'Arts face £124m extra local funding cuts', *The Stage News*, 8 August 2013 (www.thestage.co.uk/news/2013/08/arts-face-124m-extra-local-funding-cuts).

[47] Neil Elkes, 'Council urged to come clean on cost of Capita services deal', *Birmingham Post*, 12 December 2013 (www.birminghampost.co.uk/business/business-news/council-urged-come-clean-cost-6397249).

[48] 'Neighbourhood wardens cull in Wolverhampton City Council cuts', *Express & Star*, 7 December 2013 (www.expressandstar.com/news/2013/12/07/neighbourhood-wardens-cull-in-wolverhampton-city-council-cuts).

[49] Local Government Association (LGA), '£14.4 billion funding blackhole threatens to swallow public services', LGA media release, 4 July 2013 (www.local.gov.uk/media-releases/-/journal_content/56/10180/4053260/NEWS); LGA, *Future funding outlook for councils from 2010/11 to 2019/20*, July 2013 (www.local.gov.uk/c/document_library/get_file?uuid=b9880109-a1bc-4c9b-84d4-0ec5426ccd26&groupId=10180).

[50] *The Guardian* reported on a Chartered Institute of Public Finance and Accountancy report that showed accelerating rates of library closures, with 200 closing in 2012 alone. See Alison Flood, 'UK lost more than 200 libraries in 2012', *The Guardian*, 10 December 2012 (www.theguardian.com/books/2012/dec/10/uk-lost-200-libraries-2012).

[51] One in seven public toilets had been shut in the last three years, according to a November 2013 report in *The Telegraph*; see Tim Ross, 'One in seven public toilets closed by council cuts', *The Telegraph*, 17 November 2013 (www.telegraph.co.uk/news/politics/labour/10454773/One-in-seven-public-toilets-closed-by-council-cuts.html).

[52] Kirsten Besemer and Glen Bramley, *Local services under siege: Attitudes to public services in a time of austerity*, Economic and Social Research Council, April 2012 (www.poverty.ac.uk/system/files/WP%20Analysis%20No.2%20-%20Local%20Services%20Under%20Siege%20(Besemer%20%20Bramley%20May%202012).pdf).

[53] Sure Start was announced by then Chancellor of the Exchequer, Gordon Brown, in 1998 with £500 million funding for the first three years.

[54] 'Miliband hits out at closure of Sure Start', 18 November 2013 (www.itv.com/news/update/2013-11-18/miliband-hits-out).

[55] George Eaton, 'Labour targets Cameron's broken promises on Sure Start', *New Statesman*, 18 November 2013 (www.newstatesman.com/politics/2013/11/labour-targets-camerons-broken-promises-sure-start).

[56] http://childrenscentresfinder.direct.gov.uk/snapshot-childrens-centre/

[57] Patrick Wintour, 'Cameron urged to back campaign to save Oxfordshire Sure Start centres', *The Guardian*, 12 November 2013 (www.theguardian.com/society/2013/nov/12/cameron-save-sure-start-children-centres-oxfordshire).

[58] Polly Toynbee, 'Our children will inherit a far worse legacy than mere debt', *The Guardian*, 28 January 2011 (www.theguardian.com/commentisfree/2011/jan/28/children-legacy-debt-sure-start).

[59] Department for Education, *Written ministerial statement by Michael Gove on schools financial settlement – education spending*, 13 December 2010 (www.gov.uk/government/speeches/written-ministerial-statement-by-michael-gove-on-schools-financial-settlement-education-spending--2).

[60] By November 2011 124 Sure Start centres had been closed; see Nicholas Watt, '124 Sure Start centres have closed since coalition took power', *The Guardian*, 14 November 2011 (www.theguardian.com/society/2011/nov/14/sure-start-centre-closures-coalition).

[61] Family and Childcare Trust, 'Campaign for Sure Start' (www.daycaretrust.org.uk/pages/campaign-for-sure-start.html).

[62] Ibid.

[63] Anna Bawden, 'Full force of cuts hits community services', *The Guardian*, 6 November 2013 (www.theguardian.com/society/2013/nov/06/budget-cuts-hit-community-services).

[64] www.goodwintrust.org/home

[65] Kirsten Besemer and Glen Bramley, op cit.

[66] Teresa Cavero and Krisnah Poinasamy, *A cautionary tale: The true cost of austerity and inequality in Europe*, Oxfam, 12 September 2013 (http://policy-practice.oxfam.org.uk/publications/a-cautionary-tale-the-true-cost-of-austerity-and-inequality-in-europe-301384).

[67] Melissa Thompson and Rachael Bletchly, 'Women under attack: How austerity Britain is affecting females more than men', *Mirror*, 2 May 2012 (www.mirror.co.uk/news/uk-news/how-austerity-britain-is-affecting-women-814805); 'New analysis of the June 2013 Spending Review from Women's Budget Group', Fawcett Society, 25 September 2013 (www.fawcettsociety.org.uk/new-analysis-of-the-june-2013-spending-review-from-womens-budget-group); Randeep Ramesh, 'Households with lone breadwinner are biggest group living in poverty in UK', *The Guardian*, 13 November 2013 (www.theguardian.com/society/2013/nov/13/households-lone-breadwinner-biggest-poverty-uk).

[68] www.poverty.ac.uk/report-gender-tax-benefits-government-cuts-government-policy/women-'hit-worst'-austerity-measures

[69] Women's Budget Group, *The impact on women of the coalition government's spending round 2013* (http://wbg.org.uk/pdfs/WBG-Analysis-June-2013-Spending-Round.pdf).

[70] Fawcett Society, *A life raft for women's equality* (www.fawcettsociety.org.uk/wp-content/uploads/2013/02/A-Life-Raft-for-Womens-Equality-FINAL.pdf).

[71] Fawcett Society, 'The impact of austerity on women', Policy Briefing, March 2012 (www.fawcettsociety.org.uk/wp-content/uploads/2013/02/The-Impact-of-Austerity-on-Women-19th-March-2012.pdf).

[72] Family and Childcare Trust, 'Summary of the Holiday childcare costs survey 2011', 12 July 2011 (www.daycaretrust.org.uk/pages/summary-of-the-holiday-childcare-costs-survey-2011.html); Children England, *Counting the cuts: The impact of public sector spending cuts on children's charities*, March 2011 (www.childrenengland.org.uk/upload/CountingTheCutsFinalforPDF.pdf).

[73] Annex A of *Overview of tax legislation and rates*, p 33 (www.hmrc.gov.uk/budget2013/ootlar-main.pdf).

[74] Fawcett Society, *Fawcett Society analysis of the 2013 budget*, June 2013 (www.fawcettsociety.org.uk/wp-content/uploads/2013/06/Fawcett-Society-analysis-of-the-2013-budget.pdf).

[75] www.savelegalaid.co.uk/legalaidunderlaspo.html; Dina Rickman, 'Domestic violence: Women's services face "disastrous" cuts as councils slash budgets, FOI reveals', *The Huffington Post UK*, 4 November 2012 (www.huffingtonpost.co.uk/2012/10/31/domestic-violence-rape-crisis-cuts_n_2049137.html?just_reloaded=1); Sandra Horley, 'Welfare reform piles pressure on victims of domestic violence', *The Guardian*, 19 June 2013 (www.theguardian.com/local-government-network/2013/jun/19/welfare-reform-domestic-violence).

[76] 'Recession blamed for domestic violence increase', *Mirror*, 28 July 2011 (www.mirror.co.uk/news/uk-news/recession-blamed-for-domestic-violence-increase-144262).

[77] Women's Aid, 'Cuts in refuge services putting vulnerable women and children at risk', Press release, 27 November 2012 (www.womensaid.org.uk/domestic-violence-press-information.asp?itemid=2944&itemTitle=Cuts+in+refuge+services+putting+vulnerable+women+and+children+at+risk&section=0001000100150001&sectionTitle=Press+releases).

[78] Sylvia Walby and Jude Towers, *Measuring the impact of cuts in public expenditure on the provision of services to prevent violence against women and girls*, Northern Rock Foundation (www.nr-foundation.org.uk/downloads/measuring-the-impact-of-cuts-in-public-expenditure-on-the-provision-of-services-to-prevent-violence-against-women-and-girls).

[79] Women's Resource Centre, *The impact of public spending on women's voluntary and community organisations in London*, March 2013 (http://thewomensresourcecentre.org.uk/wp-content/uploads/London-report-FINAL-for-website.pdf).

[80] Mary O'Hara, 'Legal aid cuts are devastating to women, especially those suffering abuse', *The Guardian*, 3 December 2013 (www.theguardian.com/society/2013/dec/03/legal-aid-cuts-devastating-to-women-abuse-victims?CMP=twt_gu).

[81] 'Barristers threaten strike action over cuts to legal aid', *The Guardian*, 16 November 2013 (www.theguardian.com/law/2013/nov/16/barristers-legal-aid-cuts-strike-threat); BBC News, 'Legal aid: Lawyers in Wales agree strike action', 28 April 2013 (www.bbc.co.uk/news/uk-wales-22330695); 'Strike threat over legal aid cuts', 16 November 2013 (http://uk.news.yahoo.com/strike-threat-over-legal-aid-cuts-114218014.html#CLGoO6x).

[82] www.feministtimes.com/access-to-justice-for-women-in-the-uk; Fawcett Society, *Fawcett Society analysis of 2013 budget*, June 2013 (www.fawcettsociety.org.uk/wp-content/uploads/2013/06/Fawcett-Society-analysis-of-the-2013-budget.pdf); Women's Resource Centre, *Transforming legal aid: Delivering a more credible and efficient system*, May 2013 (http://thewomensresourcecentre.org.uk/wp-content/uploads/Briefing-Legal-aid-consultation.pdf).

[83] Justice Alliance, *Justice deserves Lib Dems stay changes to legal aid: Testimonials* (http://justiceallianceuk.files.wordpress.com/2013/11/ja-statements-22nov2013-2.pdf).

[84] www.legislation.gov.uk/ukpga/2012/10/contents/enacted; Garden Court North Chambers, *A quick guide to LASPO 2012 Part 3* (www.gcnchambers.co.uk/areas_of_specialisation/areas/criminal_defence/criminal_law_updates/a_quick_guide_to_laspo_2012_part_3_sentencing_and_the_punishment_of_offenders).

[85] Jon Robins, 'Government behaving like "playground bully" – peers savage LASPO again', LegalVoice, 28 March 2013 (http://legalvoice.org.uk/topstories/government-behaving-like-playground-bully-peers-savage-laspo-again).

[86] Catherine Baksi, 'Two more legal aid defeats as LASPO completes Lords', *The Law Society Gazette*, 28 March 2012 (www.lawgazette.co.uk/64954.article).

[87] Vidhya Alakeson and Giselle Cory, *Home truths: How affordable is housing for Britain's ordinary working families?*, Resolution Foundation, July 2013 (www.resolutionfoundation.org/media/media/downloads/Home_Truths_2.pdf).

[88] See www.theguardian.com/politics/2013/nov/27/boris-johnson-thatcher-greed-good

[89] Hélène Mulholland, 'Boris Johnson backs down over "Kosovo" comments on housing benefit', *The Guardian*, 28 October 2010 (www.theguardian.com/politics/2010/oct/28/boris-johnson-kosovo-style-cleansing-housing-benefit).

[90] Joseph Rowntree Foundation, *Britain's housing in 2022: More shortages and homelessness?*, 19 March 2002 (www.jrf.org.uk/publications/britains-housing-2022-more-shortages-and-homelessness).

[91] Patrick Collinson, 'Renting – Britain's social scandal that is being ignored', *The Guardian*, 4 January 2014 (www.theguardian.com/money/blog/2014/jan/04/renting-scandal-ignored-politicians?CMP=twt_gu).

[92] www.housing.org.uk

[93] Shelter, 'Shelter sees surge in demand for help from people struggling to pay for their home', Press release (http://media.shelter.org.uk/home/press_releases/shelter_sees_surge_in_demand_for_help_from_people_struggling_to_pay_for_their_home).

[94] Homeless Link, 'One in three has experienced homelessness or knows someone who has' (http://homeless.org.uk/news/one-in-three-has-experienced-homelessness-or-knows-someone-who-has#.UqIQp6U2EfM).

[95] Homeless Link, 'Welfare changes pushing young people into homelessness, report warns' (http://homeless.org.uk/news/welfare-changes-pushing-young-people-homelessness-report-warns#.Ul-sjVO66as).

[96] Pete Apps, 'Shelter warns of 80,000 children in temporary accommodation', *Inside Housing*, 4 November 2013 (www.insidehousing.co.uk/home/news/shelter-warns-of-80000-children-in-temporary-accommodation/6529333.article).

[97] Crisis, 'Research: Almost one in ten people have been homeless', 13 December 2013 (www.crisis.org.uk/pressreleases.php/583/research-almost-one-in-ten-people-have-been-homeless).

[98] Johnny Void, 'One third of homeless people hit by benefit sanctions', 23 September 2013 (http://johnnyvoid.wordpress.com/2013/09/23/one-third-of-homeless-people-hit-by-benefit-sanctions).

[99] Homeless Watch, *A high cost to pay: The impact of benefit sanctions on homeless people*, September 2013 (www.insidehousing.co.uk/journals/2013/09/23/b/w/t/A-High-Cost-to-Pay-Sept13.pdf).

Conclusion

[1] Moussa Haddad, *The perfect storm: Economic stagnation, the rising cost of living, public spending cuts, and the impact on UK poverty*, Oxfam, 14 June 2012 (http://policy-practice.oxfam.org.uk/publications/the-perfect-storm-economic-stagnation-the-rising-cost-of-living-public-spending-228591).

[2] Voluntary Organisations' Network North East, 'Surviving not thriving' (www.vonne.org.uk/campaigns/surviving_not_thriving.php).

[3] www.involveyorkshirehumber.org.uk/resources/quarterly-confidence-survey/16th-quarterly-confidence-report

[4] New Start, 'Are we gambling away the future of local high streets?', 21 November 2012 (http://newstartmag.co.uk/your-blogs/are-we-gambling-away-the-future-of-local-high-streets).

[5] David N.F. Bell and David G. Blanchflower, *What should be done about rising unemployment in the UK?* (www.dartmouth.edu/~blnchflr/papers/speech379paper.pdf).

[6] '2011 London anti-cuts protest' (http://en.wikipedia.org/wiki/2011_London_anti-cuts_protest).

[7] 'UK Uncut to stage food bank protests in HSBC branches', Liberal Conspiracy, 25 June 2013 (http://liberalconspiracy.org/2013/06/25/ukuncut-to-stage-food-bank-protests-in-hsbc-branches).

[8] BBC News, 'Lewisham Hospital: 15,000 march against closure plan', 26 January 2013 (www.bbc.co.uk/news/uk-england-london-21196758).

[9] www.boycottworkfare.org

[10] www.movementforchange.org.uk

[11] http://communitiesagainstthecuts.com/author/catc2012

[12] www.livingwage.org.uk/what-we-do

[13] www.whobenefits.org.uk/page/content/front

[14] http://falseeconomy.org.uk

[15] 'The proposed declaration and action plan of the People's Assembly' (http://thepeoplesassembly.org.uk/draft-statement).

[16] 'Reading the riots', *The Guardian* (www.theguardian.com/uk/series/reading-the-riots).

Index

Page references for endnotes are followed by n